The Wolf Files

Adventures in Weird News

Buck Wolf

The Globe Pequot Press

GUILFORD, CONNECTICUT

Text design by Casey Shain
Spot art © ClipArt.com

Library of Congress Cataloging-in-Publication Data
Wolf, Buck.
    The Wolf files : adventures in weird news / Buck Wolf.— 1st ed.
      p. cm.
    ISBN 0-7627-2853-1
        1. United States—Social life and customs—1971—Anecdotes. 2. Popular culture—
United States—Anecdotes. 3. Curiosities and wonders—United States—Anecdotes.
4. United States—Biography—Anecdotes. 5. Wolf, Buck—Anecdotes. I. Title.

E169.12. W59 2007
306'.0973—dc22

                                                                    2003059648

Manufactured in the United States of America
First Edition/First Printing

To My Little Sister, Valerie—

Who gave birth to five beautiful children in five years—about the same time it took to write the columns in this book.

And to Lisa Bitondo—

We miss you.

Contents

Schlock **Meisters** 65

Marginal **History** 99

Frightening **Beauty** 117

Patriot **Games** 139

Feral **Beasts** 165

Mundane **Thrills** 193

Acknowledgments

Anything that's lasted five years or more is as an ancient tradition, if not a miracle, at least on the Internet.

I have many people to thank, starting with Elvis Presley and my colleagues at ABCNEWS.com.

In 1998, students applying to the University of Chicago, a bastion of Nobel Prize winners, got to weigh in on that age-old question that has preoccupied America for decades—Is Elvis still alive? The venerable university posed this question to conspiracy-minded applicants, and thus began the first edition of *The Wolf Files*, "You Ain't Nuthin' but an Egghead."

A new installment has been published nearly every week since. I've tried mightily to let Elvis rest in peace—or shop undisturbed at my local Wal-Mart, if that's really where he is—and yet he's still spotted in *The Wolf Files*. I, too, am an egghead Elvis lover, and he, after all, is the Patron Saint of Weird News.

This work would not have been possible if not for Andra Varin, who painstakingly translated *The Wolf Files* into English after mastering the author's native language of gobbledygook. She is a graceful editor and a good friend.

For the last three years, Zach Young provided the art and original illustration for this work. His efforts are not included here, but they've been an inspiration.

As forces in the newsroom, Randy Stearns, Kristie Kiernan, and Scott McKenzie played an invaluable role in keeping *The Wolf Files* afloat and compensating for organizational and mental skills that I was either born without or lost through youthful indiscretions.

Steve Jones, general manager of ABC News Radio, proposed this book and played a huge role in making it a reality.

My thanks also to Bernard Gershon, ABCNEWS.com's general manager, for supporting and guiding this project.

I'm grateful to The Globe Pequot Press, and Mary Norris in particular, for this compilation.

This book is a sampling of some 250 installments of *The Wolf Files* on ABCNEWS.com. Many have been edited or abridged. I've tried to preserve as many as possible in the original form. Books, journals, and other materials mentioned in these columns are available on the Internet.

The Wolf Files regularly appears on ABC News Radio thanks to Antonia Marrero and Kathy Healy. I'm especially grateful to Ted Wygant and Ed Baxter of KGO (San Francisco), Brad Weelis of DARS (Satellite), Dave Durian of WBAL (Baltimore), Jeff Bell and Chris Lane of KFBK (Sacramento), Jim Scott of WLW (Cincinnati), Jimmy Barret of WRVA (Richmond), Dean Richards of WGN (Chicago), Joey Reynolds of WOR (New York), Charles Adler of CJOB (Winnipeg), and Bob Conners of WTVN (Columbus).

I wish to thank *Us* magazine for letting me give the likes of Jennifer Lopez, Britney Spears, and Sarah Jessica Parker a dressing down, as a member of the Fashion Police.

I must also thank my sisters Allison, Pamela, and Valerie, as well as my nine nieces and nephews, who, based on their intimate knowledge of my apparel, take my work as a fashion critic as a sign of the apocalypse.

I also wish to thank other colleagues and former colleagues and friends. They include: Bob Aglow, Alyson Aleman, Pam Ardizzone, Helen Benedict, Ana Benshoff, David Blaustein, Beau Brendler, Nancy Chandross, Carin Castillo, Bill Diehl, Andrea Dresdale, Gordon Donovan, Stefan Fleischer, Peter Fritsch, Andrew Galarneau, Brian Hartman, Chris Harder, Spencer Krull, Scott Lewis, Doug Levere, Joe Mancini, Craig Matters, Helen Mond, J. Jennings Moss, Marilla Ochis, Heidi Oringer, James Perez, Bruce Porter, Ed Mazza, Valerie Reiss, Rory Rosegarten, Betsy Schorr, Mark Schechner, Joel Siegel, Dave Tillett, Mike Warren, Barry Weintraub . . . and the Scrubbies.

Above all, I'm grateful to my mom and dad, who taught me how to laugh at myself and at the world.

Introduction

God hates me. I've outraged Bozo the Clown. And, as if I needed one more personal reference, Adolf Hittler says I'm a nice guy.

In my line of work, these things are occupational hazards. You chase weird news at your own risk. You become what you pursue—strange.

Writing *The Wolf Files* has been a singular odyssey. The Hittler I encountered was a 61-year-old retired bus driver who was named before that other Hitler (who lacked the extra "T") became infamous. Hittler said he deplored the Nazis, but didn't want to insult his parents by changing his name—a decision resulting in a lifetime of sniggers from neighbors, coworkers, and hotel clerks.

I've explored modern mummification. I spoke with one man who plans to have his cremated remains crushed into a diamond and fitted into a necklace for his wife. I also developed a chatty friendship with the last descendant of the European noble we know as Count Dracula.

Dracula, as he likes to be called, embraces his legacy and as a renowned bloodsucker, harbors political aspirations and volunteers for the Red Cross. Rest assured, he wants your blood for a very good reason.

Legendary "Gonzo" journalist Hunter S. Thompson has often said, "When the going gets weird, the weird turn pro," and I often question whether this applies to me or to the people I've written about. I sometimes suspect my continued employment at ABCNEWS.com is based on being a convenient place for other reporters to forward crank calls.

I'm also reminded of words of Kurt Vonnegut Jr., who noted, "We are what we pretend to be. So we must be very careful what we pretend."

All I can say is that these things really happened: One day the NHL lent the Stanley Cup to me and let me parade it through Central Park as a social experiment.

Another time, I got to sit in a synagogue with Michael Jackson, to witness his first experience with Judaism. I noted in a 1999 installment of *The Wolf Files* that the King of Pop had the whitest skin in temple—and he loves bagels.

Other experiences have been a mixed blessing. John Wayne Bobbitt called one Saturday night to brag about the cosmetic surgical enhancements on his one claim to fame.

Your God is probably not my God—a sixty-year-old out-of-work radio personality who was born Terrill Clark Williams and legally changed his name in 1981. The striking new sobriquet failed to inspire a following, even when he flashed his California driver's license and American Express card, both of which bear the name G-O-D.

I earned God's wrath after he announced he was planning to sue the Los Angeles Times for taking his name in vain. After he admitted that it was all a ploy to get some attention, I documented the incident in a January 2000 edition of The Wolf Files: "God's PR Scheme."

God then proclaimed he was suing me. For weeks, he called relentlessly. No lawsuit emerged, and he eventually let the matter drop. God only knows what he's doing now.

My dealings with Bozo were no laughing matter. When I first spoke to the man claiming to be TV's most famous clown, aka Larry Harmon, he told me he regretted that he didn't become a doctor. A year later I found that Harmon was indeed a bozo, but certainly not the original Bozo—and you should never clown with history.

Harmon had a disturbing practice, on occasion, of neglecting to credit Pinto Colvig, the clown who first appeared as Bozo on records and TV. Harmon's status at Milwaukee's International Clown Hall of Fame has subsequently been downgraded.

No matter how strange the story, I try to deal fairly with every subject in this book, yet still go for the laugh. It's sometimes hard to think what place offbeat stories have in a newsroom, yet nearly every news organization, including the Associated Press and Reuters, devotes a regular feature to weird news.

At their best, these stories somehow throw light on the world we're living in. I've tried to distinguish The Wolf Files by avoiding stories based on botched crimes and quirky accidents—to avoid poking fun at violence or suffering.

Of course, I make exceptions for shameless self-promoters who have turned their lives into punch lines. Hence, the occasional calls from the porn-star-turned-standup-comic-turned-sideshow-attraction better known as John Wayne Bobbitt.

As for my personal journey in the wide world of weird, it's up to the readers to decide on its merits. Let me assure you that I'm having significantly more fun than Bobbitt, and it comes at a fraction of the pain.

Fallen
Stars

And the Loser Is . . .
Oscar Goofs, Gaffes, and Blunders

MARCH 2002

The glitter, the glamour . . . and the chance to see the high and mighty fall on their million-dollar, silicone-sculpted butts. Forget who wins Best Actor. Who's this year's Oscar Bozo? You can always count on one nominee to walk off with the prize nobody wants.

In 1985 Sally Field set the modern standard for cringing, over-the-top acceptance-speech hysterics when she won Best Actress honors and told a bewildered planet, "I can't deny the fact you like me. Right now . . . You really like me."

The pixielike star isn't Hollywood's only flying nut. In that nanosecond when the envelope is torn open and the world holds its collective breath, you never know which celebrity will melt into a babbling idiot, only to return to his seat wishing that he had stayed home and watched the show on TV, like the rest of us.

No wonder in the early days the Academy Awards were held in private. "There is something embarrassing about all these wealthy people congratulating each other," Cary Grant once said.

All that changed in 1934, when the ceremony became a public spectacle, and tuxedo-clad celebrities began tripping over their own egos. Director Frank Capra was so certain he would win for *Lady for a Day*, he began his backslapping, bear-hugging march to the podium as soon as presenter Will Rogers said, "Come on up and get it, Frank."

"Over here! Over here!" said Capra, when the spotlight was thrown on the other side of the room.

Capra suddenly found the real winner was another Frank—Frank Lloyd—who directed *Cavalcade*. Capra called his return to his seat "the longest, saddest, most shattering walk in my life."

Now it's hard to imagine Oscar Night without an Oscar Bozo. Sure it's morbid to turn public humiliation into a spectator sport. But they're celebrities. That's their job.

So as we get ready to watch Hollywood's annual four-hour love-fest, let's celebrate with these classic Oscar Bozos.

The Wolf Files' Oscar Bozo Awards

The Windbag Award: To Greer Garson. According to Oscar legend, she spent ninety rambling minutes at the podium after winning Best Actress in 1943 for *Mrs. Miniver.* Cooler heads say her speech was closer to seven minutes. Predictably, she began it by saying, "I'm practically unprepared."

Fairy-Tale Disaster Award: To Rob Lowe. In perhaps the most embarrassing Oscar opening, the 1988 organizers scripted a song-and-dance routine between Snow White and Lowe, who was introduced as her "blind date." Disney was so distressed that the company sued.

Oscar D'Amore Award: To Cuba Gooding Jr., who exclaimed "I love you" fourteen times—thanking everyone from God to Tom Cruise—after winning Best Supporting Actor for *Jerry Maguire* in 1997. Even after the orchestra interrupted him, he continued: "Everybody who was involved in this, I love you! I love you! I love you!"

Brevity Is the Soul of Wit Award: To Alfred Hitchcock and Joe Pesci. After winning the Irving Thalberg Memorial Award in 1968 in recognition of his illustrious career, Hitchcock muttered "Thank you," and walked offstage. Twenty-three years later, after winning Best Supporting Actor for his work in *Goodfellas*, Joe Pesci did the same exact thing.

Save It for Therapy Award: To Gwyneth Paltrow. Winning Best Actress in 1999 for *Shakespeare in Love*, she said, "I would not have been able to play this role had I not understood love with a tremendous magnitude."

Nature-Calls Award: To Meryl Streep, who left her just-claimed Oscar for *Kramer vs. Kramer* on the back of a toilet during the 1980 festivities.

The Au Naturel Award: To actor David Niven. In 1974 a streaker ran behind him as he was announcing the Best Picture award. The nudist flashed a peace sign—not to mention the Full Monty—to a shocked audience. Without missing a beat, Niven said the man would always be remembered "for his shortcomings."

Silent Oscar Award: To Hal Roach, who received a special honor in 1991 for bringing Laurel & Hardy and many other classics to the big screen. Billy Crystal introduced him, and the audience gave him a booming ovation. But when everyone sat down, Roach, a centenarian, began speaking without a mike. The audience and TV viewers just stared for several moments, unable to hear him. Crystal quipped, "I think that's fitting since Mr. Roach started in silent film." It was Roach's last public appearance. He died six months later.

Give This Guy Viagra Award: To Roberto Benigni, the 1999 double Oscar winner (Best Actor, Best Foreign Film) for *Life Is Beautiful.* In broken English he proclaimed, "My body is in tumult . . . I would like to be . . . lying down and making love to everybody." He later added, "I am-a so happy, I want to wag-a my tail!"

Hey, Are You Guys against Me? Award: To 1964 presenter Sammy Davis Jr., who was handed an envelope for the wrong award. Representatives from Oscar's counting unit at Price Waterhouse had to rush onstage to stop him from blurting out a mistake. He quipped, "Wait'll the NAACP hears about this."

You Can See Me Now Award: To Barbra Streisand. She and Katharine Hepburn tied for Best Actress in 1969. In the excitement Babs tore her Scaasi bell-bottoms on her way to collect the statue. Then, as her outfit appeared distressingly see-through under the spotlight, she raised her Oscar and said to it, "Hello, gorgeous!"

More Outrageously Dressed than Cher Award: To costume designer Lizzy Gardiner, who wore a gown crafted out of some 200 American Express gold cards (in her name). Perhaps it was a commentary on her film, *The Adventures of Priscilla, Queen of the Desert.* Remarking on the film's $12,000 costume budget, she said backstage, "We absolutely didn't think we would win."

Excessive Sibling Affection Award: To Angelina Jolie, who won a Best Supporting Actress statue in 2000 for *Girl, Interrupted.* When her name was announced, she gave her brother a fulsome smooch with her bee-stung lips. She told the crowd: "I'm in shock. And I'm so in love with my brother right now, he just held me and said he loved me."

Inverted Oscar: To Ronald Reagan. In 1947 he narrated a silent montage of past Oscar winners. Much to Reagan's surprise, the crowd was laughing hysterically as he said, "This picture embodies the glories of our past, the memories of our present, and the inspiration of our future." What he didn't know: The reel was upside down.

Oscar Mayer Wiener Award: To Jack Palance, for dropping to the stage floor and doing one-armed push-ups to celebrate his 1992 Best Supporting Actor award for *City Slickers*.

Oscar Imposter Award: To Marlon Brando, who sent "Sasheen Littlefeather" to the stage to reject his Best Actor award in 1973 for *The Godfather* in protest of Hollywood's treatment of American Indians. Later it was discovered that her real name was Maria Cruz, that she wasn't an Apache, and that in 1970 she had won the Miss American Vampire contest.

Oscar Instigator Award: To Vanessa Redgrave in 1978, for using her acceptance speech for Best Supporting Actress for *Julia* as a diatribe against "Zionist hoodlums." Dozens of police officers had to quell a protest outside the theater. Playwright Paddy Chayefsky, who followed her onstage, quipped, "A simple 'thank you' would have been sufficient."

Must-Have-Been-Bottle-Fed Award: To director Bernardo Bertolucci. Accepting an award for *The Last Emperor* in 1988, he referred to Hollywood as the "Big Nipple."

Titanic Fool Award: To James Cameron. The *Titanic* director copped Leonardo DiCaprio's big line from the film, unabashedly shouting "I'm king of the world!" as he waved his trophy. In a halfhearted attempted to pay some tribute to the real *Titanic* tragedy, he then called for a moment of silence "in remembrance of the 1,500 men, women, and children who died when the great ship went down." Then he abruptly reverted to hyperventilating hysteria and yelled, "Now let's party 'til dawn!"

Big Sister with a Big Mouth Award: To Shirley MacLaine, who presented an award to her brother, Warren Beatty, for *Reds* in 1982, saying: "I want to take this opportunity to say how proud I am of my little brother, my dear, sweet, talented brother. Just imagine what you could accomplish if you tried celibacy." Beatty and his then-girlfriend, Diane Keaton, were not amused.

You Crack Me Up Award: To comedian Marty Feldman, for presenting the 1976 Live Action Short Oscar. Calling the two winning producers to the stage, he threw the statue to the floor, then handed a shard of the award to each one. He said, "It said, 'Made in Hong Kong' on the bottom."

Where Am I Now? Award: To Alice Brady, who won a Best Supporting Actress award for *In Old Chicago* in 1938. Brady wasn't present, but a man walked up and accepted the award on her behalf. After the show neither he nor the Oscar was ever seen again.

Who Am I Now? Award: To Spencer Tracy, who won Best Actor in 1938 for *Captains Courageous*. The inscription on his gold statue read DICK TRACY.

Get This Over With Award: To Sir Laurence Olivier. In 1985 the seventy-eight-year-old Shakespearean forgot to name the Best Picture nominees. He simply opened the envelope and proclaimed, *"Amadeus!"*

Michael Jackson Goes to Temple
King of Pop Takes Lessons in Kosher Sex

OCTOBER 1999

I always knew it would take a force larger than life to get me to go to temple. It wasn't God. It was Michael Jackson.

When the tip came that the King of Pop would be attending services at an Orthodox temple on Manhattan's Upper West Side, I snapped into action. In the world of weird news, this was the pot of gold at the end of the rainbow, and now I was a singing, dancing Munchkin.

My tipster—a stone-hearted PR maven, let's just call her "Madam X"—owed me a big favor. But she laid down the law: I could sit in the pews with Jackson and witness his first Jewish experience. But that's it. No interviews. No photos. No other reporters.

"Don't make me sorry I told you," Madam X said, jerking my leash. "Just observe. If you do anything else, if you disrupt the service, you'll pay."

For many years friends and family had tried to revive my Jewish heritage. But I knew the only thing that could revive my faith was seeing Michael Jackson in temple. I'm bad. I'm bad. I know it. I know it.

I dashed up Broadway, into the Carlebach Shul, and there he was—in a black fedora, dark sunglasses, a red silk shirt and iridescent tie—praying among 150 of New York's most religious Jews.

The unnatural red glow of Jackson's lips made my pulse race. It was just like MTV, only he was standing amid a sea of bearded men in yarmulkes as they prayed in Hebrew. Strangely, Jackson was both the only African American and the whitest man in temple.

As the rabbis chanted, the King of Pop mouthed amen at all the right moments, almost tearfully. Walt Disney would have been proud. The most plastic man alive looked so lifelike. I gazed up, searching for answers, and elbowed closer, hoping for an autograph.

Was it really so strange? Jackson lives a fad a minute. It's been reported over the years that he sleeps in an oxygen tent, collects the Elephant Man's bones, and maintains a slavish devotion to plastic surgery. One day he models one-glove fashion, the next it's germ-catching oxygen masks. So why not give Orthodox Judaism a whirl?

Jackson's host was Shmuley Boteach, better known on the daytime TV talk show circuit as "The Kosher Sex Rabbi."

Boteach promised America a plan to end the distressingly high divorce rate. "Have kosher sex," he told gentiles, just like Orthodox Jews—and that's anything but prudish. He promised that the Old Testament provided for the hottest, most volcanic form of lovemaking.

"Rabbis long ago made the female orgasm an obligation incumbent on every Jewish husband," the media-friendly rabbi advised, dispensing advice like a latter-day Dr. Ruth.

Are sex toys okay? Can you call a vibrator kosher? What about masturbation? Yes, said Boteach, as long as it increased intimacy between a husband and wife. He told

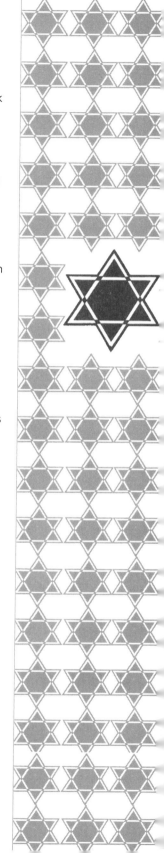

TV viewers that God's in favor of oral sex: "You are supposed to have fun and be passionate. I don't recommend oral sex if that is all you and your spouse do. God wants us to have children," he warned.

But you can't have fun every day. Boteach said the key to kosher sex was not to have sex two weeks every month, and that time must include the woman's menstrual cycle. By abstaining, the libido rebuilds. "I know that is easier said than done," he said. "But this gives love that forbidden quality that keeps it sexy. When that waiting period ends, you explode with joy."

Needless to say the Orthodox rabbi's unorthodox approach got him into enough hot water for a lifetime of matzo ball soup. He stepped down from his post at a synagogue in north London after a leading rabbinical court denounced his book *Kosher Sex*, a mix of Talmudic teachings peppered with quotes from Mae West, Oscar Wilde, Woody Allen, and Zsa Zsa Gabor.

Boteach was comfortable being perceived as a caffeine-driven ham who runs from one interview to the next. "Do I love spreading the word of God and the Talmud? Absolutely," he once told me. "Do I like seeing myself on TV? That's nice, too."

Bringing the controversial Jackson to temple certainly didn't help improve his popularity. Boteach was on the verge of becoming the latest of Jackson's gurus—a rabbi who would justify the Gloved One's strange antics, eventually heading up his Heal the Children charity, even though many thought of Jackson as more of a child feeler than a child healer.

"Michael has a sincere curiosity in Judaism," said Boteach, who came to his house, tutored him in his unique brand of Judaism, and affixed a mezuzah to his home (not the famous Neverland Ranch in California). He said Jackson was familiar with *Kosher Sex*.

"He'd listen to me for hours, and it's not that I'm such a fantastic teacher," Boteach said. "It's that Jackson is so interested in learning."

The Telekinetic Al Fayed Connection

The sex-therapist rabbi sat between Michael and me. On the other side sat the man who introduced the pop star to Boteach—the internationally renowned spoon-bending psychic Uri Geller. The evening was getting even more interesting.

A former Israeli paratrooper, Geller became world famous for his purported telekinetic powers—which he demonstrated over the years by ruining silverware on the same TV shows that would later feature Boteach.

Geller would hold up a spoon, cock his eyebrow, and it seemingly bent, as if he had magical powers. In the late 1960s, Israeli leader Golda Meir mentioned him on a radio show, and he suddenly became an international celebrity.

In one supposed demonstration of his powers, Geller claimed he stopped London's Big Ben from ticking. Another time he claimed to stop a German cable car in midflight. Millions believed in him.

At his high point Geller suggested that he was working with the CIA and Israeli intelligence on psychic espionage programs to keep the old Soviet Union in line. But his career nose-dived after a 1972 *Tonight Show* appearance. Johnny Carson's staff consulted with magician and paranormal investigator James Randi, who said he set up safeguards to prevent Geller from using sleight-of-hand magic. After fumbling for several uncomfortable minutes, Geller claimed he was simply too tired to use his powers. "A lot of magicians do things that Geller does," Randi told me later. "They just don't try to pass themselves off as psychics."

Geller retreated to England, where he kept a lower profile, but still maintained that he has telekinetic powers and could teach others. He even tutored Jackson's friend Mohamad Al Fayed, the fabulously wealthy owner of Harrods department store and father of Princess Diana's late boyfriend, Dodi.

The Jackson-Boteach-Geller triumvirate proved that celebrity—just like politics—makes for strange bedfellows. Geller turned to me at a break in the ceremony to rave about Jackson's psychic power.

"Michael has great concentration and he is a great learner," he said. "I think he has potential."

King of Pop Digs Bagels

As the evening progressed, Geller and Boteach whispered instructions to their pal. Jackson stood when they stood, sat when they sat, and clapped his discolored hands through spiritual folk songs.

The evening was ending, and Jackson's handlers started sidling him through the crowd. Madam X's warning still rang in my ears. But how could I let

go of a rare chance? I just asked the obvious—"Hey, Michael, did you have a good time?"

"This was wonderful," said Jackson in his famously spacey manner. "You people are so kind." I shook his hand gingerly, hoping his nose would not fall from his face.

Outside, Geller and Boteach congratulated each other. They clarified that Jackson never expressed an interest in converting. The entertainer just wanted to experience a Jewish prayer service. Still, the rabbi and the psychic both thought Jackson has the makings of good Jew. The King of Pop is loving, compassionate, and—Boteach said—he "really likes bagels."

Perhaps with lox. Perhaps with cream cheese. Definitely with one sparkling white glove.

Every Man (and Woman) an Elvis
Black, Asian, and 'Extreme' Elvii

SEPTEMBER 2002

Fat, white males are losing their absolute grip over the Elvis impersonation market.

As millions of fans flock to Memphis each year for Elvis Week, gay, black, and Latino clones of the King take their place on Beale Street, where a young Elvis learned to snarl his lips and swivel his hips.

Some traditionalists wring their hands at the mention of "Elvis Herselvis," the lesbian Elvis, who pulls on a Vegas jumpsuit and croons the King's hits with her rockabilly backup band, the Straight White Males.

"When this gay lady sings the Elvis hit 'Girls! Girls! Girls!' she brings connotations to the song that aren't supposed to be there," said Max Wages, a traditionalist Elvis impersonator from Phoenix.

But what would the real Elvis think of his transvestite clone, who calls herself the only Drag King? If he were alive, could he keep his suspicious mind open?

Perhaps. After all, even back in his 1950s heyday, he dyed his hair, wore eye makeup, and drove a pink Cadillac.

"Elvis was the original gender-bender," Herselvis, aka Leigh Crow of San Francisco, once told *The Wolf Files*. "In the 1950s, people were afraid of the way he danced. They thought he was gay. He broke down walls."

In recent years Presley disciples have broken down new walls. Green E—the Environmental Elvis—is singing a new version of "In the Ghetto" called "In the Landfill." El Vez—the Mexican Elvis—has turned the same song into "En El Barrio," a Latino unity hymn. El Vez speaks fondly of his south-of-the-border home, "Graciasland."

Still, Elvis doesn't belong to the people. He belongs to Elvis Presley Enterprises (EPE)—the business arm of a multimillion-dollar estate. If you try to use the King's name or likeness without consent—even on a black velvet painting—they'll sue your butt into Heartbreak Hotel.

For years impersonators were just about the only ones under Graceland's litigious radar. But by September 2002, the Presley estate had seen enough crazy clones in dangerously overstretched leather. The King's lawyers threatened to pull out of any future festival with impersonators. "We've all seen pictures of people who just should not have gone outdoors in outfits like that," said Jack Soden, chief executive officer of EPE.

But Soden overlooked one thing: Everybody wants to be Elvis. It's a force of nature impossible to stop. Elvis may have died a fat, middle-aged man strung out on drugs, but he's still cool.

After an avalanche of angry letters, Soden changed his tune, admitting that most impersonators, no matter how odd, gave "heartfelt" tributes.

So put on your white spangled jumpsuit. Whether you're a fourteen-year-old Hasidic girl or a gay cop, you, too, can proudly embrace your inner-Elvis and compete for prizes in Graceland-sanctioned competitions.

Trent Carlini, who has performed as Elvis all over the world, teaches impersonation classes in Chicago, where blacks, Asians, and women stand shoulder to shoulder with white guys.

"I'll teach anyone," Carlini said. "As long as you remember that Elvis was a king, not a court jester."

Students should be aware that Elvis swivels his hips only during drum fills. The lip curl should be used not as a sneer, but a shy smile. And when you throw a scarf to the ladies in the audience, make sure it's heavy, so it carries beyond the front row.

Carlini might not approve of all of the following impersonators. But here are some of my favorite *Elvii*:

The Elvis Gallery

The Asian Elvis—One thing makes Yoshi Suzuki stand out from hundreds of other Asian Elvis impersonators. His voice is so close to Presley's that Presley's own backup singers, the Jordanaires, recorded a whole album with him. No other latter-day Elvis of any ethnicity can say that. Another testament to Yoshi's uncanny voice: Presley's own hairdresser, Larry Geller, chose Suzuki for the audio version of his book, *If I Can Dream*.

"It started as a joke," Suzuki said. "I did *The Gong Show* as 'The Japanese Elvis,' and I won first prize." Now, it's a career.

Cop Elvis—Talk about commitment: 1 January 2001, a New Zealand policeman chose to turn in his badge rather than stop imitating his hero. Constable Brian Childs of Wellington, the reigning Australasian champion Elvis Presley imper-sonator, resigned from the force after being ordered by police bosses to choose between his blue uniform and his blue suede shoes.

Political Elvis—Bruce Borders might not be the King. But he was mayor of Jasonville, Indiana, a town of 2,500 people. "The competition tried to use Elvis against me," Borders said. "But the voters knew I was serious." He remained an Elvis performer through his eight years in office, beginning in 1988. "I was reelected to one four-year term and still did about seventy gigs a year. After that I quit to concentrate on selling insurance and being Elvis," he said. "I just didn't have the time for politics."

Black Elvis—A perennial finalist in the "Images of Elvis" contest, Robert Washington quickly makes people forget that his complexion is quite different from that of his hero. As one show business manager put it: "Washington really brings out the craft. He brings black and white people together. Can there be a higher compliment?"

Extreme Elvis—What would Elvis be like if he were alive today (and still gaining weight)? A 350-pound San Francisco performance artist, who lets fans rub his Buddha belly, said he has the answer. Presley traditionalists have complained that "Extreme Elvis" has been known to perform a grotesque striptease. "If you see the way Elvis was going with his act, you know what I'm doing is true to my hero," Extreme Elvis said, adding that he celebrated Presley's birthday by taking a cocktail of Zoloft, Viagra, and Geritol.

The Original Elvis Clone
First Presley Impersonator's Tragic End

AUGUST 2001

What happens to a man when he first pulls on Elvis Presley's gold lamé? Phil Ochs hoped to end the Vietnam War.

Historians should note that the very first Elvis impersonator to perform at a major venue was Phil Ochs at Carnegie Hall in 1970—a show that virtually ended a once promising career.

A few years earlier Phil was hailed as the second coming of Bob Dylan. A committed antiwar activist, he was omnipresent at every major antiwar rally, with such underground hits as "I Ain't Marchin' Anymore." At his height Ochs had sold out Carnegie Hall and written "There but for Fortune" for Joan Baez.

But Vietnam took its toll. Ochs had seen too many flag-draped coffins, and he sank into a major depression.

To cheer him up, his brother Michael took him to see Elvis in Las Vegas. "Elvis hadn't performed in years and he was like an uncaged animal that night," Michael recalled. "Phil was blown away with the show and the fans' reaction."

Phil was thunderstruck: What if Presley's power could be harnessed? Elvis forever changed America in the 1950s, when he fused black and white music together and reinvented rock 'n' roll. He still had the people's ear.

"If there's any hope for America, it lies in a revolution," Ochs proclaimed.

"And if there's any hope for a revolution in America, it lies in getting Elvis Presley to become Che Guevara."

Of course even if the real Elvis knew who Che Guevara was, he would have nothing to do with hippies. So, Ochs figured, he'd become Elvis. He'd dress up, play the songs, and mix in his own antiwar message.

The show was a complete disaster. Jeering fans called him a sellout. It was bad enough to be dismissed as a second-rate Dylan, it was even harder to be a fourth-rate Elvis with political aspirations.

Ochs spiraled into depression, alcoholism, and mental illness. He took his own life in 1976, living just long enough to see the war finally end.

Now, a quarter century later, Ochs's foresight demands appreciation. Every race, creed, religion, and sexual orientation has its own Elvis impersonator—an undisputed triumph of multiculturalism.

You might hear of Phil Ochs again soon. Actor and latter-day lefty Sean Penn snapped up the movie rights to his life story.

Naturally Michael Ochs is pleased his brother is still remembered, and he laughingly recalled his last-ditch effort to stop Phil's ill-fated Elvis tribute— teasing him that his pot belly protruded from his shiny suit of gold.

"I told him to think about a diet," he said. "It didn't work."

Still, historians should again credit Phil Ochs—he was a fat Elvis even before Elvis was a fat Elvis.

Everybody's an Ape
Some of Hollywood's Finest Have Worn Monkey Suits

JULY 2001

It's more than the ever-thickening tufts of hair on my back that brought me to this conclusion: Monkeys are Tinseltown star-makers.

It goes back at least as far as *King Kong*. Simians are a box office sensation, and while it may seem like cheap theater, you'd have a tough time count-

ing up all the Oscar-winning actors and familiar faces
who've taken a turn in a monkey suit . . . or alongside
costars who did.

We all remember Charlton Heston on his knees,
overemoting before the ruins of the Statue of Liberty. "Oh
my God! I'm back! I'm home . . . You maniacs!" Heston
cries out in the shocking finale of *Planet of the Apes*. "You
blew it up! Damn you! Damn you all to hell!"

But few recall the scene a few sequels later, with legendary actor/director John Huston as the orangutan law-
giver, preaching to a mixed-species congregation about the
evils of man and nuclear war in *Battle for the Planet of the
Apes*.

The man who gave us such classics as *The Maltese
Falcon* and *The African Queen*, and who tells us:

> *"Beware the beast man, for he is the Devil's
>   pawn.*
> *Alone among God's primates, he kills for sport
>   or lust or greed.*
> *Yea, he will murder his brother to possess his
>   brother's land.*
> *Let him not breed in great numbers,*
> *for he will make a desert of his home and
>   yours.*
> *Shun him, drive him back into his jungle lair,
>   for he is the harbinger of death."*

"It's hard to say why Huston put on the monkey suit,"
said David Hofstede, author of *Planet of the Apes: An
Unofficial Companion*. "According to his biography, he
needed the money for his Friday-night card game. But he
was probably joking around. He probably just had an
affection for *Planet of the Apes*, like so many of us."

The 1967 original spawned four sequels, a TV show, a

Saturday-morning cartoon, and two comic book series, and it paved the way for the sort of toy merchandising of *Star Wars* and other sci-fi film franchises.

In small, large, and sometimes unusual ways, the *Apes* have touched the careers of such show business luminaries as Sal Mineo, Edward G. Robinson, John Landis, and a host of others. With Tim Burton's remake of *Planet of the Apes*, Mark Wahlberg, Helena Bonham Carter, and a new generation of actors join the ape family. Let's just say right now that they're in good company. At least seven Oscar-winning actors, writers, and directors have engaged in monkey business.

Ape Alumni

Claude Akins—A fine veteran of the simian theater. As the evil gorilla General Aldo in *Battle for the Planet of the Apes*, he murdered Roddy McDowall's son. Later, TV audiences loved him as the bumbling Sheriff Elroy P. Lobo in *B.J. and the Bear*. Akins came along late in the *Apes* saga, and apparently saved producers money because he didn't need much gorilla makeup.

Pierre Boulle—The French author who wrote *Monkey Planet*, which eventually became *Planet of the Apes*. He also wrote the book *Bridge on the River Kwai* and won an Oscar for the screenplay.

James Gregory—The rumpled inspector Frank Luger from *Barney Miller* played the diabolical gorilla General Ursus from *Beneath the Planet of the Apes*. Memorable line: "The only good human is a dead human."

Linda Harrison—Contrary to popular opinion, Charlton Heston's cage mate in the first two ape films didn't disappear off the face of the earth. She was last seen in the Julia Roberts/Richard Gere romantic comedy *The Runaway Bride*.

Phil Hartman—The Troy McClure character on *The Simpsons* appears in the musical adaptation *Stop the Planet of the Apes, I Want to Get Off*. Inspired lyric: "I hate every ape I see, From chimpan-A, to chimpan-Z, But you'll never make a monkey out of me."

Charlton Heston—Need a good laugh? Consider Heston's best line from *Planet of the Apes*: "Take your stinking paws off me, you damn dirty ape!" Now picture some of the other actors considered for that role: Marlon Brando, Burt Lancaster, Paul Newman, Jack Lemmon, and Rock Hudson.

Kim Hunter—Hunter, who plays Dr. Zira in three *Ape* movies, won an Oscar for her portrayal of Stella Kowalski in *A Streetcar Named Desire*. Memorable line: To Charlton Heston: "You're so damn ugly."

John Huston—It's unclear why this multiple Oscar-winner donned an orangutan outfit in the last and least of the original *Ape* movies. Around the same time, he acted in Roman Polanski's *Chinatown*, which seemed much more suited to his distinguished career.

Arthur P. Jacobs—The legendary publicist, whose clients included Judy Garland, Marilyn Monroe, and Gregory Peck, produced the *Ape* series. Jacobs also brought another talking-animal movie to the big screen—*Doctor Dolittle* (the Rex Harrison version).

Gordon Jump—He played a slave auctioneer in *Conquest of the Planet of the Apes*. You probably remember him as Mr. Carlson on *WKRP in Cincinnati* and as the Maytag repairman.

John Landis—The man who directed *Animal House* played an animal—a young chimp in *Battle for the Planet of the Apes*. He was a complete unknown at the time.

Mervyn LeRoy—A true Hollywood great, he directed such classics as *Little Caesar* and *Mr. Roberts*. He is also one of the slave apes who take over Century City, California, in the apocalyptic final scene in *Conquest of the Planet of the Apes*.

Roddy McDowall—Everyone remembers him as Cornelius. But in later and lesser *Ape* installments, he played the monkey-messiah Caesar, who rescues ape slaves from oppressive humans. When the film franchise was nearly spent, he led an ape-human army against a band of mutants. Who can forget his battle cry: "Now fight like apes!" Later he emerged on the *Planet of the Apes* TV show as Galen.

Sal Mineo—The 1950s Hollywood heartthrob who played opposite James Dean in *Rebel without a Cause* was a superintelligent chimpanzee astronaut in 1972's *Escape from the Planet of the Apes*. He hated putting on the simian makeup, and his character was killed off quickly. It turned out to be one of Mineo's last performances. He was killed a few years after the movie's release.

Ricardo Montalban—Years before William Shatner would be screaming his character's name in a *Star Trek* movie ("Khaaaaaaaaan!"), Montalban played the humble circus trainer who sided against his species and helped the apes take over. Traitor. He should be banished to a desert island with the ghost of Herve Villechaize.

James Naughton—Yup. Ally McBeal's dad was an astronaut who crash-landed near Ape City in the short-lived TV incarnation of *Planet of the Apes*.

Burt Reynolds—He turned down the role of the Charlton Heston clone, Brent, in the first *Ape* sequel. It went to James Franciscus.

Edward G. Robinson—An Oscar winner for lifetime achievement, he was originally slated to play the orangutan Dr. Zaius. He even can be seen with orange whiskers in a five-minute screen test. But he hated putting on the makeup. The part eventually went to Maurice Evans.

Franklin Schaffner—The director of the original *Apes* flick went on to win an Oscar for *Patton*. He later directed *Papillon* and *The Boys from Brazil*.

Gregory Sierra—The Chicano detective from *Barney Miller* played a gorilla sergeant.

Rod Serling—The creator of *The Twilight Zone* is one of several writers credited for the original film. The shot of Heston falling to his knees before the Statue of Liberty was his most vivid contribution.

Paul Williams—When this 1970s singer-songwriter sang "You and Me Against the World," was he talking about Roddy McDowall? Perhaps. Williams, who played an orangutan adviser to Cornelius, went on to win an Oscar for writing "Evergreen" for *A Star Is Born*.

This list would get really long if it included every distinguished actor outside the *Planet of the Apes* universe who played alongside a simian. Folks such as Clint Eastwood in *Every Which Way but Loose*. And let's not forget, President Ronald Reagan was so popular playing the surrogate father of a chimp in *Bedtime for Bonzo* that he went on to do *Bonzo Goes to College*. You know what they say on *Monkey Planet*, it's human see, human do. Personally I never met a talking ape movie I didn't like.

Munchkin Carousing
Little People Under the Rainbow Make Peace with Judy Garland

J U N E   1 9 9 9

The last of the Munchkins sing Judy Garland's praise, but the Oscar-winning actress was once persona non grata among the little people of Oz. More than six decades after the filming of *The Wizard of Oz*, dwarfs are still shooting down the rumors that the actors who played Munchkins ran amok in their Culver City, California, hotel, whooping it up in wild, drunken sex orgies.

Judy Garland didn't help matters in the mid-1950s when talk show host Jack Paar asked whether the Munchkins were little kids.

"They were little drunks," she said. "They all got smashed every night."

It was a hurtful remark. But former Munchkin Jerry Maren, who welcomed Dorothy to Oz as a member of "The Lollypop Guild," remembers Garland as "an all-American teenager."

"She was nothing but nice to us on the set," says the seventy-nine-year-old, 4-foot, 5-inch actor, who devoted fifty years to show business in a colorful variety of bit parts and odd jobs. He was a baby chimp in *Planet of the Apes*, a confetti-thrower on *The Gong Show*, and Jerry Mathers' stand-in on *Leave It to Beaver*. Maren's best-paying work came in commercials, playing Buster Brown and McDonald's Mayor McCheese.

But it's often hard for Maren's generation of dwarf actors not to be bitter. Show business was one of their few chances at employment, even if that meant embarrassing roles and poor pay.

If Garland made a joke at the Munchkins' expense, it's time to forgive and forget, Maren says—and that's why he and four other Munchkin players came to Garland's hometown of Grand Rapids, Minnesota, to mark the thirtieth anniversary of her passing.

"Judy used to bring candy to the set and give it out," says Margaret Pellegrini, the 4-foot, 3-inch retired actress who played a Sleepy Head.

"She was just sixteen and she was a star, even then. But she was very friendly to us. Even if she made one negative remark, it doesn't change the way I feel."

The Underbelly of Munchkinland

Dwarfs say the filming of *Oz* in the late 1930s was a landmark event. The 124 Munchkin actors, gathered from all corners of the country, marked the largest gathering of little people.

Back then, dwarfs—primarily the children of average-size people—rarely ever met other dwarfs. Many lived in wretched isolation, wrestling with the physical hardships and stigma of their small size. Suddenly the actors who played Munchkins found a world of their own.

"I had never been in a room full of people before when I didn't have to look up," Pellegrini says. "Many marriages resulted from the film."

But Steven Cox's book, *The Munchkins of Oz* put a different spin on the Munchkin gathering. "They had sex orgies in the hotel, and we had to have police on just about every floor," he quotes *Oz* producer Mervyn LeRoy as saying.

In Chevy Chase's 1981 flop *Under the Rainbow*—supposedly inspired by the Munchkins' antics—dwarfs were swinging from chandeliers.

"It's all a bunch of B.S. People see dwarfs and midgets and they get carried away with their stories to make them funny," says Maren. "We couldn't do stuff like that. They were working us dawn till dusk, and we really weren't pulling in enough money for hard-core partying."

Looking back on those days, dwarf actors say they were treated no better than animal acts. Show business impresario Leo "Papa" Singer acted as agent for most of the Munchkins and took a whopping 50 percent commission.

"Years ago, the public conception was small body, small mind," says former Munchkin Meinhardt Raabe, who played the Coroner who pronounces the

Wicked Witch of the East "really most sincerely dead."

Just to show you *The Wizard of Oz* pecking order, Ray Bolger, who played the Scarecrow, pulled down a cool $5,000 a week. Garland made $500 a week. The Munchkins each took home $50 a week. And Toto the dog made $125 a week. "That's a lot of dog biscuits. Toto must have had a good agent," Maren jokes. "That mutt should have been working for scraps."

But the Munchkin gathering changed lives. *Oz* inspired America's most prominent dwarf actor, Billy Barty, to form Little People of America (LPA)—an organization for short people and their families to cope with their condition, meet other dwarfs, and lead happy lives.

Barty himself was already well established when the casting call came for Munchkins, having appeared regularly as Mickey Rooney's little brother in the "Mickey McGuire" comedy short series.

"I didn't work on *Oz*, but the people who did realized that it was a significant gathering," he says.

Since forming LPA in 1957, Barty landed significant roles in *The Day of the Locust, Willow,* and *Foul Play.* But like other actors of short stature, he's had his turn playing elves and leprechauns, even pulling on a monster costumer to play Sigmund in the Saturday-morning kids' show *Sigmund and the Sea Monsters.*

Now a respected old-timer, Barty looks back on a career that's allowed him to work with everyone from Tim Conway to Elvis Presley. He even worked with onetime Munchkin nemesis Judy Garland.

"We were quite friendly, although I think she was a lonely person," Barty says, recalling the years leading up to her fatal overdose on sleeping pills in 1969. "She spoke fondly of working with the Munchkins."

Why, then, did she make that remark about drunken Munchkins?

"Who knows," Barty says. "Like a lot of things about Judy Garland, it is a mystery."

P.S. Barty died December 23, 2000. Mickey Rooney went to his funeral, though he had bypass heart surgery only three weeks earlier. "I can't imagine what my life would have been like without Billy," Rooney told The Wolf Files. *"He was one of the funniest guys I ever worked with, a great friend."*

The Diff'rent Strokes Syndrome
Is Celebrity Child's Play?

It's not easy to be young, rich, and famous. Just ask any child star. "Any kid can screw up. But if you have money and fame and no privacy, you can really, really screw up," says Corey Feldman, who first got noticed in the mid-1980s when Steven Spielberg cast him in *Gremlins* and *The Goonies*.

At age fourteen Feldman vaulted to the upper echelons of child stardom in Rob Reiner's coming-of-age classic, *Stand by Me*. But just three years later, he struggled with addiction and a string of heroin-related charges.

Feldman isn't whining about being a former child star. He's singing about it—on his new album. It's called—you guessed it—*Former Child Actor*. And guess who he was getting to help him promote it: Barry *Brady Bunch* Williams, Danny *Partridge Family* Bonaduce, Todd *Diff'rent Strokes* Bridges, and perennial *Tiger Beat* cover boy Leif Garrett.

Feldman was even hoping they'd get together for an all-former-star version of "We Are the World," to raise money for charity.

"Wouldn't it be like a scene straight out of a David Lynch movie?" says Feldman.

Sadly, it seems as if quite a few child actors are real-life David Lynch movies. Some call it the *Diff'rent Strokes* syndrome, and certainly Gary Coleman, Dana Plato, and Todd Bridges are shining examples of kids who just had a miserable time growing up in public.

Plato had several brushes with the law before she committed suicide in 1999, overdosing on drugs at the age of thirty-four.

Bridges also struggled with chemical dependency and has been arrested several times. In 1990 he was acquitted after being accused of shooting a crack dealer.

Coleman earned an estimated $18 million as the star of that top-rated sit-com. But he was locked in a long legal battle with his parents. When a court finally dissolved the trust they had established, their share was worth $770,000, while Coleman himself had only $220,000.

The 4-foot, 8-inch star reached adulthood alone, working as a $7-an-hour security guard on a movie set. In 1993 he revealed on *Geraldo* that he had twice attempted suicide with sleeping pills.

After a widely publicized fistfight with an autograph-seeking fan, Coleman was fined $400. He failed to come up with the money and soon after declared bankruptcy. A Web site later held an auction of his personal items, selling his size-4½ bowling shoes ($107.50), Afro picks ($61.00), and spatula ($41.00) to keep him financially afloat.

But is Coleman's story typical of child stars, or does it just make for a better story? "If you take the word 'star' out of the equation, you will see that these child stars are just like most other children," said Joal Ryan, author of *Former Child Stars: The Story of America's Least Wanted*.

In 1997, about the same time Coleman was struggling as a security guard, Emmanuel Lewis—another diminutive young actor—was graduating from Clark Atlanta University with a theater-arts degree. Lewis has kept a low profile since *Webster* wrapped in 1987, a far cry from the mid-1980s, when he took the stage at the American Music Awards as Michael Jackson's newest sidekick.

Even the surviving *Diff'rent Strokes* kids seem to be doing better. Bridges is married with a child and preaches clean and sober living. He even played a drug dealer in the TV docudrama *After Diff'rent Strokes: When the Laughter Stopped*—and sold crack to his on-screen persona. Bridges recently took on vintage rapper Vanilla Ice in the Fox special *Celebrity Boxing* and won. He's also been appearing in soap operas.

Coleman has worked occasionally in recent years, voicing cartoons and doing guest spots on TV. He's currently running for governor of California.

One more point about child stars—a lot of what you've heard isn't true. Kirk Cameron, who played Mike on

Growing Pains, didn't die in a bowling accident; Mikey—that kid from the Life cereal commercials—did *not* die from eating Pop Rocks candy and washing it down with Coke; and Susan Olsen—Cindy from *The Brady Bunch*—never starred in a porn movie.

Olsen merely resembles the star of the 1986 X-rated skin flick *Crocodile Blondee*.

"It's just too much fun to believe stuff like that happens," said Richard Roeper, author of *Hollywood Urban Legends*. "And we just want people to fit into a particular mold."

Let's take a look at some child actors who became tabloid stars. Some of them emerged from their troubled, teenage years, just like a lot of kids. A few were really destroyed by fame.

Anissa Jones

Born: March 11, 1958

Highlight: As the pigtailed darling "Buffy" on *Family Affair*, she was the cutest thing on TV for about six years, beginning in 1966.
Low point: Turned to drugs as a teenager. Shuttled between mother and father. Died of an overdose of quaaludes and barbiturates in 1976 at eighteen. Her ashes were cast upon the Pacific Ocean.

Danny Bonaduce

Born: August 13, 1959

Highlight: Played the wisecracking, bass-playing redhead on *The Partridge Family*, one of the most enduring TV hits of the early 1970s.
Low point: Multiple arrests for drug and cocaine possession. Convicted of assaulting and robbing a transvestite prostitute in 1991.
Recently: Bonaduce took on Barry Williams, formerly of *The Brady Bunch*, in the Fox special *Celebrity Boxing*. He wrote an autobiography, *Random Acts of Badness*, last year and hosts a morning drive-time radio show, *The Jamie & Danny Show*, in Los Angeles. He's also a cohost on *The Other Half*, a morning talk show.

Rusty Hamer

Born: February 15, 1947

Highlight: For twelve years he played Danny Thomas's bratty son Rusty on *The Danny Thomas Show* (also known as *Make Room for Daddy*)—one of the longest-running TV shows of its era.

Low point: When the show ended in 1965, Hamer's career fizzled. He left Hollywood and battled with depression and alcoholism. He shot himself in the head and died at age forty-two.

Mackenzie Phillips

Born: November 10, 1959

Highlight: Arrived in 1973 with her role in *American Graffiti*. She then landed a prominent role in the sitcom *One Day at a Time*.

Low point: Arrested in the show's third season for cocaine possession. Left and returned several times. Fell asleep during rehearsals, refused to take drug tests, and reportedly appeared incoherent at points.

Recently: Advocating sobriety, she toured with her father's group, The Mamas and the Papas. She later costarred on the Disney Channel series *So Weird*.

Drew Barrymore

Born: February 22, 1975

Highlight: At age seven she rocketed to fame as Gertie in *E.T. The Extra-Terrestrial*.

Low point: Entered a rehab clinic at the age of thirteen to fight drug and alcohol abuse. In one episode she swiped her mother's credit card and hopped a plane to the West Coast with the intention of continuing on to Hawaii. She was apprehended by private investigators in Los Angeles and led back to rehab in handcuffs. On the road to recovery, she portrayed Amy Fisher in a TV movie.

Recently: She reprised her role in *Charlie's Angels* and will star in an update of the Jane Fonda sci-fi classic *Barbarella*. She's divorced from her second husband, Tom Green.

Adam Rich

Born: October 12, 1968

Highlight: Rich was the cherubic star of ABC's *Eight Is Enough* for four years, beginning in 1977. The show consistently ranked at the top of the ratings chart.

Low point: TV dad Dick Van Patten bailed him out of jail in 1991, after he was arrested for allegedly smashing a pharmacy window to steal drugs. He was arrested soon after for shoplifting and pleaded no contest to both charges. Rich battled alcohol and substance abuse, and in 1996 he participated in a hoax to fake his own death in *Might* magazine. He later said he did it to satirize the media capitalizing on celebrity funerals.

Recently: At age thirty-three he extolled the virtues of his 12-step program. In December 2002, he drove onto a closed portion of Interstate 10 and nearly struck a California Highway Patrol car. He was booked for driving under the influence of an illegal substance.

Macaulay Culkin

Born: August 26, 1980

Highlight: Culkin is considered the most powerful child star since Shirley Temple. His adorable screaming in 1990's *Home Alone* catapulted him to the top of Hollywood. A few years later he was earning $8 million a picture, more than Richard Gere.

Low point: Battling with his parents over his estate—once estimated at more than $50 million—he became a surly teen. As the highest-paid ten-year-old in Hollywood history, he told reporters, "I don't even get an allowance." He sued his father, scrawled graffiti in his New York apartment, and dyed his hair blue. He told *New York* magazine that Michael Jackson's Neverland ranch is "the only place on earth where I feel absolutely, 100 percent comfortable."

Recently: At age twenty-two, Culkin took to the London stage and received good reviews in *Madame Melville*, in which he played a fifteen-year-old American schoolboy in 1960s Paris who's seduced by his thirty-year-old literature teacher. He will soon appear in the independent film *Party Monster*, his first film in nearly a decade.

The Golden Age of Hysterical Prudishness

Network Execs: Don't Call Hitler a 'Bastard'

JUNE 2001

Pregnancy was once a dirty word—at least on TV in the 1950s.

In the age of *Sex and the City* and *The Sopranos*, it's hard to appreciate that it was once too salacious to show a husband and wife in bed together. Networks later had rules that married couples could be shown in the sack, as long as they didn't touch or kiss, and the husband kept one foot on the floor. Even by the 1970s you could drive an SUV down the space separating Mr. and Mrs. Brady in bed.

If you really want to appreciate American media's prudishness, talk to former TV writer Leonard Stern. He has a collection of TV memos, beginning from 1955 when he worked on *The Honeymooners*, a time when networks put the kibosh on anything that even sounded like sex.

"On page 7, Ed Norton says, 'va-va-va-voom,'" a senior producer wrote in one memo. "Before we can give clearance, what does it mean in English?"

Stern remembers *Honeymooners* star Jackie Gleason fighting censors every step of the way. "They even objected to Norton working in the sewer," he said. "They thought that people would be eating while they watched the show and might get grossed out. But Gleason knew that Norton just had to work in the sewer."

TV giants Norman Lear, Larry Gelbart, and Sherwood Schwartz also opened their file cabinets and sent Stern the most idiotic memos they'd received from nervous network executives. Stern published this collection in *A Martian Wouldn't Say That!!*

A few examples: When producer E. Jack Neuman was bringing *Inside the Third Reich* to TV in the early 1980s, Standards and Practices tried to stop him from referring to Hitler as a "bastard."

One memo states, "In the line, 'And that little bastard in the big pants will strut across the stage wagging his mustache,' you must delete the word 'bastard' in regards to Hitler!"

A livid Neuman had to shoot back his own memo, pointing out that Hitler was a textbook bastard.

"Hitler's mother was named Schicklgruber, and he was born out of wedlock," he wrote. "No less than two thousand prominent histories mentioned that fact, and no less than half the world's population . . . regards Hitler as a bastard."

Now, because of Neuman's convictions, we can all call Hitler a bastard on TV.

"TV execs aren't bad people," Stern says. "I think they are sometimes operating in an environment where they have no conception of what creativity is. They think everything will work out if you concentrate on the bottom line."

And that type of mentality truly scares some folks, who fear it promotes ignorance and intolerance. Producer Bruce Johnson says he received this memo on one project: "We cast a black actor as our lead, but the way you've written the dialogue you can't tell that."

Johnson wrote back to the vice president of development that he didn't intend the black character to speak differently from the white characters. The VP wrote back, "Okay, but how will the audience know he's black?"

Undying
Legends

Vampire Politics
A Real Bloodsucker Runs for Office

MAY 2002

Another blood-sucker is running for office. Dracula's last known relative is leading a tax revolt in a small German town—and to some officials, he's become a real pain in the neck. Prince Otto Rudolphe Vlad Dracul and several elected leaders in Schenkendorf are fed up with government bureaucracy. They're threatening to form their own country—The Kingdom of Dracula.

Prince Otto traces his royal roots back to the fifteenth-century Romanian lord Vlad "The Impaler"—whose legendary cruelty inspired Bram Stoker's *Dracula*. But now the prince is promising kinder, gentler vampire politics.

"I want a maximum tax of no more than 20 percent," he tells supporters, urging them to call him "Dracula," if they like.

The Schenkendorf revolt is amusing some German leaders. But Prince Otto's followers have already established a shadow government with Schenkendorf's mayor in charge and Prince Otto serving as the kingdom's official representative.

Fangs Are Tacky

The vampire legend is hardly the making of a political pedigree. Vlad the Impaler earned his nickname with a spike through the belly of countless victims—a form of execution he enjoyed so much, he'd hold lavish outdoor banquets to admire the bloody corpses as he drank wine and feasted.

But the new Dracula isn't scaring anyone. The sixty-one-year-old Prince Otto preys exclusively on tourists, and he went into business only after former Romanian dictator Nicolae Ceausescu confiscated his family heirlooms, forcing him to leave Transylvania.

At first Schenkendorf, a rural town outside Berlin, didn't seem vampire friendly. Prince Otto complained that skinhead gangs were vandalizing his eighteen-acre estate. But when he opened Dracula's Castle, he became a local celebrity.

If you make it there, check out the castle's beer garden, coffin museum, and gift shop, which offers "Blood Red" and a *Songs of Dracula* CD. Tourist dollars have made this Dracula a local hero, and the prince enjoys hamming it up for the kids with a black cape and vampire shtick.

"I don't wear fangs," he says. "That's a little tacky."

A Good Reason to Suck Blood

Prince Otto actually cares about his image, and he's using his name for more than a fast buck. As a Red Cross volunteer, he led a local drive to aid war-torn Bosnia, by hosting "bloodlettings."

"I want your blood," Dracula said in an ad campaign, "for a very good cause."

He'd kick off the events by rising from a coffin, thrilling thousands of donors and resulting in the collection of more than 3,000 liters of blood.

Politics, however, makes mincemeat out of nice guys, and Prince Otto must be prepared for the scrutiny. Already the vampire has at least one skeleton in the closet—he wasn't born to royalty. That's right Dracula fans, Prince Otto isn't a blood relative. He's adopted.

Back in the 1970s, when Prince Otto was a mere commoner who sold antiques, he befriended Katharina Olympia Caradja, a Romanian princess who owned two palaces in Bucharest but had no male heir to inherit her family fortune.

Under Romanian law, a male heir was necessary for the rights of royal inheritance, and Otto was more than happy to be adopted. "I waited until after my parents died [in 1987]," he said. "Then I began a new life."

Now Prince Otto is the last link to old Vlad, a legacy he wants to protect. He's been trying to stop a conglomerate from opening a $30 million "Dracula

Land" amusement park in Romania with carnival rides—claiming the attraction exploits his name. Some Germans are saying that Prince Otto is the one who's exploiting Dracula, calling his political movement a silly ploy to promote his tourist attraction.

But the prince and his followers say they're making a point. Although they may have no chance of winning seccession, they say Germany has to make changes. "We're serious," says Prince Otto. "This Dracula plans to leave a very different legacy."

But just in case they do succeed, Prince Otto is ready. He's printed maroon-colored "Kingdom of Dracula" passports, complete with the Kretzulesco family crest. If you're not thinking of relocating, perhaps you can purchase a facsimile at Dracula's gift shop.

P.S. The Schenkendorf tax revolt subsided. But Prince Otto won an important victory in January 2003 when Western consultants drove a stake through the heart of Romania's plan to build a theme park near Dracula's birthplace.

Modern Mummification
A Pyramid Scheme in the Funeral Business

MAY 1999

Here's good news for anyone who feels too tightly wrapped: A Salt Lake City burial service will mummify your remains for only $60,000 (crypt not included).

Sure, that is a little Tutankhamen. But the latest status symbol might just be a bronze sarcophagus with you inside, pickled and preserved for all eternity. More than 140 people have signed up with the Summun company—and one of them is Dodi Fayed's dad, according to founder Corky Ra.

"If you want a loved one preserved in perfect condition, mummification is a sensible alternative," says Ra, age fifty-four, once known as Claude Nowell. He took the name "Ra" in honor of the Egyptian god of the sun. "We go to the gym, try so hard to look good in life. Why not cherish the body in death, too?"

New Plastic Mummies

Modern mummification borrows heavily from ancient Egyptian techniques. The organs are removed from the body, cleaned, and put back in the body, which is soaked in preservatives for seventy-seven days (Ra consulted the *Book of the Dead* to arrive at that number).

But you wouldn't mistake modern mummies for the one Boris Karloff portrayed in the 1932 horror classic. These days, in the final steps, the body is wrapped in cotton gauze and coated with polyurethane and fiberglass.

Summun can't offer its clients a pyramid, but it does make a customized sarcophagus. "We can build a sarcophagus with an Art Deco look," Ra says. "We can even build a sarcophagus that looks like an Oscar statue."

A Pet Project

In 1980 Ra performed his first mummification on his own cat, which died of feline leukemia. A few years later he would do the same to his Doberman pinscher, "Butch." The pooch is now posed in Ra's office, forever at his master's side as he works, ears perked.

"When I mummified Butch, it made me realize that I'd always be able to appreciate the luster of his fur and his beauty," Ra says. "I knew this would be a business and a service I could offer others."

At a funeral directors' convention in Las Vegas, Ra met Dr. John Chew, head of the mortuary science department at Lynn University in Florida. Chew also had a lifelong interest in mummification, and they were soon in business. But like many start-ups, Chew and Ra haven't yet kicked into high gear. The only humans they've worked on are thirty bodies donated to medical science at Lynn University.

"We're ready to go," Ra says. "But our clients are very young and we must wait."

For now, pets pay the rent. Summun has mummified thirty-seven dogs, cats, and other critters. They charge $1,700 for a parrot and $28,000 for a large dog, such as a 135-pound mastiff. "We've even had inquiries for pet tarantulas," Ra says.

But why would anybody want to be a mummy? The Egyptians believed that their souls would someday return to their bodies. Modern mummies, it seems, are motivated more by earthly desires.

"Let's face it, our bodies are important to us," Ra says. "When you are covered in dirt in a cemetery, you are forgotten." And, the theory goes, the first mummified American, for good or ill, will go down in history.

Modern-day mummies also have one advantage over their ancient counterparts. Today's methods preserve the body's tissues, so that you'll be nice and fresh just in case you want to clone yourself in the future.

Houdini's Annual Reappearing Act
Death's Great Escape

OCTOBER 2001

If there's a way to cheat death, Harry Houdini vowed he'd send a message from the Great Beyond. Each Halloween, loyal followers of the famed magician try once again to summon his spirit. Don't be confused by cheap imitators, folks. If the world-famous Houdini is going to grace us with his ghostly presence, it's going to be at the Official Houdini Séance. It's even trademarked.

"I think the chances to make a connection this time are excellent. We have friends and family of Houdini who will join the séance, and they will create the necessary spiritual vibrations," said Rev. Raymond Fraser, age fifty-six, of Canton, Michigan, in October 2001. "I have spoken to many spirits. I have a 70 percent success rate."

Training at the Spiritualist Correspondence School

Houdini was a famous debunker of table-levitating spiritualists and often exposed them as flimflam artists who used simple parlor tricks to exploit the gullible. But Fraser, who was ordained through a correspondence course by the National Association of Spiritual Churches, says Houdini's low opinion of clairvoyants like himself doesn't matter.

"Folks like that are only nonbelievers when they are alive," he says. "When they are dead they know that we are all spirits who can exist outside the body."

Through séance, Fraser says he's helped dozens of people make contact with dead relatives. The communication can occur in many ways, he says. Sometimes it's a materialization—a milky-white haze of the departed spirit hovers over the room. Sometimes it's a disembodied voice. Sometimes the spirit will speak through the body of a séance participant.

"In 1978 I was a salesman for IBM," Fraser says. "I went to a séance, a frail old woman went into a trance, and the spirit of a man spoke through her body. That's when I knew there was something here."

Yet Fraser admits there are fakes in his field. Beware those who claim they've spoken to famous people. "You hear all these claims that someone made contact with the spirit of Abraham Lincoln," he says. "Those people are full of crap."

Secret Code from the Netherworld

Leave it to the great showman Houdini to die on Halloween. This year (2001) marks the seventy-fifth anniversary of his passing. Perhaps now—with psychics preparing a séance in Detroit—the great escape artist will speak, as he promised his wife he would.

Houdini became obsessed with the occult after his mother died. He consulted with psychics to contact her, a common practice in his day, and found they were employing the same sleight of hand and stage magic that he was using.

The magician made headlines going from town to town, daring psychics to prove their powers onstage. In 1922 Houdini even joined a panel, sponsored by *Scientific*

American, that offered a $2,500 cash prize to any medium able to produce a true physical manifestation. Several mediums came forward, but none could pass the panel's test.

Sir Arthur Conan Doyle, creator of the famous Sherlock Holmes character, was a great admirer of Houdini. But Doyle was also a true believer in the occult, and the two often clashed on the subject. "My opinion of Sir Arthur Conan Doyle is that he is a menace to mankind," Houdini once wrote.

But as an escape artist, Houdini couldn't resist the challenge of coming back from the dead. This is a man who risked being chained to a wooden crate and dumped in New York's East River to thrill audiences.

In his most famous stunt, the water torture cell, he'd hang by his ankles, locked in chains, as he was lowered headfirst into a glass tank. As the clock ticked, the audience could see Houdini's eyes bulge as he seemed to run out of breath. He was, at the time of his death, one of the most famous performers in the world.

But just in case, he and his wife Bess even worked out a special code so that she wouldn't be fooled by a fraud.

'Ten Years Is Enough to Wait for Any Man'

Bess honored his request. For ten years she held séances, the last one in 1936, broadcast over radio from London. She finally stopped, she told friends, because "Ten years is enough to wait for any man."

A protégé of Houdini's brother—a lesser-known escape artist known as "Hardeen"—picked up the tradition. Sidney Radner, now age eighty-two, of Holyoke, Massachusetts, has been holding the séances since 1940.

Many of Houdini's greatest magic props sat in Radner's garage for more than 40 years. "Hardeen gave me some," Radner says. "But I'm a fan. I bought some, too."

Radner wouldn't describe himself as a believer. "We're open-minded. We're honoring a tradition," he says. But some spooky things have happened at these things.

At a séance at Niagara Falls in the 1970s, when a medium called on Houdini to make his presence known, there was suddenly a crashing sound, Radner recalls.

Heads turned to a bookshelf. A flowerpot and a book on Houdini's life had suddenly fallen to the ground. "It was spooky," Radner says. "The book fell open to a page where Houdini asks, 'Do the dead return?'"

But was the dead magician sending that long-awaited signal? Radner says he wasn't convinced.

The Ghost Who Couldn't Spell

A sure hoax came to a New York séance one Halloween in the 1980s, conducted in Houdini's Manhattan residence on 113th Street, when a medium began channeling the spirit of the great escape artist.

Unfortunately, the ghost of Houdini couldn't spell his own brother's name. "You'd expect a little more from the world's most famous magician," Radner said. This year he's bringing turn-of-the-century handcuffs that Houdini used in his act. "If they suddenly open, we'll know something supernatural is happening," he says.

But the bigger test, Radner says, might be getting the cuffs to Detroit. "With all the security concerns," he says, "who knows if they'll let me take them on the airplane. Just getting them there might require a Houdini act."

Trailer-Park Ghosts
Untraditional Spooks

OCTOBER 2002

It's bad enough to be undead. But what if you're damned for all eternity to a dump? You can only hope that when you shuffle off this mortal coil, you'll have a decent place to haunt—a Gothic mansion, with cobwebs, creaky steps, and tastefully placed trapdoors—straight out of *Martha Stewart Living Dead* magazine.

Can't you see the Versace leather-upholstered coffin? And in the kitchen, a stainless-steel cauldron bubbling up a traditional blood daiquiri for the sobbing hag who materializes on the staircase at midnight, pining for the man who stole her heart two centuries ago?

You'll have a squalling black cloud of bats over the roof and, for hours of

family fun, a torture chamber in the dungeon. Is that too much to ask?

Sadly, for many ghosts, it seems that the modest dream of having a house to haunt will never be anything more than a Stephen King novel. Perhaps it's just a sign of the times. Now even ghosts have housing issues.

Today ghosts are being reported in trailer parks, tollbooths, fast-food restaurants, and laundry rooms.

Couch Potatoes of the Damned

"You'll be surprised all the places you'll find a ghost," says Leslie Rule, author of *Coast to Coast Ghosts* (Andrews McMeel)—who documents haunted toy chests, TV studios, and brewpubs.

But let's not be bleeding hearts. Perhaps these ghosts are just underachievers—couch potatoes justifiably damned for all eternity to a McDonald's. Maybe if they had done more with their lives, they'd be doing more with their afterlives.

This Halloween, *The Wolf Files* looks at some nontraditional hauntings.

Unhappy Campers: Is there an unnatural feeling of unrest in your doublewide? Does the simulated-wood paneling sometimes sweat blood . . . even when you're not drinking malt liquor?

When a real tear streams down the face of your velvet portrait of Elvis and his eyes start to move, you know your trailer might be haunted—and not by regular ghosts.

Redneck apparitions are giving a whole new meaning to "white trash," according to Larry Weaver of Durham, North Carolina, who lived in a trailer for seven years and founded trailerghost.com.

A redneck ghost is just like any other, except he drinks more beer, leaves chewing tobacco canisters lying around, and may insist on midnight offerings of Cheetos.

"We know ghosts haunt locations—not just houses, so why not?" says Weaver. He says he started the Web site as a joke, only to find that many trailer-park residents really believe they own a rolling haunted house that's propped up on cement blocks.

"You have a lot of strange accidental deaths in trailer parks—and that's the makings of a haunting. I heard of one guy who was killed when he was hit in the head with a nail gun. That has to make for an unhappy spirit."

The Express-Lane Horseman: Here's the best reason yet to travel with plenty of quarters. Motorists in Richmond, Virginia, are reporting the disembodied spirit of a Native American on horseback chasing them as they cross the east-bound tollbooth on the Pocahontas Parkway.

The ghostly rider whoops and hollers a war cry, and sometimes he carries a torch.

"The reports started in May, as soon as the tollbooth opened, and they've continued," says Sara Cross of the Virginia Department of Transportation.

Is the haunted tollbooth merely a gimmick to get motorists to sign up for electronic tags for express-lane service?

"No," Cross says. "Actually the ghost is so popular, the troopers are warning ghost hunters not to get out of their cars. It's hazardous."

The Cappuccino Choker: What do you do when a sudden, strange chill runs through your coffee shop, and your employees feel unseen fingers around their throats?

Reports of "The Cappuccino Choker" at Java Jive coffeehouse in Centre Hall, Pennsylvania, led to an investigation by local psychics. Rather than move, owner Rose Sweeney decided negotiation was better for business than outright exorcism.

Sweeney decided that "The Cappuccino Choker" needed a PR makeover, so she decided to rename the apparition. He's now known as Harry, and if you feel his presence there late in the evening, it's only because he's had too many refills.

The Phantom Shoe Bandit: In the Puerto Rican countryside, mysterious monsters known as *chupacabra* slaughter goats. In the wilds of Northern California, Bigfoot's mournful cry fills the night.

And in Hanover Township, Indiana, 60 miles southeast of Chicago, a mysterious pile of shoes, sometimes more than a hundred, accumulates on a country road near a cornfield—and no one knows how or why.

"It started six years ago with one woman's boot at the side of the road," says Jim Ambroziak, age fifty-six. "It stood there for a week. Then, mysteriously, a man's boot appeared. Then, we saw children's boots. Then it all went out of control."

Residents now call it "Shoe Corner." It's a mysterious mishmash of footwear—sneakers, highheels, slippers—of all sizes. Some seem brand-new. Some are so old and foul, they can't be donated to charity.

As soon as residents cart off the shoes, more appear. Even the local highway department is a bit confused. Where would a prankster get all these shoes? Nobody in town will admit to it.

"Last week, I saw floppy, red clown shoes," Ambroziak says. "It's very sick and disturbing."

If it is some ghost with a foot fetish, perhaps we can soon explain the real mystery plaguing humanity—missing socks.

An Unhappy Meal: At the McDonald's in Lewiston, New York, you sometimes get a shake, even if you order a coke. It's haunted.

What angered the ghost of William Morgan, who died in 1826? Was it a bad Filet-O-Fish Sandwich? A Not-So-Happy Meal?

In the mid-1970s, the restaurant manager said he saw apparitions and heard strange voices. A terrified cleaning woman claimed a ghostly old man materialized in the pantry and then vanished. After another sighting, a maintenance man quit.

Ghost hunters say Morgan was supposedly murdered long ago after a few run-ins with the Freemasons, although mystery surrounds his death.

The McDonald's is located in Lewiston's Frontier House—where the Masons used to hold meetings. That may be why Morgan's forever ordering takeout. The current manager says everyone in town knows about William Morgan's ghost, but there are fewer sightings now. Maybe he's decided to try Wendy's.

Killer Material: Talk about dying onstage: Many longtime performers at The Comedy Store in Los Angeles are not kidding when they say the nightclub is haunted.

The ghost of Sam Kinison is said to be heard screaming in the night about politics, sex, and religion—much as he did when he was alive. The preacher-turned-shock-comic was on his way to a gig in 1992 when he was killed by a drunken driver.

Even before Kinison, paranormal investigators have been homing in on The Comedy Store as a paranormal hotbed. The club was formerly Ciro's, a 1950s gangster hangout. So many ghosts have been spotted that Comedy Store–owner Mitzi Shore had a team of ghost busters investigate the premises. "For years, we just took it for granted that spirits were hanging out—especially late in the evening," says Argus Hamilton, a longtime performer. "And you could expect Kinison to haunt any comic who even thought of getting married."

Laundry Room Gremlins: If you're a spook, you need a clean white sheet over your head. So you have to do laundry regularly.

With that in mind, don't make a fuss if you're in Eureka Springs, Arkansas, and an unearthly presence is hogging the dryers in the Crescent Hotel laundry room.

In the 1930s cancer patients from across the country came to Eureka Springs for an experimental treatment. But the doctor who promised them a cure turned out to be a quack, and they died miserable deaths.

Now these detergent demons are said to rudely shove people out of the way. They've ripped jewelry from women's necks.

"The laundry room is right across from where the hospital morgue was," says Dana Petty, a ghost researcher. "So it was once an unhappy place."

Don't feel bad for the hotel operators. It's known in the resort industry that thrill-seeking tourists love ghosts. Many inns—such as the Crescent Hotel—even boast that they're haunted, giving a whole new meaning to the "spirit" of capitalism.

At the Lizzie Borden House in Fall River, Massachusetts, for $200 a night, guests can sleep in the very room where Lizzie allegedly took an ax and gave her stepmother forty whacks. Of course, that room is booked solid every Halloween.

Should we pity all those unfortunate hotels that weren't built atop a morgue? Do you need real bloodstains on the carpet to attract Halloween tourists?

The Hard Rock Hotel in Orlando, Florida, is trying to scare up business this Halloween. If you dare, ask for a "guaranteed" haunted room. Blood oozes from the showerhead. Mirrors mysteriously crack in the middle of the night. And whatever you do—don't check under the bed. You may never check out.

These rooms are $585 a night, and that's scary enough for me. Even if the blood is just ketchup.

Ernie and Bert's Forbidden Love
Muppet Pals Deny Sex Rumors

A P R I L   2 0 0 2

Just like Tom Cruise, Muppet stars Ernie and Bert are threatening to sue to prove that they're not gay. Rumors have long dogged those two *Sesame Street* legends. They live together. They sing silly songs. They bicker like husband and wife. One has a curious obsession with his rubber ducky.

Not that there's anything wrong with being a gay Muppet, but the Children's Television Workshop (CTW) insists that it's simply not true—and it's no laughing matter.

Sesame Street has threatened to take legal action against Peter Spears, the director of *Ernest and Bertram*, an eight-minute spoof on hot puppet love. It ends with a distraught Ernest taking his own life.

At Sundance several weeks ago, *Ernest and Bertram* generated some buzz and seemed destined to play at similar film festivals. But with CTW lawyers threatening, Spears says that's in serious jeopardy.

Rumor Mongering and Puppet Love

Spears declined to speak with *The Wolf Files*, hoping to negotiate one more showing of the film. Lawyers for Ernie and Bert would do no more than acknowledge that they've targeted the filmmaker.

But even before this incident, Ernie and Bert have been under constant attack.

In 1993 *TV Guide* received dozens of letters railing against *Sesame Street* for condoning a homosexual relationship. Shortly afterward, a North Carolina preacher began a campaign on his radio show to ban them for their immorality.

In *Hollywood Urban Legends*, critic Richard Roeper traced the rumors of Ernie and Bert's sexuality to *Spy* magazine founder Kurt Anderson.

"Bert and Ernie conduct themselves in the same loving, discreet way that millions of gay men, women, and hand puppets do," Anderson wrote. "They do their jobs well and live a splendidly settled life together in an impeccably decorated cabinet."

Of course, some people didn't get the joke. The situation grew so unpleasant that the Children's Television Workshop had to issue this 1993 press release:

"Bert and Ernie, who've been on *Sesame Street* for 25 years, do not portray a gay couple, and there are no plans for them to do so in the future. They are puppets, not humans. Like all the Muppets created for *Sesame Street*, they were designed to help educate preschoolers. Bert and Ernie are characters who help demonstrate to children that despite their differences, they can be good friends."

Bert's Taliban Connection

Sex rumors aren't Ernie and Bert's only PR crises. Just after the September 11 bombing, Osama bin Laden's supporters marched through the streets of Dhaka, the capital of Bangladesh, waving posters of bin Laden side by side with a sneering Bert—who seemingly lost his little felt head and joined Al Qaeda.

But Bert was still a loyal American puppet. It turns out that bin Laden supporters downloaded a manipulated photo posted on the Internet as a joke.

The "Bert Is Evil" Web site ties the *Sesame Street* legend to the great crimes of the twentieth century, mocking various conspiracy theories—showing pictures of the mysterious, unibrowed Muppet marching with Hitler as a Nazi storm trooper, smoking dope with Charles Manson, and plotting to kill John F. Kennedy.

Site manager Brad Fitzgerald, a college student with apparently lots of time on his hands, offers reports that Bert was a founding member of the Ku Klux Klan. "The Klan's pointed cowl was actually patterned after Bert's head," the site claims.

Fitzgerald's site had actually been closed several months before September 11, after lawyers for the Children's Television Workshop threatened to sue him. However, the twisted pictures of Bert are still floating around the Internet.

"I still think I had the right to do what I did. It was all in fun, just parody," he said. "But I'm just one guy and I can't take on a multimillion-dollar corporation."

Fitzgerald says he's not surprised that the Children's Television Workshop is after a filmmaker who wants to take on Ernie and Bert's sexuality. But he thinks the Muppet should be free to choose his own lifestyle.

"There's no doubt Bert had a role in JFK's assassination," Fitzgerald said. "But I don't think Bert did it because he's gay. He had deeper, darker motivations, and the folks at Sesame Street can't keep this conspiracy covered up forever."

P.S. After Ernest & Bertram was screened at the Sundance Film Festival, it became a word-of-mouth hit. There were, however, no subsequent public screenings. Ernie and Bert are still living together. There are whispers on Sesame Street, but some things are better left unspoken.

Even in Death, Groucho's Still Grouchy
A Marxist Conspiracy

AUGUST 2002

If Groucho Marx didn't have reason to be grouchy in life, he has one in death—he died on the wrong day. Talk about a comic with lousy timing: Groucho passed away just seventy-two hours after Elvis, on August 19, 1977. And every year since, he's been forgotten.

In life Groucho graced the cover of Time twice—once in 1932 and again in 1951. Yet editors pushed his obituary (a few measly lines) to the back of the magazine to make way for Elvis. As Groucho used to say, "If that isn't an insult, I don't know what is."

Now every August, as the media recycles the well-worn details of Presley's life and thousands of fans flock to Graceland for "Elvis Week," you may well ask, what does Groucho get? A rubber chicken? Let's not forget, he's a whole lot more than a greasepaint mustache, a big cigar, and funny glasses. Groucho is one of the most frequently quoted men in American history—and he seldom gets credit.

Although Woody Allen made sure in *Annie Hall* to acknowledge Groucho for his most famous quip, "I'd never belong to a club that would have me as a member," he used that line to explain his own endless chain of failed relationships. After all, how could he like a woman who likes him? A fair point.

But Groucho—a subversive master of the absurd—was aiming much higher when he made this remark. In the roaring '20s, Groucho was finally a star. The Marx Brothers were the toast of Broadway, with the hits *The Cocoanuts* and *Animal Crackers*. After struggling for years in vaudeville, suddenly Paramount Pictures had signed them to a fat contract.

It was then that an exclusive country club in Sands Point, New York, invited Groucho and his family to join. Of course that invitation was withdrawn when they found out Groucho was Jewish. Club officials explained that Jews weren't allowed in the pool.

"What about my son? He's only half Jewish," Groucho said. "Can he go into the water up to his knees?"

Years later another ritzy country club offered Groucho membership—that's when he refused to join any club that would include members like him. Perhaps it was the greatest statement ever made about social climbing.

Marx Not a Communist

Groucho—born forty-five years before the King, in 1890—always knew how to offend anyone worth offending. That brash attitude vaulted him from the stage to the screen with his brothers, and then to radio and TV as a solo act, in a career spanning six decades.

"I've got a good mind to join a club and beat you over the head with it," Groucho tells his rival in *Duck Soup*, voted by the American Film Institute as one of the top-five comedies of all time.

In it, Groucho plays Rufus T. Firefly, the leader of Fredonia, a mythical country on the verge of war, and his brothers Harpo and Chico play spies. Can Groucho negotiate a peace plan? "It's too late," he tells a foreign diplomat. "I've already paid a month's rent on the battlefield."

It's no wonder that *Duck Soup*, released in 1933, became a cult classic in the Vietnam era, or that FBI chief J. Edgar Hoover kept close tabs on Groucho, apparently fearing Americans would be corrupted by Marxism. Interestingly,

Groucho's 186-page FBI dossier, released just a few years ago, revealed that the Communist Party was just one more club that Groucho didn't join. Gee, I wonder why?

Perhaps it didn't help Groucho's reputation at the FBI that he's also credited with this observation: "Military intelligence is a contradiction in terms."

Lydia the Tattooed Stock Broker

So many Americans have lost fortunes on Wall Street. Perhaps they can take comfort that Groucho, too, was cleaned out in the great stock market crash of 1929.

An extremely frugal man, Groucho saved for years but weathered three costly divorces after the Great Depression. As he would say, "I worked myself up from nothing to a state of extreme poverty."

Years later, in the 1950s, he was invited to take a tour of the New York Stock Exchange. Suddenly, while in the observation booth, he grabbed the public address system and began singing "Lydia the Tattooed Lady" and "When Irish Eyes Are Smiling."

Trading stopped as a sergeant at arms tried to wrest control of the microphone.

"Listen, you crooks," Groucho yelled out to the trading floor. "You wiped me out of $250,000 in 1929. For that kind of dough, I'm entitled to sing if I want to."

So for about fifteen minutes, Groucho got his money's worth, singing, dancing, and telling jokes, as the Wall Street stock ticker ran blank and traders cheered.

Equal Opportunity Offender

More often than not, Groucho was a man of inspired nonsense. This is a man who once shot an elephant in his pajamas. How the elephant got in his pajamas, we'll never know.

And this self-educated, voracious reader became one of America's greatest wits. "Outside of a dog, a book is a man's best friend," Groucho said. "Inside of a dog, it's too dark to read."

By the time he was emceeing the game show *You Bet Your Life* on radio and TV, contestants were lining up to subject themselves to Groucho's abuse, and he was an equal opportunity offender.

He once asked a tree surgeon, "Have you ever fallen out of a patient?" He told an author, "It won't do you any good to plug your book on my show, because none of our listeners can read."

Groucho, it seemed, could say anything to anybody, and he couldn't be flattered.

"Mr. Marx, I'd like to thank you for all the joy that you've put into this world," a Catholic priest once said.

"And I'd like to thank you," Groucho replied, "for all the joy you've taken out of this world."

Elvis 'The Stubbed Toe' Presley

Ironically, in the late 1950s, the president of the Elvis Presley Fan Club appeared on *You Bet Your Life*. True to form, Groucho was duly unimpressed and refused to talk to the woman about her hero. Here's what happened:

Groucho: Are you interested in matrimony?

Fan Club President: Indeed I am.

Groucho: Do you have any other interests?

Fan Club President: You haven't mentioned Elvis Presley.

Groucho: I seldom do, unless I stub my toe.

Needless to say, the Elvis Presley Fan Club never had Groucho Marx as a member.

Grouchoisms

Here are some oft-quoted lines attributed to Groucho. Marx fans should note that some of these classics come from movies to which a variety of writers contributed.

"Marriage is a wonderful institution. But who wants to live in an institution?"

"Middle age is when you go to bed at night and hope you feel better in the morning. Old age is when you go to bed at night and hope you wake up in the morning."

"She got her good looks from her father. He's a plastic surgeon."

"I never forget a face, but in your case, I'll make an exception."

"A man is as young as the woman he feels."

"Anyone who says he can see through women is missing a lot."

"Time wounds all heels."

"Now there's a man with an open mind—you can feel the breeze from here!"

"I find television very educating. Every time somebody turns on the set, I go into the other room and read a book."

"Paying alimony is like feeding hay to a dead horse."

"From the moment I picked your book up until I laid it down I convulsed with laughter. Someday I intend reading it."

"When I take a woman out to dinner, I expect her to look at my face. That's the price she has to pay."

"I was married by a judge. I should have asked for a jury."

"I'm sick of these conventional marriages. One man for one woman was good for your grandmother. But who wants to marry your grandmother? Nobody. Not even your grandfather!"

"Those are my principles. If you don't like them I have others."

"I've had a perfectly wonderful evening. But this wasn't it."

Take My Skull, Please
Comic Ends Life as Theater Prop

It's hard to crack a good joke when you're dead. But Del Close always knew how to get the last laugh. Close taught improv at Chicago's Second City to the likes of Mike Myers, Bill Murray, and John Belushi. He died at age sixty-four last month, but he will go on playing the fool for all eternity—as a theater prop.

The comic willed his skull to Chicago's Goodman Theater, to be used in productions of *Hamlet*, as the court jester Yorick, whose skull is unearthed, prompting Shakespeare's famed line, "Alas, poor Yorick! I knew him, Horatio."

Del's skull, missing a few front teeth, was presented to the theater July 3 on a velvet cushion. Alas, poor Del, who suffered from emphysema. He was a showman to the very end.

"Del wasn't fussy," said his personal and professional partner, Charna Halpern. "He wanted his skull used in Hamlet, but he was also willing to have it just lie around in some desert scene. . . . Dell was always willing to take smaller parts."

Welcome to My Pre-Wake

Drug addiction and mental breakdowns thwarted his own chance at stardom, but Close will be remembered for the careers he launched. John Belushi called him "my greatest influence."

"Del was . . . the single most powerful force in improv comedy in America," actor-writer-director Harold Ramis told the Associated Press. "He's the intellectual and moral standard that guides us all in our work. He taught everybody the process."

A jeweler's son from Manhattan, Kansas, Close left college to become a fire-eater with a traveling carnival, turning to comedy in the 1950s, when he worked with a trailblazing improvisational group that featured Mike Nichols and Elaine May.

In the 1960s he emerged as founding member of Second City—matching his onstage discipline with offstage debauchery. He was kicked out of the comedy troop in 1965 and traveled with Ken Kesey's Merry Pranksters before returning to Chicago.

Ramis recalls driving to the psychiatric hospital where Close was living while appearing at Second City.

Belushi reportedly used Close's apartment as one of his drug lairs. It was Belushi's death from a drug overdose that apparently convinced Close to finally give up heroin. But he never became a Boy Scout. He used to joke that his drug use started in the 1950s, when the U.S. Air Force used him as a guinea pig in LSD research.

As the story goes, doctors monitored his rapid eye movements and recorded his dreams. Years later he said he received a letter from the air force, saying: "You still owe us one dream."

He and Halpern founded the Improv Olympic workshop, which honed the stage skills of Myers, Chris Farley, and Andy Dick. Close is credited for developing longform improvisation, which he famously called "Harold."

The pain of the last few months sapped the comic's joy. Confined to a wheelchair and struggling to breathe, he decided to take himself off his respirator, but not before throwing his own "pre-wake" party.

"Bill Murray and I called everyone we knew," Halpern says, gathering Ramis and other close friends, some of the biggest names in comedy. "We had white chocolate martinis, and he had the time of his life."

The next day Close called for some morphine and met his fate. His last words: "I'm tired of always being the funniest one in the room."

Bozo Unmasked
The Controversy Behind TV's Most Famous Clown

JULY 1999

Larry Harmon might be a Bozo. But he certainly isn't the original Bozo.

Larry Harmon owns the rights to Bozo—and many times he's taken credit for creating the most famous clown character and bringing him to TV. But just because you own a Picasso doesn't mean you can claim you've painted the masterpiece.

A *Wolf Files* investigation concludes that Harmon is better described as a marketer who seems to have a habit of sticking a red, floppy Bozo-size shoe in his mouth.

On TV, Bozo told kids, "It's nice to be important, but it's more important to be nice." Maybe it's time for Harmon to listen to his own, internal Bozo.

Clowning with History

Harmon, age seventy-four, denies he ever tried to rewrite clown history, and he refused to be interviewed for this article. But in a written statement, he said he's simply a victim of sloppy news reporting.

"In some of those articles, I have been misquoted and blatantly misrepresented," the statement said. "I cannot be responsible for misquotes or incorrect information printed by the media and routinely recycled over and over a long period of time."

But to believe Harmon, we must also believe the Associated Press, the *New York Times*, the *Los Angeles Times*, and at least six other major newspapers misquoted or misunderstood him, oftentimes repeatedly.

Moreover, Harmon offered no explanation for a 1996 licensing brochure copyrighted by his production company and titled "50 Years of Clowning Around with Bozo." It begins: "Bozo. You can't even say it without smiling. Bozo the Clown, *created by Larry Harmon half a century ago*, has gone from children's recording star to international TV star, joining the American vocabulary along the way."

The Father of Bozo Speaks

To Bozo's true creator, former chairman of Capitol Records, Alan W. Livingston, Harmon's claims have been hurtful, though somewhat amusing. Livingston's distinguished career includes signing Frank Sinatra and the Beatles.

In 1946 Capitol asked Livingston to write and produce a children's record. He delivered *Bozo at the Circus*, the first read-along recording. "Kids, whenever I clap my hands, you turn the page," Bozo would say. It sold more than a million copies, and a clown legend began.

Livingston worked with an artist to develop Bozo's basic look. The clown's name, now a household word, was born during a late-night brainstorming session. Circus folk had long used "bozo" to refer to tramp clowns.

Pinto Colvig—not Larry Harmon—was hired to be the voice of Bozo. He was so successful, he took the act to TV in 1949 on KTTV, channel 11 in Los Angeles.

Capitol copyrighted the clown and turned him into a small franchise. With a call for Bozo in supermarkets, schools, and community events, several Bozos were employed for publicity purposes. Enter Larry Harmon.

"He was an out-of-work actor at the time, and now he is taking credit for my work," Livingston says. "It is such a joke."

Harmon's Bozology

In his letter to *The Wolf Files*, Harmon says that he's always credited Livingston. But a review of newspaper articles attributes elaborate quotes to Harmon about his inspiration to create the great clown.

In an August 29, 1990, edition of the *Chicago Tribune*, Harmon says he based Bozo's name on a famed Gypsy humorist named "Bozolowski."

"What stuck with me was those four letters," he told the paper. "It was a name everyone can pronounce. I tried it in all the languages. It came out the same."

Harmon then went into detail about how he designed the hair and other characteristics: "I knew I wanted sort of a cotton-like fabric that I curled up and brought out to the sides," he was quoted as saying. "Red is one of my favorite colors. Red, white, and blue I love. That's America."

Livingston says he was aware that Harmon was making these statements over the years. "I was angry," he said. "But I had a million things going on at Capitol. Once I moved on from Bozo I figured, why look back. I didn't think anyone would take Harmon's claims seriously."

Capitol closed its TV operations in the early 1950s. Harmon and some partners subsequently bought the rights to Bozo and went from market to market, selling the Bozo concept of a live clown show for kids in the dawn of the TV age.

The Bozo you saw on TV depends on where you grew up. Harmon raised an army of more than 200 Bozos for TV shows in every sizable American city, and as faraway as Thailand, Greece, and Brazil.

The most famous Bozos: Willard Scott in Washington (yes, the NBC *Today* show weatherman), Frank Avruch in Boston (whose show has been syndicated in markets with no local Bozo), and Bob Bell (and, later, Joey D'Auria) in Chicago (one of the longest and most successful kid shows in TV history). Altogether, Bozo shows have logged more than 50,000 hours of recording time, a *Guinness* record.

Harmon never portrayed a TV Bozo for an extended period. He did take some plumb gigs, training with Apollo astronauts at zero gravity, riding a float in the Tournament of Roses parade, and providing the voice of Bozo in cartoons.

The cartoons reportedly once bore a credit line for Livingston as Bozo's creator. That has been deleted over the years. A videocassette in the mid-1990s pictures Harmon in greasepaint with the caption describing him as "The Original Bozo."

Harmon has maintained that he trained his Bozos and their writers. But some people involved in the shows and their families feel he overstated his involvement. In a 1984 magazine article in the *Chicago Tribune*, Harmon admitted that Bell was self-taught. "He was a natural Bozo," Harmon said. "Bob was able to jump into my soul. . . . He was able to reach into my mind and my emotions, because Bozo was me. . . . And Bob has my love for the children, my sensitivity, my understanding."

But, in the same article, Bell, now deceased, described a much cooler relationship with Harmon. "I haven't seen him for years. He never calls. He never comes around," he said. "Even when he's at the station, contracting for his cartoons, he never stops in and says hello. Never."

Sharing credit doesn't seem to be Harmon's strong suit. When Bell was inducted into the International Clown Hall of Fame in 1996, Harmon made it difficult for Bell to attend the ceremony in his Bozo greasepaint and rubber nose—and after a tiff, according to family members, Bell wore a suit, surely a disappointment to fans, who were expecting to see Bozo's famous orange-wing hairdo.

"My father was seventy-four and frail," Bell's daughter Joan said. "It was outrageous."

Hall of Fame Downgrades Harmon

After *The Wolf Files* began its Bozo investigation, the Clown Hall of Fame took down Harmon's Lifetime in Laughter award and changed Harmon's credit on its Web site from Bozo's "creator" to his "franchiser."

"I now regret that we gave him that award," says Bill Lange, founder of the Clown Hall of Fame. "Personally, I think Larry Harmon is a jerk and other clowns deserve some credit for Bozo."

Livingston is now campaigning to have the Hall of Fame induct Colvig, who died of lung cancer in 1967. Colvig lived the quintessential clown's life. As a teenager he ran off and joined a circus, eventually working for Ringling Bros. He also served as the voices of Goofy and Grumpy in Walt Disney cartoons and helped songwriter Frank Churchill write "Who's Afraid of the Big Bad Wolf."

"Pinto did a great job," Livingston said. "He got Bozo's voice down perfectly, and he really knew how to make kids laugh."

Recalling the first *Bozo* show, stage manager Lee Carrau, age seventy-six, described it as a great experiment in the dawn of TV. "It was a live show, two cameras in a small studio, with animals and screaming kids. We never knew what would happen, monkeys jumping around every-where," he says. "Every week was absolute pandemonium."

Carrau remembered Colvig well. "He used to go to the bar after the show in Bozo costume for laughs," he said. "He was a fun, fun guy."

Asked about Harmon, Carrau said, "Never heard of the gent."

P.S. Harmon campaigned in 2001 for a star on the Hollywood Walk of Fame. Some Bozo lovers objected. Harmon was turned down, although no reason was cited.

Fear of Clowns
Coulrophobia Is No Laughing Matter

MAY 2002

What evil lurks behind a greasepaint smile? Who are these orange-haired strangers folding balloons for our kids? What could be worse than when clowns go bad? The fear of clowns is no laughing matter. It's a clinical disorder called coulrophobia—and it destroys the horn-honking, tricycle-riding, throw-a-bucket-of-confetti fun of going to the circus. In some cases it's a lifelong condition.

P. Diddy: I'm No Clown-Phobe

Anyone can be coulrophobic. Sean "P. Diddy" Combs once issued a denial that he had a "no-clown clause" in his contracts, demanding that there be no harlequins at his concerts. Did the rap star ever get pummeled silly with a rubber chicken?

Certainly everyone remembers stories about bad clowns, just as they remember stories about bad scout leaders.

"Perverts and bad people have all sorts of rackets," said Kathryn Keyes-O'Dell, executive director of the International Clown Hall of Fame in Milwaukee. "It's no wonder they dress as clowns. Children trust clowns."

Perhaps the venerable art of clowning is still haunted by the memory of serial killer John Wayne Gacy, who tortured and killed thirty-three young men and boys. In his spare time Gacy strapped on oversized shoes and performed as "Pogo the Clown" at birthday parties.

Nevertheless, there are some 30,000 entertainers in the United States who work at least part-time as clowns, and the vast majority are interested only in throwing custard pies and piling into cars. The sickos are few, and they stand out like a red rubber nose.

Still, as the mother of a twelve-year-old, Keyes-O'Dell can relate to skeptical parents. "If you see a clown at the park or on a street corner folding balloons by himself, don't trust him," she said. "He's a stranger." She also said she wouldn't hire any entertainer without rigorously checking out his references and profes-sional associations.

The Krusty Legacy

Popular culture is awash with the image of the evil clown. For many of us it began with the menacing Joker in *Batman* comics. Then there's the demonic toy clown in the 1982 movie *Poltergeist* that wrapped its candy-colored arms around a little boy to choke him to death.

In *It*, Stephen King gave us the horrifying image of "Pennywise the Clown," who hid in sewers and ate kids. Cult-movie fans point to *Killer Klowns from Outer Space*. And then there's the dark comedy *Shakes the Clown*, staring Bobcat Goldthwait as an alcoholic birthday-party entertainer. The widespread condemnation of the film once prompted Goldthwait to remark, "Clowns have no sense of humor." That image could only be reinforced by the cynical, hardened Krusty on *The Simpsons*.

Clowns were once the most revered of entertainers, and they trace their history to ancient Egypt and China. They were the truth-tellers in Shakespearean theater. There's an old vaudeville joke that even cannibals won't eat clowns . . . because they taste funny. But now they're easy targets.

In Britain, "Coz the Clown" said he was assaulted by a group of ten-year-olds who mangled his magic wand, tore his clothes, and popped his balloons as their parents watched in apparent amusement. He's since started a campaign to stop what he calls "Clown Abuse."

On the corporate front, even the Golden Arches' beloved hamburger huckster has been targeted. In Billings, Montana, a Ronald McDonald statue was stolen from a local restaurant and found the next morning, lynched, hanging from a tree.

To be sure, for every bad clown, there are hundreds of good clowns. *The Wolf Files* has dug around for a few examples of each. The good ones are devoting their lives to entertaining sick kids, reforming juvenile delinquents, even traveling to war-torn countries. The bad ones, well, they speak for themselves.

Good Clown, Bad Clown

GOOD CLOWN: Mr. Yoowho

In lands ravaged by war, "Clowns without Borders" performed in the streets, entertaining child refugees. Moche Cohen, the mime clown known as "Mr. Yoowho," said his group has traveled to such places as Bosnia, Turkey, North Africa, Nepal, and Afghanistan. The group's motto is "No Child without a Smile."

BAD CLOWN: Ouchy the S&M Clown

If you need a little more thrill than a squirt of seltzer down the front of your pants, Ouchy the Clown of San Francisco is at your service. He'll discipline you with a rubber chicken, or worse. In his own defense, he said, "I don't do children's parties." However, "If you're an open-minded adult, I'd like to meet and beat you."

GOOD CLOWN: Dr. Stubbs

Who's the biggest clown on staff at the renowned Memorial Sloan-Kettering Cancer Center? It's Dr. Stubbs, aka Michael Christensen, a cofounder of the Big Apple Circus Clown Care Unit. Cynics assume entertainers pay highly publicized hospital calls scripted by public relations experts. But since 1986 Christensen has spearheaded a program that's placed ninety-three clowns on the clinical staffs of seventeen hospitals around the country. They make about 200,000 bedside calls each year. Some convalescing kids might be a little freaked out by Christensen's hairy-legged, hobo clown. "It happens," he said. "The key is to wait at the door for the child to invite you in. It sometimes helps to let the child watch the clown put on his makeup."

BAD CLOWN: Koko the Killer Clown

Koko the Killer Clown, a featured attraction at a Coney Island sideshow, has spent recent years folding balloons in a soiled prison cap, mumbling caustic remarks to the audience through the smudged greasepaint on his lips. Koko (né Tony Torres) was once a Ringling Bros. and Barnum & Bailey Circus clown. But when he caught his best friend in bed with his wife, he shot the man sixty-nine times. Since Koko was a dwarf—and both men were standing—many of the bullets were lodged in the victim's crotch. Koko tells audiences at his Coney Island performances that he served six years of a fifty-year sentence.

GOOD CLOWN: Dr. Hunter "Patch" Adams

The doctor portrayed by Robin Williams in 1998's *Patch Adams* is sending 30,000 pounds of donated medical gear to Kabul, Afghanistan, along with a troupe of clowns to help hand out the goods.

BAD CLOWN: Coco the Cop

In a purple wig and light-up nose, Coco the Clown busted four hookers in Tampa, Florida. Officer Tim Pasley, posing as Coco, engaged women in conversation until they offered him sex for money, when backup officers would swoop in to make the arrest. You'd think that would make him a good clown, but real clowns have been offended that Officer Pasley played off the bad-clown image, making their jobs harder. Pasley admitted to a local newspaper that the idea for Coco came from a producer for Fox's *COPS* TV show.

GOOD CLOWN: Earnest Desire

Michael Fandal might be a clown in prison, but he's on the right side of the law. This fifty-three-year-old retired New York City policeman works at Horizons, a juvenile detention lock-in facility, as a teacher, showing troubled youths how to have good clowning fun. He started performing while still on the force, sometimes tying balloons to the girdle holster that concealed his pistol. "I could stand on my head without my gun falling out," he said. "The kids never knew. It was hidden under my clown suit."

BAD CLOWN: Insane Clown Posse

Members of the hard-core rap group wear clown makeup while singing about sodomy and promising beatings for their enemies.

GOOD CLOWN: Onionhead

The Universoul Circus endeavors to bring circus entertainment to minority communities. Star Onionhead developed his clowning skills on the mean streets of the Bronx, incorporating rap music, basketball, and traditional clowning skills. "My clown's a 'playa clown,'" he said. "I give respect and I get respect."

BAD CLOWN: Flasher the Clown

Flasher never really exposed himself. Bob Manion, sixty-one, had entertained thousands of parade watchers for more than twenty years in the annual Walnut Festival in Walnut Creek, California. In his act he'd rip open his trench coat to reveal his pet dog sitting inside his pants. There was no flashing of skin. But two years ago he got booted after someone complained to police that clown peekaboo acts were offensive. Festival organizers say Flasher will be invited back this year as long as he changes his act and obeys the rules. So, at least for this bad clown, there's hope.

GOOD CLOWN: Mr. Twister

Even if you don't find clowns the least bit funny, you have to appreciate a guy who runs down the street ahead of meter maids, feeding coins into parking meters in downtown Santa Cruz, California, to help forgetful motorists. The folks watching Mr. Twister's street act sure laughed, but not some city officials. They want local merchants to enjoy a high turnover of shoppers. And, of course, parking tickets are a source of city revenue.

A cop told him his act was illegal, and he was later given a summons. But council members embraced Mr. Twister's plight and, in a show of solidarity, they donned red rubber noses as they voted to repeal the law.

The Party-Hardy Stanley Cup
Hockey's Top Award Gets Around, Even to a Strip Club

MAY 2002

What single object is the world's most famous champagne cup, potato chip dish, and dog-food bowl, while doubling on occasion as a baptismal font? It's the Stanley Cup.

The Stanley Cup has partied longer and harder than Ozzy Osbourne over its 109-year reign as hockey's Holy Grail. In a tradition unique in professional sports, every player on the championship team gets at least twenty-four hours to do virtually whatever he wishes with old Stan.

The cup has visited the White House and Lenin's tomb. It's also visited churches, bars, and strip clubs. It's been to the tops of mountains and the bottoms of pools. It's been strapped to a Harley, a dog sled, and a golf cart. And along the way it's been kissed, hugged, and admired by countless millions. Many, undoubtedly, are not hockey fans. They wait on line for more than an hour simply to enjoy a moment in awe of Stanley's grandeur.

This is what the best in the NHL fight for each year: a 35-pound, 3-foot-high polished silver trophy with five removable rings at the base. Each one lists thirteen teams and their players, which remain on the cup for sixty-four years. The older rings are retired and on display at the Hockey Hall of Fame in Toronto.

'Yes, You Can Sleep with the Stanley Cup'

After the winning team takes their victory lap, the Stanley Cup really begins its travels, clocking more than 100,000 miles a year, raising millions of dollars for charity, and acting as hockey's foremost celebrity.

For Mike Bolt, the thirty-two-year-old keeper of the Stanley Cup, it's the days with the players, who often take the cup out for some rowdy partying, that presents the biggest challenge. Last year Rob Blake of the Colorado Avalanche insisted that the cup be taken to Simcoe, Ontario, where it was perched atop the roof of the combine on his family's farm.

Once a player enjoys his twenty-four hours, the cup's off to a new teammate.

As long as it does no damage to the cup, Bolt doesn't mind. He can't even name all the players who've taken the cup to bed. Mostly though, it's just good-hearted celebration: a trip to a favorite restaurant, an old high school, a retirement home, a night out on the town.

Several players have taken the trophy to a cemetery to show their parents what they've achieved.

"It's really an honor to do my job," Bolt said, after The Wolf Files requested that he bring the sporting world's most famous trophy down to ABCNEWS.com, where we promptly took it on a little visit to nearby Central Park.

Bolt arrived in a blue blazer with the crest of the Hockey Hall of Fame, toting a blue trunk on wheels. Whenever he presents the cup, he wears white gloves, even though the players can get downright personal with Stanley. He stays with the cup twenty-four hours a day, more than two hundred days a year, making sure it comes home safely to the Hockey Hall of Fame.

The full-time job of cup keeper emerged in the mid-1990s, when demand for the cup began pouring in from all over the world.

Before then the Stanley Cup endured all sorts of mishaps and misadventures. Poor old Stanley had been dented, dismantled, submerged in swimming pools, kicked into a canal, and used as a flowerpot and a dog-food bowl.

Some would call it disrespect. But certainly Stanley has emerged from it all as the most famous of all sports trophies. And perhaps one reason why the cup is so popular is the players' personal relationship with it, which shows all manner of human expression.

Here are some of the strangest Stanley Cup tales:

Stanley Cup Misadventures

Baptism—Talk about a great save: In 1996 Colorado Avalanche defenseman Sylvain Lefebvre had his daughter baptized in the cup.

Dog-Food Bowl—In 1980 New York Islander Clark Gillies allowed his dog to eat from it. Ranger Ed Olczyk did Stanley a little more honor when he let 1994 Kentucky Derby winner Go for Gin eat from it.

Out for a Swim—In 1991 Stanley was found at the bottom of Pittsburgh Penguin Mario Lemieux's swimming pool, a feat later duplicated by Avalanche goalkeeper Patrick Roy.

Strip Club Runway—Gentleman that he is, Stanley has been spotted on several occasions at topless joints. When the Edmonton Oilers took the championship in 1987, the cup ended up on the runway with an exotic dancer at the Forum Inn, just across from the Northland Coliseum.

Mark Messier, who has a reputation of getting pretty rowdy with the cup, reportedly let fans drink from it. Stanley graced another strip club when the Rangers took the cup in 1994. After a wild night in New York City, it was the one time the strip club clientele wanted to touch something other than the dancers.

The Flower Vase—In 1906 members of a Montreal club took the cup to a local photographer. Pictures were taken but the cup was forgotten. It wasn't until weeks later that hockey officials found that the photographer's mother was using the cup to plant geraniums, which were decorating the studio window.

Drop-Kicked into a Canal—In 1905 some Ottawa Silver Seven players, reveling in their championship, decided they could punt the cup over the Rideau Canal on the Ottawa River. The water was frozen, and at the time the cup didn't have so many rings around the bottom, so it wasn't much larger than a football. The trophy was recovered the next day on the ice.

Stranded at the Side of the Road—In 1924 some Montreal Canadiens left old Stan for roadkill. They were en route to the team owner's house for a victory party and pulled over to fix a flat tire. They didn't realize until after they arrived that they had left the cup roadside. After a frantic ride back, they found it untouched, a mile and a half from the party site.

Bowling Alley Trophy Case—In the early 1900s a member of the Montreal Wanderers who operated a bowling alley supposedly stuck the cup in a trophy case, heaping gum and cigars in the chalice to impress the clientele and, presumably, to boost sales.

Junk Drawer—When the Ottawa Senators won in 1927, King Clancy supposedly found the Stanley Cup to be a handy holder for junk mail, stray pencils, chewing gum, even cigars.

Meet My Silver Lover—Did they need a new teddy bear? Were they looking for love in all the wrong places? Players regularly take the Stanley Cup to bed for reasons that might best be left unspoken. New York Islander Bryan Trottier once said, "I wanted to wake up and find it right beside me. I didn't want to just dream of this happening." In another act of strange intimacy, Stanley took a shower with Steve Yzerman of the Detroit Red Wings.

A Strange Trip—During a 1962 playoff game between the Canadiens and the Chicago Blackhawks, a fan took the cup out of the Chicago stadium display case, telling police outside that he was merely returning it to Montreal, "where it belonged."

Santa's Driver's License

Forget Flying Reindeer,
Father Christmas Can Drive

DECEMBER 1998

Yes, Virginia, there is a Santa Claus. And I can prove it. He has a driver's license in twenty-nine states. A *Wolf Files* investigation has identified 102 Santas listed in motor vehicle department databases across our great country, from Florida to Alaska.

Some scrooges might tell you that states just create honorary motorist records for Santa, to keep in the holiday spirit. And they are right. This explains the Kris Kringle on 1 Noel Drive in North Pole, Ohio.

But take heart, Virginia, many license holders are living, breathing Santas, who are jolly and plump—and ready to listen to your Christmas wish.

"What's the surprise? I filled out a form, changed my name, and I'm Santa," says the Santa Claus of Oakley, California, who claims his checks and credit cards bear his new legal name.

"You don't want to take my check because it's from Santa? That's your problem," he says. "My credit's good."

Born Robert K. Neilsen Jr., this retired Teamster changed his name in the mid 1970s, when he developed a second career, filling little hearts with joy at $12 an hour (the mall rate).

Billionaire Developers Don't Pay

"I don't do malls anymore. These billionaire developers don't want to pay," he says. "Charity I gladly do for nothing. I love making people happy."

Unlike other states, in California you don't even need to change your name. For a small fee you can register to assume an alias on your driver's license, a practice that affords some comfort to movie stars, even though a special task force this year warned that this could be abused. The Golden State boasts nine Santas, as well as an Easter Bunny in Hollywood. However, you'll have to go to Florida, Nebraska, or Wisconsin to meet the Tooth Fairy.

If you are changing your identity—and toying with becoming another of America's Santas—the pros warn of stiff competition under the mistletoe.

"When I changed my name to Santa Claus, I made sure it was Santa A. Claus," says a retired school bus driver from Catasqua, Pennsylvania. "This way, I could be listed in the phone book in front of any other Santa and rightfully claim my spot as this country's leading Santa."

With two reindeer in his backyard, the Catasqua Santa says he does his best to live up to the Father Christmas image. Mall work helps with the bills, affording him time to work with the handicapped.

"When a smart-aleck little kid calls me a fake," he says, "I can pull out my driver's license or American Express card and I say, 'Do you know me?'"

P.S. Not every "S. Claus" in the phone book is a Santa. Just ask Sandy Claus of Baltimore. "We get calls like this all the time," says her husband, Robert. "But my wife doesn't complain. Her maiden name was Zuromski."

Schlock
Meisters

The Spy Who Gonged Me
The Secret Life of Chuck Barris

JANUARY 2003

Talk about the unknown comic: If you believe Chuck Barris, he had a secret life as a CIA assassin.

Barris is certainly guilty of many offenses. He was a pioneer of reality TV, bringing to life *The Dating Game*, *The Newlywed Game*, and other unscripted programs designed to allow participants to humiliate themselves before a national audience. He then stepped in front of the camera with his most infamous creation, *The Gong Show*.

But while Barris was destroying American culture, was he also executing enemy spies? In *Confessions of a Dangerous Mind*, a 1980 autobiography, the TV legend offers this self-assessment: "My name is Charles Hirsch Barris. I have written pop songs, I have been a television producer. I am responsible for polluting the airwaves with mind-numbing puerile entertainment. In addition, I have murdered thirty-three human beings."

Now George Clooney, in his directorial debut, is bringing the Barris story to the big screen—depicting the funny man as a hit man. The movie stars Clooney, Julia Roberts, Drew Barrymore, and Sam Rockwell as a gong- and gun-wielding Barris.

Clooney isn't sure whether the spy games are all in Barris's head. "I made it a point never to ask Chuck," he says. "I thought if I was going to tell the story, I should do it without knowing the answer. It's a fascinating story either way."

Sure, Barris may have created the CIA gimmick to drum up interest in the book. Not a bad idea, as it's hard to check. The CIA doesn't comment on questions about its personnel. Maybe I'm a special agent, too. Prove I'm not.

However, Barris offers disturbingly detailed accounts in the book. Describing one mission, he writes: "I jammed my automatic into his mouth. The front of the silencer broke teeth as it went in. . . . I pulled the trigger three times. The man's eyes remained surprised while the back of his head splattered against the wall of the church."

It's also a little odd that winners on *The Dating Game* received free trips to "Swingin' West Berlin" and "Beautiful Helsinki." Why not Miami? Barris purportedly chose the vacation destinations and traveled as a chaperon to create a cover for his cloak-and-dagger games.

Would a man really talk about concealing microfilm in his rectum just to create interest in his life story? Then again, remember who we're talking about. When dog acts were on *The Gong Show*, Barris claimed he'd rub Alpo on his suit, because an unscripted snout in the crotch was good for a laugh, every time.

Barris, now age seventy-three, won't elaborate on his supposed spy past, even as he promotes the movie. All he says is, "I can't."

He can't? Why not? Is it too painful? Is the government putting a gag on him? He leaves that to our imagination. That's Chuckie Baby, as the world once knew him, selling the show. Truth or fiction, you decide.

Chuck might not be a spy, but he has made some lasting contributions—and he has done some good in the world. *The Dating Game* brought the swingin' sexual revolution to TV. Back in 1965, TV shows didn't even acknowledge that husbands and wives slept in the same bed. But with *The Dating Game*, suddenly men and women were engaging in frisky over-the-top dialogue:

Bachelorette: Bachelor No. 3, make up a poem for me.

Bachelor No. 3: Dollar for dollar, and ounce for ounce, I'll give you pleasure cause I'm big where it counts.

The Newlywed Game, started a year later, allowed TV to acknowledge that, indeed, there was sex after marriage.

Host: What household chore will your wife say you do exactly the way you make whoopee?

Husband: Wash the dishes.

Host: Your wife said, "Take out the garbage."

An Unusual Place for Whoopee

From the very start, the contestants needed no prodding to talk dirty. "The second week's shows were more horrendous than the first," Barris said. "Angelic little girls and seemingly benign gentlemen were metamorphosing into garbage pails."

The most salacious *Newlywed Game* moment has long been considered an Urban Legend, appropriately titled, "Where's the most unusual place you've made whoopee?"

As the story goes, in 1977 host Bob Eubanks put that question to a couple named Olga and Hank. One might anticipate that she would say something like, "The backseat of a Buick Skylark."

To put it politely, Olga thought "unusual spot" meant a part of her body where she had sexually experimented. And she answered with slang, referring to her posterior.

"No, no," Eubanks said. "What I'm talking about is the weirdest location."

For many years, TV researchers claimed that this story was untrue. Even Eubanks had his doubts. But Clooney unearthed the tape of that controversial broadcast.

Tom Selleck Can't Score

In 1968 a United Airlines trainee, Tom Selleck, failed twice as a bachelor contestant on *The Dating Game*. But don't feel too bad. A casting agent saw him and Twentieth Century Fox signed him to a $35-a-week contract. He grew that *Magnum P.I.* mustache, and the rest is history.

Other future stars who tried to score on TV: Arnold Schwarzenegger, Farrah Fawcett, Steve Martin (before his hair went gray), and Andy Kaufman, who pretended to be a confused foreigner and refused to answer any questions.

Gong Show Rejects

The Gong Show was originally supposed to be a real talent show, with one or two offbeat acts to spice things up.

"All the acts—the winner and losers—would love the show because they would be getting what they wanted more than money," he says. "Exposure."

But Barris quickly changed plans, finding that TV viewers had an endless appetite for kooks who sang dreadful versions of "Feelings."

Here are some *Gong Show* legends:

- Count Banjula, a banjo-playing vampire, who would wear a black cape and fangs, hang upside down, and strum down-home folk songs.
- A 300-pound lady in a bikini singing "Your Cheating Heart."
- A pair of boys dressed as a vagina and umbilical cord singing "You're Having My Baby."
- A woman standing on her head while singing "Life Is a Dream."
- The stripping accountant.

The panel of B-list celebrity judges disposed of each act accordingly, and Barris would come on stage, top hat pulled over his squinty eyes with an obnoxious introduction: "Our next act says he's only semi-professional. That's okay, because we're only quasi-interested."

And if things ever got slow, Barris had regulars: Gene Patton, a fat stage-hand with two left feet, better known as "Gene Gene the Dancing Machine," and Murray Langston, aka "The Unknown Comic."

The Popsicle Twins

The most infamous of all *Gong Show* acts was The Popsicle Twins—a pair of young women in skimpy outfits who sucked on orange Popsicles in a suggestive manner, to the tune of "I'm in the Mood for Love."

Amazingly, the judges didn't break out the gong. Phyllis Diller gave them a "0" and Jamie Farr gave them a "2." But Jaye P. Morgan gave them a perfect "10," adding, "That's the way I started."

Morgan would later get booted for flashing her breasts on the show.

Pee-Wee's Big Embarrassment

Before Paul Reubens became a national sensation as Pee-Wee Herman, he won first prize on *The Gong Show* as part of a duo that did an impression of a dripping water faucet. He later would describe the incident as his most embarrassing moment in show business. Of course that was before he was busted at an X-rated theater by Florida authorities for indecent exposure.

Ironically, when Reubens won his *Gong Show* trophy, along with a check for $512.32, judge Arte Johnson remarked that we'd be "seeing a lot more" of this kid. Perhaps, too much.

Reubens, age fifty, is currently fighting charges in California for allegedly possessing child pornography.

Another famous clown who got his start on *The Gong Show*: Joey D'Auria, better known as Bozo the Clown. D'Auria, who portrayed Bozo on local TV in Chicago, kept his *Gong Show* trophy sandwiched between his two Emmys. He faced the gong as "Dr. Flameo," who held his hand in a fire while singing a frenetic version of "Smoke Gets in Your Eyes."

If some of *The Gong Show* acts seem a lot like David Letterman's Stupid Human Tricks, just guess who was one of the celebrity judges in the show's final days.

P.S. Apparently fed up with Barris and his joke and dagger games, the CIA broke its legendary wall of silence over personnel and issued this statement to ABC News:

"Chuck Barris never worked for the CIA. The notion that he was an assassin for the CIA is utterly ridiculous. Mr. Barris used to host The Gong Show *and . . . he may have spent too much time next to the gong."*

Kramer Keeps Partying
Jerry, Elaine, and George Not Surprised

JUNE 2001

The guy who inspired *Seinfeld's* Kramer character wants to be a whole lot more than the master of his own domain. He's running for mayor of New York.

Before you completely laugh off Kenny Kramer, I have two words for you: Jesse Ventura.

Up to now Kenny Kramer's celebrity was largely based on living next door to *Seinfeld* cocreator Larry David in New York's Hell's Kitchen. It was there that David and Jerry Seinfeld conceived of the blockbuster sitcom—with David basing the Kramer character on the slacker who lived down the hall, who never had a job and was always mooching.

"I've been inspired," Kramer told *The Wolf Files* at Yankee Stadium, where he was spreading the word about his run for office as the Libertarian candidate. "If a wrestler can become governor of Minnesota, why can't I become mayor of New York?"

Indeed, New Yorkers will most certainly have the "Kramer option" when they step into the voting booth. At a state-wide convention in April, Kramer won the Libertarian nod by a 20-to-5 margin, running against "None of the Above."

"I'm glad I pulled it out," says Kramer. "Imagine if I lost and had to call up 'None of the Above' to make a concession speech?"

Living Off Electric Disco Jewelry

The TV Kramer glides through life happily unemployed, forgoing a conventional career for such life goals as building a Jacuzzi in his cluttered Manhattan apartment or writing a coffee table book about coffee tables.

The real Kramer is a fifty-eight-year-old Bronx native who has supported himself as a purveyor of glow-in-the-dark disco jewelry and as a voice-over artist for X-rated CD-ROMs, among other things.

"That electric jewelry lasted years after disco died. I built a little nest egg there," Kramer says. "Unlike the TV Kramer, my harebrained schemes work."

When *Seinfeld* came along, Kramer had the presence of mind to retain the rights to his name. He didn't make a dime off the show, but he makes a living marketing himself, with books, T-shirts—and a "reality" bus tour through *Seinfeld*'s New York. If you must see the cranky chef better known to TV viewers as "The Soup Nazi," Kramer is your man. So many tourists in New York raved about the *Seinfeld* bus ride, former Mayor Giuliani lent his name to the project, videotaping an official greeting.

'Why Shouldn't I Live Off My Name?'

"Why shouldn't I live off my name? Isn't that the American way?" Kramer says. "I make a good living off this. And I don't work hard," he proudly boasts. "I'm milking it for all it's worth."

But is it enough to become mayor?

With the Yankees frittering away an early six-run lead, fans in the upper deck grew frustrated with the home team and began chanting, "Kray-mer! Kray-mer! Kray-mer!" The would-be mayor nodded approvingly and munched popcorn.

Certainly New Yorkers have seen other celebrities and fringe characters run for office. Al Lewis, better known as "Grandpa" from *The Munsters*, has run for governor on the Green Party ticket. Howard Stern also threw his hat in the ring, on the 1994 Libertarian lineup.

This time, the Libertarians think they're backing the right horse. "We've elected many amateur comedians as mayor of New York," says the party's New York chairman, Richard Cooper. "Why not finally have a professional?"

Kramer's already got more recognition than any of the Democratic challengers. Term limits bar Giuliani from running again.

The Candidate Who Inhaled—Deeply

But what are Kramer's positions? And how do they jibe with the free-market ideal of libertarianism?

The gap isn't as wide as you'd think. Kramer's hippie roots certainly jibe with the Libertarian plan to decriminalize drugs. As you'd imagine, this candidate would never deny inhaling. "In my day I collected enough marijuana seeds to fill a beanbag chair," he says.

These days he's sworn off drugs. "That's a personal decision," he says. "You should have a right to make that decision."

He's pro–abortion rights, anti–death penalty, and supports education vouchers.

But Libertarians, of course, oppose price controls and government intervention. That might be hard for some New Yorkers, who, like Kramer, have rent-stabilized apartments.

Kramer says he pays only about $1,700 for his two-bedroom, two-bathroom apartment. That's a steal in midtown Manhattan, and certainly something he wouldn't enjoy if the Libertarians scrapped the city's Rent Stabilization Law.

On top of it all, Kramer's apartment is the very source of his fame. If not for his proximity to Larry David, he'd be just another unemployed schmuck.

"That's a law that's not in the mayor's hands," says Kramer. "So I'm not going to take a position on it."

And Kramer's slacker reputation might suit the Libertarian ideal. After all, he'll reduce the size of government, if only by not working that hard. In fact a Kramer administration might return New York to its colonial roots, when holding office was a part-time job for gentleman farmers.

"If elected," he says, "the first thing I plan to do is put my feet up on the desk, light up a cigar, and laugh my ass off."

P.S. Republican Michael Bloomberg replaced Giuliani. Kenny Kramer won a disappointing 2,621 votes, significantly less than the Marijuana Reform Party candidate. The Libertarians were disappointed, but Kramer succeeded at what he does best—keeping himself in the news.

Rubber Chicken à la King
America's Foremost Practical Joke Maker

APRIL 2000

What's so funny about a rubber chicken? Gene Rose has no idea—even though it's been his meal ticket for sixty-one years. Oh, there's plastic doggie poop, fake puke, and joy buzzers. But almost nothing tops the good old rubber chicken when it comes to turning a cheap joke into big bucks.

"I've seen it all," says Rose, a seventy-seven-year-old gag monger from Salt Lake City who has a 70,000-square-foot warehouse teeming with whoopee cushions, chattering teeth, Groucho glasses, edible panties, fart whistles, electronic nose pickers, anatomically altered pantyhose for men, fur-lined jock straps, and gag condoms.

In this business, "gross is good," Rose says. And on April Fools' Day, Rose and his family are laughing all the way to the bank.

Rose and his father-in-law started Loftus International as a novelty store in

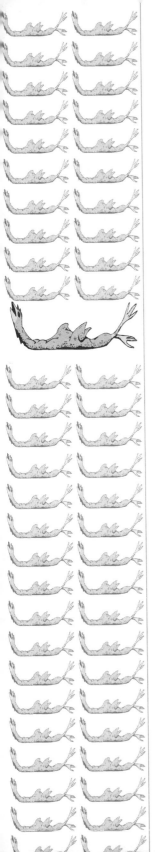

1939. Now a major wholesaler and exporter with forty-seven employees, it's also America's only manufacturer of floppy fowl.

"Salt Lake City is the headquarters of the Mormon Church and the rubber chicken capital of the world," says Rose.

Flight of the Floppy Fowl

These days Rose is slowly turning over the reins of the business to his son Jim and reflecting on a novel life. He doesn't count himself as much of a joker, but he does his best to encourage them, along with magicians, clowns, college freshmen, and coworkers who are just itching to be reprimanded.

"Gag gifts and practical jokes come and go. But the rubber chicken is forever," he says, although he doesn't know why.

Loftus has an inventory of rubber pigs and rubber turkeys, but they're minor hits. A rubber gator is good for some tourist dollars in Miami. Not much more.

"I don't question the magic of the chicken," he says. "As long as it sells, I'm happy with the sweet mystery of it all."

Nobody is quite sure when the first rubber chicken took flight. Its history might go back to the dawn of the rubber age in 1839, several show-business historians say.

Kathryn Keyes-O'Dell of the International Clown Hall of Fame says the legendary Joseph Grimaldi is widely credited with incorporating fake food into his act to delight British audiences—and he is widely hailed for developing the often dubious art of prop humor.

"In the early 1800s, gluttony was very fashionable. It was a sign of affluence," says Keyes-O'Dell. Grimaldi, a white-faced clown, would take the stage with food props stuffed in his pocket to lampoon the upper class.

But Grimaldi was a little before his time, passing away nearly a decade before the advent of rubber—and presumably, the rubber chicken.

"Contemporary clowns can't say why they pull out rubber chickens. It just works," she says. "And, of course, they're easy to carry around."

Baseball, Hot Dogs, and Rubber Chickens

These days, Americans buy the most rubber chickens. Outside of a few crates each year to Australia, Rose says it's a domestic chuckle.

Rose travels the world—largely to international trade shows—to look for the latest in two-bit laughs. "There's a guy in Sweden who wanted to sell me edible napkins," Rose says. "I don't get it. Maybe the joke just doesn't translate into English."

But you never know what works. When Rose saw his first gob of plastic puke, he scoffed. Of course it went over like a stink bomb. And in this line of work, that's a pretty high compliment.

Just like most other industries, Rose and the old guard in the novelty business are being confronted by the computer age. Chattering teeth and joy buzzers are still windup, and a $2.00 whoopee cushion still exists, but today's degenerates are opting for cutting-edge, electronic poo-poo cushions.

Unlike the old-fashioned fart gag, the electronic poo-poo cushion doesn't need to be sat upon. It can be remotely detonated and needs no filling. Maybe to some people it's not the same good old dirty fun. But when Rose tried it out on his wife, "It drove her crazy," he said.

Yes, Loftus is changing. The company had a national sensation on its hands a few years ago with "The Final Word," a pocket-size gizmo that spits out cuss words. "We had a version that wasn't dirty," he says. "It didn't sell as well."

How about an electronic rubber chicken? "Impossible," he says.

What cheap joke will Rose saturate America with next? The next pop culture fad is out there. He'll have to look into his Ouija board or Magic 8 Ball to find out.

Celebrity Garbage Pickers

One Man's Trash, Another Man's Treasure

MARCH 2000

When do you know you're a star? That's easy: when Dumpster divers sell your old socks for big bucks.

A half-eaten piece of Justin Timberlake's French toast, pulled from a radio station trash can, sold on eBay for $1,025.

The winner, nineteen-year-old Kathy Summers of the University of Wisconsin, said she would freeze-dry the toast and place it on her dresser, to prove her devotion to the boy-band legend. With any luck she'll get Timberlake to personally autograph his discarded breakfast. Maybe something like, "Kathy, Never forget the most important meal of the day. Or the maple syrup—J.T."

If you doubt that the garbage of the rich and famous is now collectible, go to eBay and plug in your favorite celebrity's name—along with words like "rare," "collectible," or "one of a kind." You'll see there's a fortune in filth—as long as it's the right kind. To know how this all got started, meet Ward Harrison, the granddaddy of celebrity trash.

Harrison, who liberally describes himself as a "septuagenarian antique dealer," has sifted through Hollywood's most famous dustbins and pulled out such treasures as Tori Spelling's report card, Milton Berle's empty prescription vials, and Jimmy Stewart's Hertz rental-car receipt.

"It's a way of life," Harrison said. "Garbage is a window into the soul, and it is one of the few ways we can really get to know celebrities."

Over the years Harrison has gotten his greasy paws on such gems as Barbra Streisand's cooking utensils, love notes from Joanne Woodward to Paul Newman, Ann Miller's dancing shoes, and Peter Lawford's FBI file.

It all started in 1973, when Harrison came across Cher's trash. "Makeup, birth control, financial records," he said. "It was like I had her whole world in my hands."

Soon he began shuttling from his Utica, Indiana, home to Beverly Hills. In those early days there was no money in it. It was just an obsession, a way to get close to the stars, some of whom didn't mind his obsession with their garbage. He even married actor Wendell Corey's daughter after they met while he was going through her dad's trash, looking for memorabilia from Alfred Hitchcock's *Rear Window.*

But the world has grown more garbage-savvy, and less friendly. "These days shredders eat all the fun," Harrison said.

Jacko's Never-Landfill

Today's biggest stars clamp down on their garbage cans. Michael Jackson even installed a landfill at his Neverland Ranch, according to celebrity bodyguard Don Crutchfield, who has watched over the likes of Frank Sinatra and Marlon Brando, and their refuse.

"It's a bad practice to just throw things away if you really want privacy," Crutchfield said.

One time two guys in a Lincoln Town Car drove down Roseanne's street and pulled over just beyond the house. Crutchfield thought they were burglars, but before he could break out his billy club, they started dumping trash into the trunk.

"They didn't even have the right trash," Crutchfield said. "They got the address wrong."

The moral is to never underestimate star power. If celebrities are now charging for their autographs, why won't they sell their garbage? The answer is, some do.

Lesser luminaries—those who need the dough—take their garbage directly to the people. When Joey Buttafuoco wore out his size 10½, double-E rattle-snake skin boots, he auctioned them off on scandalagency.com for $600.

"If they have them and the people want them, why not?" said Sherri Spillane, a talent agent who specializes in notorious clients. The boots, of course, come with a history. Buttafuoco was supposedly wearing them when he was arrested for soliciting a prostitute on Hollywood's Sunset Strip.

Or there's the red lycra stretch top and pleated skirt that Divine Brown was wearing the night she was arrested with Hugh Grant on Hollywood's Sunset Strip, which fetched more than $5,000.

Garbage Intellectuals: 'It's Not about the Money'

When the stars won't take their garbage to collectors, their families will. "We will negotiate with a celebrity's estate for their personal effects, canceled checks, almost any document with a big name on it is worth something," says Michael Kronick, president of Startifacts, an on-line memorabilia purveyor.

Startifacts is selling a square inch of green shag rug from the jungle room of Elvis Presley's Graceland home for $600. You can rest assured it isn't any old carpet remnant. The Elvis Presley Estate—the folks who say they preserve the King's good image—provides a letter of authenticity.

The commercialization of celebrity trash really irks A. J. Weberman, the man who claims he coined the word "Garbology," which is listed in the new *Encarta* dictionary.

"I go through garbage for derogatory information," he said. "That's it."

Weberman's life in trash began on a September night in 1970 when he and a friend passed Bob Dylan's town house and peeked into his trash, finding an unsent letter to Johnny Cash and other goodies.

Weberman used these questionable finds to write about Dylan's career and became a popular figure in fringe publications as well as a member of the Rock Liberation Front, dedicated to saving rock from commercialization.

According to one report, Weberman once confronted Dylan at a concert with his findings: "Dylan, you've got to live up to your responsibilities as a cultural hero, You're Dylan, man. Dylan, Dylan, Dylan."

Dylan answered: "I'm not a myth to myself, only to others."

Weberman went on to write about the trash of Muhammad Ali, Neil Simon, and Nixon Attorney General John Mitchell, among others, in fringe publications. But the world has changed.

"Garbology is still relevant," Weberman says. "But good garbage is harder to get your hands on."

Confessions of the World's Loudest Snorer
A Proud Man Sleeps His Way to the Top

M A Y   1 9 9 9

If you've been married to the world's loudest snorer for nearly four decades, you're either a saint or you're deaf. Julie Switzer is a little of both. The sixty-one-year-old British homemaker recently celebrated her fortieth anniversary with her husband, Mel, a cab driver whose snoring has been measured at 92.5 decibels—louder than a police siren or revving motorcycle.

Until he found a treatment, flight attendants would ask him not to sleep on planes. In one ten-year period, eight of his neighbors sold their homes. Only his wife stood by his side.

Mel can't really account for what landed him in the *Guinness Book of World Records* fifteen years ago with this dubious distinction. He just tries to laugh it off.

At least he found the perfect match. "My wife and I love each other," he says. "And she is deaf in one ear."

Julie's condition had no connection to her husband's strident snoozing. But even with diminished hearing, she found it hard to sleep—and tough to get up each day to get their two boys off to school. "I just thought most men sound like an electric saw in the bedroom," she says.

Dubious Fame

After two decades of sleeplessness, Julie entered Mel in a local contest, sponsored by a British tabloid in 1984, to find the loudest snoring husband in the United Kingdom. Until then Mel had not realized the scope of his snore.

"He just complained of a dry mouth when he woke up," Julie says.

The contest turned out to be the best thing she ever did. In one brave stroke, Julie turned her husband into an international celebrity of sorts. Suddenly she and Mel were flying to Japan so doctors could measure his snoring on national TV.

"I guess there are better reasons to be famous," Mel said. "But if people are sending you to Tokyo, why fight it?"

Sensing he might be a fraud, the Japanese measured his brain waves before recording his thunderous sleep habits. But doctors essentially certified him a genuine fluke of nature. The folks at *Guinness* were quick to certify Mel, and all the attention brought hundreds of would-be remedies—including one that finally worked.

About four years ago, New York entrepreneur Robert Ross gave Mel a Chinese herbal concoction that he now markets throughout North America as Y-snore.

"I had tried everything," Mel said. "One person even sent me a John McEnroe-type headband with two hooks hanging down to prop open my nostrils."

Y-snore—a mixture of ginger, yams, and a variety of herbs—changed the Switzers' life. Just a few drops in the nose and Mel is silent as a lamb. Finally, a peaceful night for his wife.

But after being an international curiosity, can he really ever be normal again?

"The best part of my new life is that I can go back to my old ways if I just stop taking the drops," Mel said. "You wouldn't believe the demand for me on TV."

"My life really changed for the better," Mel says. "I snore only when I want."

Snoring as Guy Stuff

Ross and the folks at Y-snore hope Mel Switzer will go from being a curiosity to an inspiration. "Snoring is actually a big problem," Ross says. "Two in every five married people suffer from it, and that means a lot of people are losing sleep."

Most snoring conditions are the result of sleep apnea, a condition that arises when the tongue drops back in the throat, causing it to vibrate with each muffled breath. Lady snorers are outnumbered ten to one. As a result of their noisy partners, married women are more often losing sleep—and, presumably, are more fatigued than their male counterparts at work.

Doctors take sleep apnea quite seriously. About 3,000 people die from it every year. It's a condition that affects mostly men. Other forms of snoring, while less lethal, also can cause great discomfort.

A Mayo Clinic study released in early October just confirmed what Julie and many other sleepless wives have been saying for years—while their partners snore away, they are left counting sheep.

Researchers studied ten married couples in which the husband was being checked for obstructive sleep apnea, a disorder in which breathing recurrently stops and starts as someone snores.

When the husbands were fitted with an oxygen mask–like device that stopped snoring and irregular breathing episodes, wives on average got more than one hour's extra sleep.

The clinic considers the plight of snoring spouses serious because the bedroom racket raises blood pressure and strains the cardiovascular system.

Mel says his problem got worse a few years after he was married, when he had an abscess removed from a tooth and a cyst removed from his cheek.

"I can't explain how I am who I am," he says. "But I guess it is nice to be the best at something."

Shortly before her July 4th anniversary, Julie told *The Wolf Files* that she couldn't imagine what her life would be like had her husband not been the world's greatest snorer. "It really allowed us to see the world," she says.

"But given a choice, I would have rather won the lottery."

P.S. That 92.5-decibel level is still a world's record. The Switzers, still happily married, continue to snore their way around the world.

In Praise of a Liar
The Art of the Hoax

J U N E   2 0 0 1

Should we believe Joey Skaggs when he brags about what a good liar he is? Skaggs likes to call himself a hoax artist. Over the past thirty-five years, he's

convinced journalists that he operates a celebrity sperm bank, and a canine bordello, which he called a "cathouse for dogs."

Skaggs once emerged on TV and radio as a would-be Sy Sperling with an outrageous plan to restore the hairline of balding men—follicle transplants from cadavers. Another time he posed as the first man to windsurf from Hawaii to California.

There's a simple point, Skaggs says. Journalists are hopelessly lazy and gullible. "I've never had a hoax that failed," he says—and, like a good journalist, I write down everything he says.

Believe Skaggs when he says he's an artist, not a scammer. "A scammer is trying to do someone out of money," he says. "That happens all the time. I'm using humor to show the system for what it is."

For most of these pranks, Skaggs says he merely sends out a simple press release or makes a few calls. Journalists simply never bothered to verify their facts, he says. By the time the truth comes out, he's once again a multimedia star.

With the Toyota Comedy Festival in New York showing a Skaggs retrospective, here is the hoax artist at work.

Skaggs at Work

Hair Replacement from the Dead

Hair Today Ltd. gleaned a substantial amount of airtime and ink in 1990 as a firm specializing in a cure of baldness through hair transplants from the dead, much the way doctors would transplant a kidney. Skaggs said the ideal recipients would be salesmen or TV news anchors who needed to "look their best" and could afford the $3,500 price tag. The *Boston Globe* was among the news organizations fooled on this one.

The Fat Squad

Skaggs assumed the role of Joe Bones, a former Marine Corps drill sergeant determined to wipe out obesity. He told ABC's *Good Morning America* in 1986 that for "$300 a day plus expenses" his commandos would disarm any dieter who tried to sneak a cookie before bedtime. Host David Hartman later told the press: "We were had, in spades." The *Philadelphia Inquirer* was also duped.

The Miracle Roach Hormone Cure

Remember Kafka's *Metamorphosis*? Skaggs emerged in 1981 as Dr. Josef Gregor, an entomologist who extolled the virtue of consuming cockroach hormones as a cure for colds, acne, anemia, and menstrual cramps. WNBC-TV's *Live at Five* featured an interview with the doctor, who claimed to have graduated from the University of Bogotá in Colombia. Skaggs says no one checked his credentials. The newscasters only seemed to become suspicious when Skaggs played his organization's theme song—"La Cucaracha."

Gypsy Moth Anti-Defamation League

In a 1982 *New York Times* article, Jo-Jo the Gypsy protested the political incorrectness of the term "gypsy moth" at a time when the little critters were devastating trees in the Northeast. Jo-Jo, another Skaggs incarnation, railed against the injustice of associating the pesky moths with Gypsies, a downtrodden minority that has long suffered from discrimination. Jo-Jo suggested the buggers should be called "Hitler Moths." The *New York Post* gleefully reported the esteemed newspaper's mistake, in an article headlined "*Times* falls for the old switcheroo."

Celebrity Sperm Auction

Attention ladies: Interested in "certified and authenticated rock star sperm?" Posing as Giuseppe Scagolli in 1976, Skaggs appealed to women who wanted children with sperm provided by the likes of Bob Dylan, John Lennon, and Jimi Hendrix. Several wire services and *Ms.* magazine picked up the story of a sperm-bank robbery.

The Dog Bordello

Finally a place for frustrated pooches—a cathouse for dogs! Skaggs planted an ad in New York's *Village Voice* newspaper in 1976 that promised "a savory selection of hot bitches" for your sexually deprived mutt, with the warning: "dogs only." Skaggs posed as a dog pimp, promising every Rover satisfaction for only $50. The media lapped it up, and the story hit all the wire services and local cable shows. Even ABC's New York affiliate covered the event.

The point is rather apparent. We ask so much from the news organizations we trust. If a poor artist with few resources can fool the media into believing outrageous lies, what hope do we have against a well-funded, malicious liar?

Professional Pigs
America's Newest Full-Contact Sport: Competitive Eating

JANUARY 2002

Grab a fork. Loosen your belt. And open wide. The fame and fortune of competitive food eating is coming your way. Gluttony is not just a growing health problem. Now it's a sport, complete with a sanctioning body and championship matches all over the world, where fans watch their champions devour hot dogs, pizza, sticks of butter, pickles, matzo balls, and chicken wings, all in mass quantities.

Top eaters from around the world will compete for $25,000 in prizes this February at *The Glutton Bowl*, a two-hour event on Fox Television. This championship comes after more than 3,000 gathered in Coney Island for last year's hot dog–eating contest.

"The sport is really coming into its own," says Richard Shea, president of the International Federation of Competitive Eating (IFOCE), a sanctioning body that organizes events like the Philly Wing Bowl and the Nathan's Famous Hot Dog Eating Contest.

The Burger Meister's Thrills

For folks like Don "Moses" Lerman, the former owner of a day-old bread shop from New York, it's a dream come true. Lerman is the reigning burger meister, having wolfed down 11¼ burgers in ten minutes last year.

"I'll stretch my stomach until it causes internal bleeding," he says. "I do it for the thrill of competition. Some people are good at math. Some people are good at golf. I'm good at eating."

Lerman, age forty-two, says he trains every day to stay in top shape. Like most competitive eaters, he drinks massive amounts of water, more than a gallon at a time, to stretch his stomach. Only rookies think that fasting helps.

"You don't have to be big. You just have to want it," he says. "When you've eaten your twelfth matzo ball in under three minutes, you have to reach deep within yourself to finish number thirteen."

Don't Worry: Size Doesn't Matter

Eating is another one of those activities where boastful men say size doesn't matter. A legend of the eating circuit, Takeru Kobayashi of Japan, weighed in at only 131 pounds last year when he shattered the Nathan's Famous Hot Dog Eating Contest record, devouring fifty dogs in twelve minutes.

In Japan, where food eating is taken very seriously, competitive eaters can earn hundreds of thousands of dollars in prize money. The sport has not evolved that far in America. The winner of the Ben's Kosher Deli's 2002 Matzo Ball Eating Contest, Oleg Zohornitskiy, walked off with a modest $2,500 prize, after eating a record-breaking 16¼ matzo balls in 5 minutes, 25 seconds.

But the matzo ball event was more for charity (and, of course, publicity for Ben's), raising $10,000 for the Interfaith Nutrition Network, an organization that fights famine.

However, the big bucks are out there. *The Glutton Bowl* will offer eating challenges with a $25,000 top prize.

Now, guys like Ed "Cookie" Jarvis, who won a contest last year by inhaling a 17-inch pizza in three minutes, can't get over the recognition he's getting. "In the last year, I've traveled all over the country, and I can't believe how many people have come up to me and said, 'Aren't you that food guy?' "

Some people may not have wanted to stand too close to another contestant, Jed Donahue, after he ate 152 jalapeño peppers in 15 minutes. Still, fame comes in strange ways these days.

The Hot Dog Augusta

The IFOCE has a mandate to keep the sport clean and verify records. "Nobody has ever been hospitalized at one of our events," Shea says. "There's an EMT there, just like a football game."

Shea and his brother got involved as the governing body of food fests fifteen years ago, but the Nathan's contest has been running since 1916. There are now more than 300 registered IFOCE members.

And many of those members are multifaceted. Jarvis and Lerman, for instance, are "cross-eaters" who gorge themselves at many different types of eating contests. The 2002 IFOCE calendar includes events for chicken wings, matzo balls, jalapeño peppers, oysters, burritos, onions, pickles, and hamburgers. But the hot dog contest is still "our Augusta, our big tournament," Shea says.

With the sport now coming into its own, here's a look at some of the prominent "athletes."

Big Names in Gluttony

DONALD "MOSES" LERMAN

The reigning hamburger champ and former matzo ball champ is 5-foot-8 and weighs 185 pounds.

Family Status: Single.

Training: Lerman drinks a gallon of water in 2½ minutes.

Inspiration: "It's the recognition, not the money. It's the pat on the back from friends and family."

Advice: "You don't have to be a big fat slob. I weighed just 145 until I started training for ice cream and french fries. And I'll lose that weight again."

Greatest Moment: "When the press gathered around after the matzo ball contest, it was like a presidential press conference."

Realization of Greatness: "As a kid we'd go to all-you-can-eat hotel restaurants in the Catskills and I'd be the last to leave. No buffet ever made a cent off me."

"KRAZY" KEVIN LIPSITZ

The reigning pickle champ is president of a magazine subscription service on Staten Island. He's 6 feet tall, 42 years old, and weighs 185 pounds.

Records: Lipsitz faced off with New York radio personality Curtis Sliwa for the pickle championship and took the title by consuming 2½ pounds of sour pickles in five minutes.

Family Status: Recently married Lorraine "Lorraineasaurus Rex" Lipsitz. They met at a singles event, and she soon joined him in the competitive-eating circuit. "It was my mother-in-law's worst nightmare," he says.

Training: If Lipsitz eats like a starved animal, it's for good reason. He trains with his two German shepherds, Sabrina and Rascal. "I cook up a family pack of forty hot dogs and we race. . . . We don't eat out of the same bowl."

Advice: "This is like a lot of other sports. It's about training and God-given talent. A lot of the people enter these contests for a free lunch; then they realize they were blessed."

Greatest Moment: "When I picked up my gold-plated pickle for becoming the pickle champ. A lot of people want that trophy."

Realization of Greatness: "When I was ten years old, I could eat ten ears of corn in one sitting."

ED "COOKIE" JARVIS

This pizza, french fry, and ice-cream champ is a thirty-five-year-old real-estate salesman on New York's Long Island. He's 6-foot-6 and weighs 380 pounds.

Achievements: His pizza crown came when he downed an eight-slice pie in three minutes. He earned ice-cream honors in Manhattan by devouring six pounds, fourteen ounces in twelve minutes.

Family Status: Married for four years to wife Elyse. They have a twenty-two-month-old child.

Training: "I drink a gallon and a half of water in under two minutes. The first two gallons go down in a minute and five seconds. The last two cups take a minute. That's when you start to sweat."

Inspiration: "The Food Network."

Greatest Moment: "Just three days after my dad died, I won the french fry title. I dedicated that to my dad."

Wife Says: "She'd like me to lose weight. I want someone to sponsor me like the Subway guy. I want to drop one hundred pounds."

Realization of Greatness: "Coming from a large Italian family, if you didn't eat quick, you wouldn't get seconds."

CHARLES "HUNGRY" HARDY

The 2001 matzo ball champ and the American hot dog champ is a 360-pound, 37-year-old New York City corrections officer.

Records: The hot dog crown came when Hardy downed 23½ dogs in 12 minutes. In last year's matzo ball contest, he tied Jarvis with 13 matzo balls each. In a 1-minute, 25-second "eat-off," Hardy prevailed, swallowing 2½ matzo balls to Jarvis's 1.

Family Status: Married to wife Valerie for seventeen years. They have a daughter and two sons.

Wife Says: "Bring home the bacon!"

Training: "I won't say. Would a magician teach you his tricks?"

Inspiration: "I set a sushi record in Japan and kids there on the street all shout out my name. This sport is international."

Advice: "You have to pick the right food. For me, matzo balls are the hardest. They expand in your stomach. It's like eating five pounds of sponge. Or even cement . . . I won't do ice cream. All that coldness is traumatic on the body."

Realization of Greatness: "I was called by my union in 1998 to enter a hot dog contest on the World Trade Center. I had never done this sort of thing before and I didn't want to make a fool of myself. But my wife said, 'Just think of it as free lunch.' The rest is history."

The Trials of Robo-Bear
Man in Iron Suit Seeks Grizzly Confrontation

DECEMBER 2001

Two events shaped Troy Hurtubise's life: nearly being mauled by a grizzly bear in 1984 and watching the movie *RoboCop* three years later.

Now, the scrap-metal dealer from Ontario is constructing a $100,000 armored suit, constructed from titanium, iron mesh, galvanized steel, and thousands of feet of duct tape.

Call him fearless. Call him stupid. Hurtubise has strapped on his 150-pound contraption and withstood point-blank blasts from a 12-gauge shotgun. He's intentionally fallen from the 150-foot Niagara Falls escarpment. He's been run over by a truck, hit by a moving car, smashed in the shins with a sledgehammer, scorched with flames, and hacked at with chain saws.

But can Hurtubise, age thirty-seven, face the ultimate test—standing paw-to-toe with a grizzly? The largest and most lethal land mammal stands 10 feet tall, weighs 1,500 pounds, and move at speeds of up to 30 miles per hour. We may soon find out.

'I've Waited Fifteen Years for This'

Hurtubise's story was originally told in *Project Grizzly*, a 1996 Canadian National Film Board (NFB) documentary directed by Peter Lynch. It grossed more than $30 million. And *Pulp Fiction* director Quentin Tarantino raved about it.

Unfortunately, after an NFB film crew followed Hurtubise into Alberta's Rocky Mountains, he never got to test the suit. The lone grizzly that showed up just lumbered past him.

Now Hurtubise will try again. He'll test his seemingly indestructible bear suit against fang and claw on December 9 at some secret location in western Canada, pitting himself against a 1,300-pound Kodiak bear, a close relative to the grizzly. It's being brought in by an American animal trainer and will be lured out of its cage with fresh meat.

"I've waited fifteen years for this," he told the *Canadian Press*. "I've tested the suit against bullets, knives, arrows, trucks, logs, rocks, and cars to see if I could handle the power of a bear. And now I'll find out against the real thing and see if I can put my critics to rest."

Don't Expect a Fight

Hurtubise might look like RoboCop, but he doesn't want to wrestle grizzlies. He wants to study them. The armored suit is for protection, much like the steel-cage observatories that shark researchers use. Hurtubise hopes to crawl into a den and watch a grizzly mother give birth.

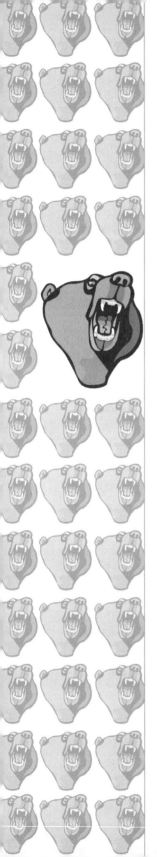

To get that close he'll need to put the suit to the ultimate test. "We're hoping that when I enter the trigger zone of the bear, it will attack, pin me to the ground, and throw me around like a rag doll," Hurtubise said. "Claws, teeth, ripping at the suit for ten seconds."

This incredible life mission began when Hurtubise was a nineteen-year-old, panning for gold on Humidity Creek in British Columbia. Down from a mountain meadow came a great beast that knocked him to the ground with a single, solid snout shove.

Haunted by his brush with death, Hurtubise got passionate about grizzlies, a little-known species. They're simply too dangerous to study up close. He took courses in "forest recreation technology" at Ontario's Sir Sanford Fleming College and dedicated himself to wildlife research.

But his big breakthrough didn't come in the textbook. It didn't come in field research. It came in the movie theater. When he saw *RoboCop*—the story of a half-man, half-machine—the idea of antibear attire took hold. And as a former scrap-metal merchant, he put his professional skills to use.

While he aspires to be Canada's Jacques Cousteau, he's also something of a comedian. In 1998 Harvard University gave him the dubious honor of an Ig Nobel Prize. It's a joke award given to inventors and researchers for achievements "that cannot or should not be reproduced."

Another Ig Nobel winner that year, Peter Fong, a Gettysburg College biologist, was honored for finding that clams reproduce at ten times their normal rate if Prozac is dumped in the water. The research apparently gave new meaning to the expression "happy as a clam."

At the time, Hurtubise was so far in debt, his bear armor had been repossessed. His creditors were gracious enough to let him take his suit to Harvard so that he could have his moment of glory at the lectern.

But Hurtubise just might have the last laugh. The Ursus Mark VI may have some commercial use for firefighters, policemen, emergency workers, even hockey players. Fourteen years of research and testing might just amount to something, and Hurtubise may ultimately prove he's smarter than the average bear. And perhaps much richer, too.

Of course there's a 10-foot-tall Kodiak waiting for him that might want to prove otherwise.

P.S. Hurtubise is now working on his next bear suit—the Ursus Mark VII—featuring a built-in video screen, a cooling system, pressure-bearing titanium struts, advanced protective airbags, and shock absorbers. It is valued at $200,000. He still hasn't had close contact with a grizzly. He's tried many times, but the bears just aren't interested in him.

The Pee Peddler's Crusade
Laws Put Urine Salesman's Business in the Toilet

OCTOBER 2000

Kenneth Curtis has the perfect business. He has no competition. His markup is sky-high. And when he's low on merchandise, he restocks his warehouse simply by chugging a couple of beers and letting nature take its course.

You see, Curtis sells his own urine—clean and unadulterated—to nervous prospective employees who must face a dreaded drug test. The price: $69 for 150 milliliters.

Do you think that's a little steep? Consider that you also get an easy-to-conceal, strap-on vinyl pouch that fits in your pants and dispenses from your crotch.

"This is really foolproof. Even if you are observed, you can use our kit in a natural urinating position and they won't catch you," Curtis says. "And that goes for women as well as men."

Things were going great until last year when South Carolina became the first state to ban the sale of human urine if it is used to undermine drug testing.

"You operate heavy machinery, you drive kids to school, you shouldn't be able to skirt the drug-testing laws," says state Senator David Thomas, who helped write the law Curtis is now challenging.

Curtis contends that the law is unfairly directed at him and violates his constitutional rights. He also says he's protecting the privacy of his clients, because urine tests can be used for more than detecting drug use.

"They say they test for illegal drugs," says Curtis. "But I'm afraid these tests are being used to keep pregnant women, cigarette smokers, and users of prescription medicine from gainful employment."

Even if the court rules against him, Curtis is vowing to stay in business. "I sometimes think there's going to be a big raid," he says. "And the cops are going to beat down my door, open my freezer, and haul away all my frozen pee. To them, it is just urine, to me it is liquid gold."

'I Don't Drink, I Don't Smoke'

Curtis says he doesn't advocate drug use, even though his Web site—PrivacyPro.com—links to marijuana advocacy sites. In fact, becoming his company's chief urine supplier has required him to live squeaky clean.

"I don't drink, I don't smoke, I don't even use prescription drugs," he says. "Since I supply urine to thousands of customers, I think there is no doubt, I've passed more drug tests than any other person in America."

The kits come complete with a chemically reactive heat source and monitoring system that allow you to foil the temperature-sensitive strip many test centers attach to specimen cups.

"You don't want to leave a 'fresh' 40-degree urine sample," Curtis says. "That makes 'em suspicious." Your parents might have warned you not to refreeze hamburger. But Curtis says he supplies enough urine for two tests. Just pop any unused urine back into the ice box. Curtis says, "It'll stay fresh forever."

Labs have caught workers going to all extremes to cheat on drug tests. People have been caught using dog urine and dehydrated urine. But there have been no reports yet of cheaters being caught using Curtis's device.

Insurance companies specializing in worker's compensation say that if cheaters become more sophisticated, random testing will become more prevalent.

P.S. Curtis tried to take his case to Washington, but the U.S. Supreme Court refused to review the South Carolina ban on the sale of urine.

The Frail Male Bladder

When it comes to summoning the courage to use a public toilet, men are the weaker sex.

You might think a guy can "go" anywhere. But nine out of ten sufferers of paruresis—better known as shy-bladder syndrome—are male. These guys find it difficult, if not impossible, to urinate if someone else is close enough to see or hear. Hell, to them, is a public urinal.

Mental-health experts say this phobia troubles an estimated seventeen million Americans to some extent. But few will talk about it.

"Paruresis can ruin lives and careers, even end marriages," says Steven Soifer, a professor of social work at the University of Maryland, who last year opened the first shy-bladder workshop. "Many people think, 'I'm the only one,' and they suffer in silence."

Since urinals offer less privacy than rest-room stalls, men tend to be more susceptible to this disorder. But as paruresis enters the public consciousness, more women are likely to come forward.

At his workshop Soifer admits that he, too, has wrestled to overcome a shy bladder. Participants then begin loading up on water, tea, and other liquids, working with a therapist as well as a "pee buddy" to use a variety of public rest rooms.

P.S. An optional graduation is held at Baltimore's Camden Yards baseball park. After all, big sporting events are the ultimate nightmare for the bathroom squeamish.

God's PR Scheme
Heaven Help This Attention Seeker

JANUARY 2000

When I changed my name to Buck, I worried that people wouldn't take me seriously. Then I spoke with God, and I felt much better. God is a long-winded, sixty-year-old chain-smoker from Los Angeles with bad hair and a potbelly. Maybe that's not your God—but that's the guy I interviewed: Terrill Clark Williams, who legally changed his name in 1981 to G-O-D.

If you don't believe in God, he'll show you his California driver's license and American Express card, both of which bear his heavenly name. At one time he was even listed in the Los Angeles directory. I actually dialed 4-1-1 and, after nearly hanging up on me, a Los Angeles operator asked if God was a business or a residence.

"That's a deeply philosophical question that I'm not prepared to answer," I told her. "Why don't you check both?"

I contacted the former Mr. Williams after reading that he planned to sue the *Los Angeles Times* for defamation after a reporter profiled him as a slovenly old man with a bad toupee, an "unfortunate" haircut, and a "basketball-size pot-belly," living in a run-down apartment, which he called "Heaven."

"God," I asked, "has the *L.A. Times* taken your name in vain?"

"Yes," he told me. "I'm asking for $10 million, and I have a message I want to get out. I need your help."

Holy mackerel! Suddenly Buck Wolf was on a mission from God—I had to spread the word.

God's Wrath

When God was known as Terrill Clark Williams, he was a radio personality. After surviving an auto accident in 1976, he vowed to devote his life to public service—and he decided that the best way to inspire people was to change his name.

Williams did slam his head pretty hard into the windshield, and he did say that he started to hear voices. Nevertheless, a Los Angeles Superior Court judge allowed him to change his name.

To receive a social security card, you must have a first and last name, so Williams simply listed his first name as "G," his middle name as "O," and his last name as "D." The card reads G.O.D.

For a while Williams as God was a big hit on fringe radio shows. But the novelty died down. He managed the apartment building where he lives for a while, and now he's unemployed.

God had once been friendly with the *Times* reporter who profiled him. He was unclear what specifically offended him and what statements might be libelous.

Then a day after we spoke, he admitted that he never intended to sue. It was a hoax to create publicity. Talk about a God who works in mysterious ways.

What did God really want? He wanted to prove he exists. "I have evidence," he told me. "The *L.A. Times* piece didn't include it. In fact the mainstream media has been ignoring it for years. I had to get it out somehow."

God has made himself known before. He's moved mountains, parted a sea, changed water into wine, according to various sources. Still, even after all these miracles, we're looking for a sign—and this God had an utterly contemporary plan to reassure his humble flock.

"I've passed a lie detector test," he proudly said. "What more proof do you need?"

I thought of telling him that most courts refuse to admit polygraph tests as evidence in a criminal trial. They've been proven fallible. But these days polygraphs are often a requirement if you want a job flipping burgers. So it's something.

In the polygraph report, prepared by Chapman Investigations of Los Angeles, God says that he is the one God, that he belongs to no religion, and that he has God-like powers. He denies he's all-knowing or all-powerful, but he says he has no hidden motives.

"I've never asked people for money," he says. "I just wanted the world to know that I'm God and all of us could be Gods because God is in everything."

Of course, to spread that benevolent, if somewhat puzzling message, he's not above creating a little ruse like pretending to sue a major newspaper in the name of the Creator.

God Knows What He Does All Day

In the end there are a lot of people using God's name. You'd think there might be a law against it, but database research shows more than twenty-five Gods listed in phone books across the country.

The former Mr. Williams says he shouldn't be confused with the God in San Rafael, California, who bared a little more than his soul in a local coffee shop.

The San Rafael God, who came to earth as Enrique Silberg, is a sixty-eight-year-old Cuban immigrant. He allegedly stripped while waiting in line for service so that women "could have some type of awareness of God," according to police reports obtained by the Associated Press.

The L.A. God says he leads a quiet life. The *Times* article describes him as living in a small apartment, one floor above his mother, whom he calls "Holy Ramona, Mother of God." Neighbors say God helps them with the groceries and pets, he vacuums, and he gathers clothes for the homeless.

Other than that, God only knows what he does all day. For recreation he has a coin-operated Asteroids video arcade game in his bedroom. And he gathers his mystical powers by meditating under a pyramid, assembled over his bed.

It's good to know that God is alive—even if he has been on disability for a few years.

"Some say the world is going to end," says God, speaking of his hopes for the new year. "I say the world already ended and we are all survivors. Great things are in store for us."

Bobbitt Still a Whack Job
The Anatomy of a National Joke

FEBRUARY 2002

John Wayne Bobbitt, the owner of America's most famous penis, would be happy to live out his life as a national joke. But he now contemplates a far worse fate—being forgotten.

It might not be everyone's dream to wake up each morning as a walking, talking punch line. But Bobbitt turned it into a paying career, at least for a while.

Who knew, back in 1993, when Bobbitt's wife, Lorena, cut off his penis and chucked it out her car window, that a tabloid star would be born?

Ms. Bobbitt was acquitted, in a nationally televised trial, on grounds of insanity, claiming that she was driven over the edge after years of abuse. He was acquitted on charges of sexual assault. But there's no doubt who won. Mr. Bobbitt—or perhaps I should say, his reattached manhood—became an international celebrity.

Everybody wanted a look. His first movie, *John Wayne Bobbitt: Uncut*, set porn video sales records and spawned the sequel, *Frankenpenis*. Screen work came along with a gravy train of personal appearances on every radio and daytime TV show, where he'd chitchat about his one claim to fame.

But the show's over. Bobbitt has been jailed several times on a variety of charges, his second wife left him after only three months, and he has been serving five years probation for attempted grand larceny.

What's more, Bobbitt has finally milked his status as America's leading freak. These days he can't get work as a circus sideshow attraction. Even a Las Vegas–area brothel threw him out for his boorish behavior.

"I tried pretty hard to help that guy out, but he really is a stupid, low-life creep," said Dennis Hof, owner of the Moonlite Bunny Ranch in Carson City, where prostitution is legal.

Bobbitt had a $50,000-a-year job as a bartender/chauffeur/handyman. He wasn't particularly good at anything but had some "face value" with his customers, Hof said.

Bunny Ranch guests frequently asked Bobbitt one question, employees recall: "Does it still work?"

Apparently it does. Perhaps too well. The Bunny Ranch madam regularly warned him to keep his hands off the ladies. "We had an agreement," says Hof. "He wasn't supposed to drink, leave town, or sleep with my girls—and he did all three."

Even Bobbitt's celebrity was a liability. Guests frequently asked to see Bobbitt's penis and Bobbitt became more amenable—after he had enlargement surgery. "I had to tell him, 'Dude, this isn't a petting zoo,'" Hof said.

Still, Hof posted a $10,000 bond in 1998 when Bobbitt was charged in connection with the theft of $150,000 of clothing.

"He is a nice, pleasant person—with absolutely no brain," says Hof. "Even with everything he's gone through, he's still a boring oaf."

After leaving the brothel for good, Bobbitt tried to hook up with the Jim Rose Circus—trying to join a traveling menagerie that includes transvestite wrestlers; a contortionist who can squeeze through the head of a tennis racquet; a professional insect-eater; and "Lizardman," a tattoo artist with a split tongue.

"We tried to involve him in a knife-throwing act, since he knows all to well what it's like to be cut," said Jim Rose.

We'll assume someone other than Lorena was doing the knife throwing.

"All Bobbitt had to do was stand still, really, and he couldn't do that."

For the last few years, Bobbitt has drifted between Las Vegas and upstate New York, where he was convicted of battering a former girlfriend.

Bobbitt still appears on talk radio, but the paying gigs are few and far between. His former manager, Robert Yates, tricked him into doing another porn movie a few years ago, setting up hidden cameras in a Nevada hotel room. Bobbitt threatened to sue but, in need of money, cut a deal for the film to be released.

Back in Vegas Bobbitt married for a third time, exchanging vows on his thirty-fifth birthday with Joanna Ferrell. He proclaimed the event a new beginning, looking forward to becoming a father.

"My other marriages were marriages of convenience," he told the *Las Vegas Review-Journal*.

"I put it in God's hands," he said of the March 2002 union with his new wife. "She made deviled eggs today and I told her, those aren't deviled eggs, they're angel's eggs."

Only six weeks later, police were summoned to Bobbitt's home, and once again he was slapped with an order of protection. In the mess, Bobbitt lost his last stab at a national spotlight—trading punches with Joey Buttafuoco on *Celebrity Boxing*.

Another missed opportunity. But have no doubt, by tomorrow Bobbitt will find things to do to himself that Lorena never could.

Marginal
History

Hittler's Pride
Don't Judge Adolf by His Name

SEPTEMBER 1998

Adolf Hittler is alive and well. But he's probably not the guy you're thinking about. Unlike the Nazi leader, this gentleman spells his last name with two Ts, disdains fascism, and never aspired to take over the world. He's a sixty-one-year-old retired school bus driver from Landeck, Austria, and he doesn't like to be teased.

"My whole life this has been a problem," he says. "Just try checking into a hotel with my name."

After refusing interviews for years, he decided to speak out at a conference for folks with problematic names September 28 in Braunau, Austria—infamous birthplace of the infamous Hitler.

"I'd get calls in the middle of the night from jokers who wanted to say, 'Heil Hitler' and other stupid jokes about gas chambers," Hittler says.

"But it is in part my choice. I decided not to change my name. I thought it would be an insult to my parents."

Hittler was a young boy when the notorious fascist came to power. He says his name caused tensions in his marriage, which ended in divorce, and that one of his two sons uses his ex-wife's maiden name.

Also in attendance at the Braunau conference was a bricklayer named Heinrich Himmler—just like the Nazi S.S. chief. He claims he once lost his job because of his name.

Hittler's problem is rare. Only about 2 percent of German men before World War II were named Adolf, according to German historian Tomas Breckenmacher. And during his reign, Hitler forbade Germans to name children after him.

Since the war, the surname 'Hitler' virtually disappeared. "All the better," Hittler says.

On occasion, Hittler has used an alias. A few years after WWII, a hotel insisted that he call himself "Adrian Heller" when transporting an Israeli tour group. He agreed.

P.S. In the United States, an "Adolf Hitler" was listed as recently as 1997 in the telephone directory of Bossier City, Louisiana.

Real Urban Legends
When Lawn Chairs Fly

F E B R U A R Y 2 0 0 1

A woman on a flight from Scandinavia to the United States had to be pried free by a rescue team after a high-pressure vacuum flush sealed her to the toilet seat of a Boeing 767.

At least that was the story in mid-January, when it was featured in dozens of newspapers, Web sites, and TV reports. According to Reuters the unnamed woman had filed a complaint with Scandinavian Airlines System.

"She could not get up by herself and had to sit on the toilet until the flight had landed so that ground technicians could help her get loose," an airline spokeswoman said. "She was stuck there for quite a long time."

Only days later the story turned out to be untrue. The airline claimed it mixed up a fictional exercise from staff training with the real thing. No woman ever filed such a complaint.

But the "Sky Toilet" story won't die. It's likely to live on as an urban legend that will haunt gullible air travelers for years to come—just like the tale of the tourist who was drugged by organ thieves and woke up with both kidneys missing. Great story. Never happened.

But just because a story is an urban legend, doesn't mean it's not true. Some of the strangest tales are nonfiction.

Here's a bone-chilling story that's undeniably true: On the day that American Airlines Flight 587 crashed in New York, both of New Jersey's winning Pick 3 lottery combinations included the numbers 5, 8, and 7. The morning drawing was 5-7-8. The later drawing was 5-8-7.

"Urban legends are not the same thing as fictional tales; a story becomes a legend when it is circulated widely and regarded as the truth. Whether they actually occurred or not is irrelevant," says Barbara Mikkelson of Agoura Hills, California, who runs www.snopes.com, one of the leading Web sites that investigates urban legends.

Still, it's important to separate fact from fiction. Coca-Cola did, in fact, once contain cocaine. But the brassiere was not invented by Otto Titzlinger.

With the help of snopes.com's terrific database of some 1,500 urban legends, here are some unbelievably strange but verifiably true tales. You may have heard variations that have fictional embellishments. But at least this much is for real.

True Urban Legends

The Leaping Lawyer—A lawyer demonstrating the safety of windows in a Toronto skyscraper deliberately threw himself at a pane of glass—and crashed through it, plunging to his death. Garry Hoy, age thirty-eight, fell from the twenty-fourth floor of the Toronto Dominion Bank Tower in 1993 as horrified witnesses watched.

Cadaver Kin—In 1982 a student at the University of Alabama School of Medicine recognized one of the nine cadavers taken to her class for dissection. It was her great aunt, who had at one time discussed the merits of donating one's body to medical science.

The Flying Lawn Chair—In 1982 Larry Walters of Los Angeles soared thousands of feet in the air on a lawn chair tethered to forty-five weather balloons. He got so high he disrupted air traffic and was eventually fined $4,000 by the Federal Aviation Administration. The thirty-three-year-old Vietnam veteran purchased the chair from Sears, hoping to fly it 300 miles from his home to the Mojave Desert.

What a Dord!—For five years *Webster's New International Dictionary* mistakenly included an entry for "dord," a nonexistent word. In the mid-1930s, dord could be found on page 771, nestled between Dorcopsis (a type of small kangaroo) and doré (golden in color). It was defined as "density."

Funhouse Funeral—A prop corpse hanging in a Long Beach, California, fun house turned out to be the real remains of an outlaw. In 1976 scenes for the hit TV show *The Six Million Dollar Man* were being shot at the Nu-Pike Amusement Park. When a production worker moved the fun house "hanging man," the prop's arm came off. Inside was human bone—the remains of train robber Elmer McCurdy.

Pure As Ivory—Early in her career, porn queen Marilyn Chambers appeared on Ivory Snow boxes, holding a baby. As her screen legend grew, Ivory sought out a cover girl that better reflected its image of 99$^{44}/_{100}$ percent purity.

You might not believe everything on Mikkelson's site. It's always best to get your information straight from the horse's mouth, unless, of course, if that horse is the famous Mr. Ed—who has been rumored to be a zebra.

The Man Who Stole Summer
The Political Blunder That Shortened Your Vacation

S E P T E M B E R   2 0 0 0

If you feel cheated out of summer fun again this Labor Day, don't blame yourself. Blame Grover Cleveland.

In 1894 the president proclaimed the first Monday in September to be a tribute to the American worker. And it has since become summer's last hurrah, the final barbecue before the kids suffer back-to-school jitters, work rips into high gear, and political campaign commercials give us all migraines.

But if you think summer ends too soon, that's not just a wistful feeling. That's a fact. Consult any calendar. The Northern Hemisphere's autumnal equinox, better known as "the first day of autumn," does not officially begin until September 22.

Clearly if President Cleveland wanted to be a true hero of the American worker, he would have not cut the summer short with that three-day buzzkill known as Labor Day weekend. In fact if he had only pushed back the holiday to, say, October 1, he would stand shoulder to shoulder in history books with Lincoln, Jefferson, and Washington.

How is Grover Cleveland remembered? Was he the inspiration for that lovable, royal-blue Muppet?

Many people with just a casual acquaintance with history remember the campaign scandal over Cleveland's illegitimate son and the Republican jeer it gave rise to, "Ma, Ma, where's my Pa? Gone to the White House, ha, ha, ha."

Cleveland's daughter—not the fearsome New York Yankee slugger—was the namesake of the Baby Ruth candy bar. But this is hardly the making of greatness.

Indeed Cleveland had a shot at immortality and blew it. Let's not beat him too hard. He did give us all a day off. Let's give him one, too. But, my fellow Americans, let's not give up.

New Labor Day: September 22

Ultimately, political power rests in voters' hands. It's time WE THE PEOPLE stop getting cheated out of the end of summer. We can move Labor Day. It's our country, our calendar.

The Wolf Files hereby proclaims a national movement to move Labor Day to September 22. As an employee of ABCNEWS.com, I humbly refuse monetary donations. But I urge all sympathetic souls to e-mail me at buck.n.wolf@abcnews.com. As the self-proclaimed leader of what I call The Endless Summer Party Campaign (ESPC), I pledge to collect all e-mails and submit them to the appropriate leaders in Washington. I will report back on our progress and I urge all of you to get involved.

The Beach Boys, of course, will be entreated to lend their star power to this movement. Tom Hanks? Alec Baldwin? If you are out there and this reaches you, get involved. You are always looking for a good cause. Here is a great one.

Move Thanksgiving: More Shopping

You might think the "Move Labor Day" movement has no chance. I say you are wrong. America has created, moved, and removed holidays at the mere stroke of a pen for reasons of much less import.

George Washington proclaimed November 26 a day of Thanksgiving. Lincoln declared it to be a national holiday, but moved it to the fourth Thursday in November. Then came Franklin Roosevelt, who declared Thanksgiving to be celebrated one week earlier because he wanted to extend the Christmas shopping season.

Government documents said the new Thanksgiving would allow Americans to "make proper provision for the Christmas rush."

Republicans and Roosevelt-haters trounced the idea. After two years Thanksgiving was moved back to its familiar date. But take heart, ESPC supporters! A precedent has been set. We can move Labor Day.

This war is winnable. We must be allowed to celebrate summer until it truly ends.

I'm sure big business will be less than thrilled if folks keep summer hours through September. I'm sure opponents will launch a "Rush to Autumn" campaign. But we must rise above their propaganda and spread the truth.

When you gather 'round to roast that final weenie, don't let anyone kid you that each season has its own beauty. Would you be happy if your loved one compared you to a winter's day? Just imagine walking to your car in the freezing cold and saying, "Boy, this winter is just flying by!"

Louis Farrakhan Sings
Nation of Islam Leader's Calypso Follies

DECEMBER 1998

Nation of Islam leader Louis Farrakhan has blasted Michael Jackson as an "unwholesome, effeminate sissy." But now

Farrakhan's musical past is catching up to him, and it seems he didn't always take gender bending so seriously. Farrakhan's stint as a calypso singer has been unearthed on a new CD from Bostrox Records, and it features a rollicking ditty on transsexuality.

The minister, who now preaches strict gender roles, donned a frilly white shirt as he sang:

> With this modern surgery,
> They change him from he to she.
> But behind that lipstick, rouge, and paint,
> I got to know, is she is, or is she ain't?

Farrakhan performed under the pseudonym "The Charmer" in the early 1950s and was considered a contemporary of Harry Belafonte, although his music was decidedly more risqué. The future minister wrote much of his own material, including, "Is She Is or Is She Ain't."

"Of course we realize there's a lot of interest in it because it is Farrakhan," says Bryan Jarrett, president of Bostrox Records in Austin, Texas. "But this is very good music. He had a legitimate career going."

As a nervous sixteen-year-old in 1949, Farrakhan claimed a prize for his violin playing on TV's *Ted Mack's Amateur Hour*. He was touring in the "Calypso Follies" in 1955 when he attended a Chicago meeting of Nation of Islam and heard his calling.

Apparently The Charmer was charmed, and his new life left little time for music. The lighthearted, sexually daring young man has recorded since his spiritual awakening, but as a fulminating minister.

In "A White Man's Heaven Is a Black Man's Hell," recorded after his conversion to Islam, he sings:

> Though you are pregnant black woman, you pull the plow,
> Like a horse, like a mule, sweat from your brow.
> He filled your womb with his wicked seed.
> His half-white children you were made to breed.
> Ah my friends, it's easy to tell,
> A white man's heaven is a black man's hell.

Jarrett says Farrakhan's recordings from the early 1950s are in the public domain. But the Nation of Islam declined to comment. His ministry does offer one recent single for sale, "Let Us Unite," recorded in 1984. There's even a dance mix.

O. J. Steak Knives
The Battle to Un-Trademark Simpson

AUGUST 2000

If you think O. J. Simpson's proposed pay-per-view lie detector test marks a new low in shameful self-exploitation, just consider O. J. cutlery.

What gift would a woman like less from a man than official O. J. steak knives? That's like trying to sell "Extra Chunky" Jeffrey Dahmer soup.

And yet in 1994, when Simpson was languishing in a Los Angeles jail, thinking up ways to pay his all-star legal team, he attempted to trademark "O. J.," "O. J. Simpson," and "Juice" so he could hawk personalized jigsaw puzzles, squeeze toys, comic books, jewelry, action figures—and yes, knives.

O. J. as Intellectual Property

A man charged in the stabbing deaths of his ex-wife and a bystander might feel a bit self-conscious about being associated with anything pointy, even if he were acquitted. But O. J.'s bid to trademark various permutations of his name outlasted his more celebrated legal battle and ended only a few weeks ago, thanks mostly to Bill Ritchie—a crusading intellectual-property lawyer.

"It was a moral issue," says the fifty-seven-year-old New Hampshire resident, who had no connection to Simpson before he heard that the gridiron legend was making an end run to the U.S. Patent and Trademark Office.

"It's clear that the O. J. Simpson name stands for violence against women," Ritchie says. "And I don't want the government to reward or endorse that with a federally registered trademark."

What gave Ritchie—an adjunct professor at the Franklin Pierce Law Center in Concord—the right to sue? That's what O. J.'s lawyers demanded to know.

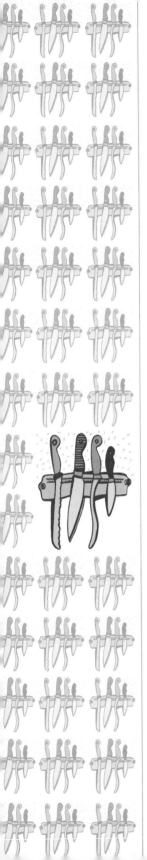

Ritchie contended that Simpson's proposed trademark would damage him and others like him because the trademarks have a connotation that makes it offensive to anyone who believes in common moral values.

"If a strange man says to a woman in an elevator, 'I'm going to O. J. you!' it would be frightening," Ritchie says. "The O. J. name has come to mean something horrible. You shouldn't be able to trademark scandal."

The Value of Sinatra's Toupee

Simpson has been moving on several fronts to capitalize on his notoriety since his acquittal in 1995. But even before a civil jury held him liable for the deaths of Nicole Brown Simpson and Ronald Goldman, his value as a marketable image had diminished. And while he still makes headlines, people are hesitant to do anything that might line his pockets.

Celebrity memorabilia dealer Michael Kronick—who supplies the Planet Hollywood and Hard Rock Cafe chains—says Simpson's autograph was once worth about $300. But since his acquittal, that price has dropped to $15—the same amount you'd pay for the signature of Gary Coleman or Pauly Shore.

It's hard to put a price on nostalgia. Kronick's Startifacts company will sell you a used Frank Sinatra toupee (which comes with a letter of authenticity) for $15,000, or you can have Al Capone's letter opener for $8,500 and a letter signed by Charles Manson for $399. If those guys can be worth big bucks to memorabilia dealers, couldn't anybody?

"I think the difference with O. J. is that those people got punished," Kronick says. "There's a feeling out there that O. J. got away with murder and is trying to cash in on it."

Nicole Nuggets

Of course some people will buy Simpson souvenirs—to destroy them.

Chicago shock jock Mancow Muller paid $3,250 for a nearly 6-foot-tall Simpson statue, which he then melted down into "Nicole Nuggets." These souvenirs were sold to benefit a fund established by Goldman's family.

Christian-radio talk host Bob Enyart of Denver did the same thing—torching some $16,000 worth of the football star's belongings, including two No. 32 football jerseys and a Professional Football Hall of Fame induction certificate.

But the man who paid $255,500 for O. J.'s Heisman Trophy last year, Tom "Juice" Kriessman of Fort Lauderdale, Florida, said he mostly wanted to impress his girlfriend.

"It represents the story of a man who rose to be a superstar and lost it all overnight," the forty-seven-year-old sheet-metal dealer told the Associated Press.

"I bought it for everything it represents: the trial of the century, O. J.'s whole career, what happened—you know, the tragedy that was his life."

He added, "I think in the future it's going to be worth a lot of money."

A Living, Breathing Counterfeit Warhol
The Pop Art Doppelganger

A U G U S T   1 9 9 8

Everybody gets fifteen minutes of fame. But how many people get to be Andy Warhol, for even a second?

For six crazy months back in 1967, Allen Midgette—who looks nothing like Warhol—got to be the man who turned the tomato soup can into an art form. He traveled the country, posing as Warhol, speaking at colleges, and trading intellectual barbs at cocktail parties.

"It was all Andy's idea—just the sort of joke he loved," says Midgette.

Deciding that the college lecture circuit was a farce, Warhol decided that he could send anyone in his place and nobody would know the difference. He only knew Midgette in passing as an underemployed actor who appeared in a few of his films, including *Lonesome Cowboys* and *Nude Restaurant*.

"I think Andy chose me because he thought I was better looking than he was."

On one day's notice, Midgette jetted to the University of Rochester. Students and teachers simply assumed Midgette's makeup and cheap silver wig were the accoutrements of an eccentric artist.

Barely knowing anything about Warhol actually helped Midgette pull off the scam. "Andy was always evasive in interviews," Midgette said. "I just did the same thing."

Midgette spoke throughout the Midwest, earning about $1,200 for five lectures. The charade came to an end when one of Warhol's friends revealed the hoax.

For the last twenty years, Midgette, age fifty-nine, has been a painter and leather designer in Manhattan's Greenwich Village. He recalls his brush with fame fondly. "There were lots of offers for drugs and sex," he said. "It was the sixties and I was a part of it. But I played it cool when I was playing Andy."

P.S. After Warhol died of heart failure in 1987, Sotheby's auctioned a Warhol android prototype that he was developing to appear in his place on TV talk shows.

Mr. Smiley's Frown
Did Harvey Ball Ever Have a Nice Day?

APRIL 2001

Harvey Ball gave the world a smile, and all he got was a lousy $45. Ball, a graphic designer who died last week at the age of seventy-nine, created a 1970s sensation—that little yellow smiley face that became the omnipresent "Have a Nice Day" slogan on stickers, T-shirts, and magnets. Can you even imagine *The Partridge Family* era without Mr. Smiley? It would be as if John Travolta never danced the hustle in dangerously overstretched polyester.

Unfortunately Ball didn't have a nice day when he contacted the U.S. Patent Office. "By 1973 the smiley face was everywhere," he told *The Wolf Files* in

1998. "They told me, 'Tough luck, it's in the public domain.'"

At first Ball let it slide. He had created this symbol of cheer as part of an in-house morale program for a Massachusetts insurance company. "I never thought it was my ticket to easy street," he says. He took his meager $45 free-lance fee and went on with his life.

What really burned Ball was that French entrepreneur Franklin Loufrani managed to trademark the smiley in eighty foreign countries and threatened to sue any U.S. company that exported Mr. Smiley without paying a royalty.

"The guy even claims he created the smiley," said Ball, momentarily losing Mr. Smiley's perpetual cheerfulness. "He's got a lot of nerve."

"I'd like the money," he told *The Wolf Files*. "But I want the credit, too."

Eventually the World War II veteran—who won a Bronze Star for his heroism at the battle of Okinawa—resisted bringing a suit against Loufrani, even as Mr. Smiley's insipid yellow grin showed up in Wal-Mart ads. Instead he settled for seeing Mr. Smiley commemorated on a U.S. postage stamp.

Ball also instituted World Smile Corp. to compete with Loufrani, selling prints of Mr. Smiley with his signature for charity. He ran a modest art and advertising company in Worcester, Massachusetts, and is survived by a wife, three sons, and a daughter.

A fortune slipped through Harvey Ball's fingers, but at least, as corny as it sounds, Ball really did try to have a nice day.

Great Moments in the History of Toilet Paper
American TP Technology Felt All Over the World

APRIL 2001

You really have to appreciate the little things in life. Consider this: The average American uses 57 sheets of toilet paper a day and more than 20,805 sheets a year. That's a lot of sheet.

You really don't appreciate toilet paper until you don't have it. Then you think about the alternatives. Perhaps it's a commentary on American journalism that just a little more than a hundred years ago, today's newspaper was tomorrow's toilet paper.

And in a good part of the world, TP is still a luxury.

America is still the world's leader in toilet paper. We're the biggest producer, the biggest consumer. And while foreigners might laugh at our cars and shoddy consumer goods, most of the world agrees we're world-class when it comes to wiping.

The U.S. toilet-paper market is worth about $2.4 billion a year, and the leading manufacturers—Kimberly-Clark and Procter & Gamble—are recognized worldwide, powering our exports beyond those of Japan and China, who still trail us in TP production.

And now the history of this very American product is at your fingertips, thanks to the Toilet Paper Encyclopedia on the ToiletPaperWorld.com Web site.

The Scott Paper Co. was once so embarrassed that it was manufacturing toilet paper that it wouldn't put its label on the product. That was about one hundred years ago. "Maybe they thought toilet paper was just a fad," says Kenn Fischburg, CEO of ToiletPaperWorld.com. "I guess you could say it caught on."

Fischburg—a second-generation paper goods and cleaning-supplies vendor—is trying to make a go of it on the Internet, promising retail customers wholesale prices.

It's more than just toilet paper he's selling. And it all comes with a story.

Early American settlers used everything from leaves to corncobs to wipe their bottoms, he says. French royalty wiped with lace. The Vikings used discarded wool. And when in ancient Rome, you did as the Romans did—with a sponge.

With some help from Fischburg, here are some of the great moments in toilet-paper history.

Toilet Paper Time Line

ca. 100 B.C.: Roman So-Called Civilization—All public toilets feature a stick with a sponge attached to its end, soaking in a bucket of brine. Citizens use the tool to freshen up.

1391: The King's Pleasure—Chinese emperors begin ordering toilet paper in sheets measuring 2 feet by 3 feet.

1596: A Royal Flush—Sir John Harington, a godson of Queen Elizabeth I, invents the first flushing toilet (a distinction often attributed to plumber Thomas Crapper).

1700s: Damn Niblets!—Colonial Americans wipe with corncobs, later switching to old newspapers, catalogs, and almanacs.

1857: Every Sheet Bears My Name—New York entrepreneur Joseph C. Gayetty manufactures the first packaged pre-moistened sheets of bathroom tissue—called "therapeutic paper"—in packs of 500 for 50 cents. Gayetty is so proud of his innovation that he has his name imprinted on each sheet.

1861–1904: The Gifts of Thomas Crapper—British plumber Thomas Crapper revolutionizes the toilet with a series of plumbing-related patents.

1872: Kimberly Meets Clark—Charles Benjamin Clark, a twenty-eight-year-old Civil War veteran, recruits John A. Kimberly to join him in building a paper mill in Wisconsin.

1890: On a Roll—Scott Paper introduces toilet paper on a roll. But the paper-goods company is somewhat embarrassed to be associated with such an "unmentionable" thing and refuses to put its name on the product. Instead

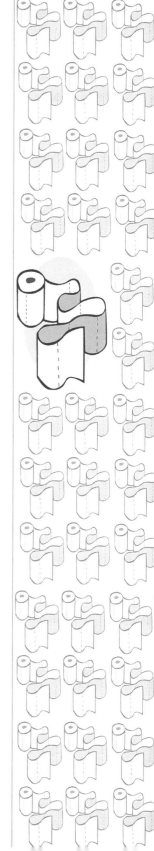

the toilet paper bears the name of intermediaries. As a result, at the beginning of the twentieth century, the Waldorf Hotel in New York becomes a leader in the toilet-paper business.

1902: Enter the Green Bay Giant—Northern Paper Mills, the company that later becomes Quilted Northern, opens, producing Northern Tissue.

1916: Gas Masks Become Sanitary Napkins—Kimberly-Clark begins concentrating on a special wadding paper. With World War I brewing in Europe, this product, Cellucotton, was adapted for use as a filter in gas masks and bandages. Nurses began using it as sanitary pads. Cellucotton was renamed "Cellu-Naps," and then "Kotex."

1920: The Tissue and the Pop-Up Box—Kimberly-Clark introduces the Kleenex tissue. Nine years later, this product is marketed in the patented Pop-Up box.

1928: From Charming to Charmin—Hoberg paper introduces Charmin. The logo—a woman's head from a cameo pin—was designed to appeal to feminine fashions of the day. A female employee called the packaging "charming," and the product's brand name was born.

1932: Wiping Away Depression—Charmin tries to mitigate the pain of the Great Depression by introducing the economy-size four-roll pack.

1935: Who's Got the Tweezers?—Northern Tissue is hailed as one of the few splinter-free toilet papers on the market.

1942: A Softer World—St. Andrew's Paper Mill in England introduces two-ply toilet paper.

1944: Patriotic Toilet-Paper Duty—The United States honors Kimberly-Clark with an "E" Award (for excellence in commercial services) for its heroic effort supplying soldiers fighting in World War II.

1964: Enter Mr. Whipple—He appears for more than twenty years in TV, radio, and print advertising. The real George Whipple was the president of the Benton

& Bowles advertising agency, which came up with the "Please, don't squeeze the Charmin" ad campaign. He sold the rights to his name to Procter & Gamble for $1.00. Dick Wilson, the vaudeville veteran who portrayed Mr. Whipple on TV, later recalled his agent calling him about the project.

"My agent asked me, 'What do you think of toilet paper?' And I told him, 'I think everybody should use it.' "

For his role in making Charmin the No. 1 toilet paper in America, Wilson's salary grew to $300,000 a year, and Procter & Gamble promised him a "lifetime supply" of toilet paper.

1973: The Johnny Carson Toilet-Paper Scare—Johnny Carson makes a joke about the United States facing an acute shortage of toilet paper. This prompts viewers to run out to stores and begin hoarding. Carson apologizes the next day for causing the scare and retracts his remark.

1991: Covert TP—The U.S. military uses toilet paper to camouflage its tanks in Saudi Arabia during the Gulf War.

1995: The Great Toilet-Paper Caper—A Philadelphia city employee is charged with stealing $34,000 worth of toilet paper from Veterans Stadium just before an Eagles football game. The accused, Ricardo Jefferson, was fired. City spokesman Tony Radwanski said: "We don't really know how long this was going on. We only looked at a ten-month period from October 1994 to August 1995, but man, he really wiped that stadium clean."

1999: Paperless Toilet—Japanese inventors unveil the paperless toilet. The device washes, rinses, and blow-dries the user's bottom with a heating element.

2000: Men Are from Folders, Women Are from Wadders—A Kimberly-Clark marketing survey on bathroom habits finds that women are "wadders" and men are "folders." Women also tend to use much more toilet paper than men.

P.S. What toilet paper does Fischburg use? "It's like fine wine," he says. "It depends what mood I'm in."

Bathroom Reading—Good, Clean Fun

Say what you will about reading in the bathroom, it's not dirty—even if you're reading Playboy.

According to University of Arizona microbiologist Chuck Gerba, the average desktop is crawling with 400 times more bacteria than the average toilet seat. Your telephone and computer keyboard, in particular, are germ havens.

"Think about it: Desktops are rarely cleaned," Gerba says. "If you're eating at your desk, it's a veritable cafeteria for bacteria."

It turns out that newspapers and magazines aren't bacteria friendly. Gerba says you're more likely to be contaminated by *E. coli* or fecal matter when you touch the sink faucet handles.

"The toilet seat has gotten a bad rap," he says. "I'm not saying you should take your office work into the bathroom or eat your lunch there. But it might be better for your health."

Gerba has spent years investigating public potties. If you think it's hard work for a microbiologist to do research in bus-station bathrooms, you're right. "I was once kneeling behind a bathroom stall on some occasions and folks called the police, thinking I'm doing God knows what," he says.

"Then I have to stand up and tell the officer, 'I'm a scientist,' and he's like, 'Sure, you are.' "

In one study Gerba and a team of other researchers attached microprocessors to toilet-paper dispensers in public rest rooms all over the world, concluding that Americans, by far, use more toilet paper than any other people—seven sheets of TP for each trip to the bathroom.

The British use the least. "It could have something to do with the coarse quality of their paper," Gerba says. The Germans and French fell somewhere in the middle.

You might think it's silly to contemplate potty time, but the average American spends about an hour a day in the bathroom, according to a survey by the National Association for Continence. That adds up to fourteen days a year—the length of most Americans' annual vacation.

If you reach the ripe old age of eighty, you will have spent nearly three full years in the bathroom.

Frightening
Beauty

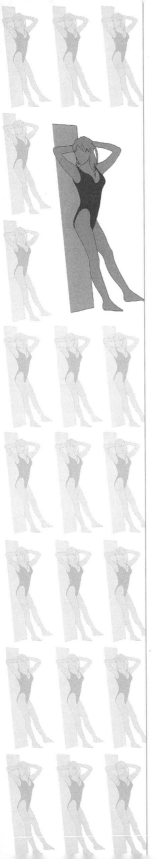

Plastic Surgeons Salute
Baywatch
The Breast of Times for Augmentation

J A N U A R Y   2 0 0 1

When Pamela Anderson Lee bounced her way to *Baywatch* babedom, cosmetic surgeons everywhere rejoiced. Now that the show is jiggling off into the sunset—with the last episode scheduled in May—cosmetic surgeons everywhere are raising their scalpel in a crisp salute to the TV show that revolutionized the face-lift and tummy tuck industry.

"We were blessed with *Baywatch*," plastic surgeon Dr. Leonard Grossman said. "It is the most vivid form of advertising. It's like an hour-long plastic-surgery commercial."

When the show was at its height in the early 1990s, prospective patients would bring in pictures of Anderson in her Speedo grandeur and ask to be lifted, sculpted, and lipo-sucked to perfection, Grossman recalled.

"*Baywatch* may have slipped out of the public eye in recent years. Now people are looking at Britney and other stars," the doctor said. "But *Baywatch* and Pam Anderson brought our business to a whole new level."

Americans went through some 4.6 million surgical and nonsurgical cosmetic procedures in 1999, according to the American Society for Aesthetic Plastic Surgery.

Breast augmentation alone is up 51 percent over last year, and 500 percent since 1992, when Americans still worried about the dangers of leaky silicone pouches.

A Deflated Legend

Even though Anderson removed her implants in 1999, she became the benchmark of all boob jobs. "Some people want to look exactly like her," said Dr. Mark Berman of Santa Monica, California. "Others want to make sure they don't get that artificial look."

Of course other *Baywatch* alumnae have inspired many a scalpel. Surgeons say many women pay for eyebrow lifts to mimic the deep-set eyes of Yasmine Bleeth, or cheek implants so they can look like Nicole Eggert.

Knowing this, Dr. Daniel Man of Boca Raton, Florida, said he has to warn patients against unrealistic expectations. "If you want to have a face-lift to become a star and you don't have potential, it is not the right attitude," he said.

Man is the author of *The Art of Man: Faces of Plastic Surgery*, a guidebook with real-life before-and-after shots. "I think some of the stars of *Baywatch* have really shown what cosmetic surgery can do," he said. "Of course, these stars are very nice looking to start with."

Discovered on the Jumbotron

We must remember Anderson's own humble start. As a high-school student in Vancouver, British Columbia, she wanted nothing more than "to be a beach bum," according to her yearbook.

Then, at a football game in 1989, a cameraman flashed Pam in a dangerously overstretched Labatt's T-shirt on the stadium Jumbotron. The brewer soon hired her to do commercials. *Playboy* called. Then, somewhere in there, she opted for that world-famous antigravity chest.

Suddenly she was wearing a white thong bikini at a surfside wedding to Motley Crüe drummer Tommy Lee.

"Pam was very frank. She made strides in taking plastic surgery out of the closet," said Dr. Robert Ersek of Austin, Texas, who says he's operated on just about every part of the human body.

"I've even performed toe-liposuction," he boasts.

Nowadays, you can even watch plastic surgery live on the Internet on sites such as celebritydoctor.com, where comedian John Byner's May 1999 face-lift was broadcast into cyberspace.

Dr. Richard Ellenbogen of Los Angeles, who describes himself as "the father of fat transplant surgery," performed the honors on Byner. "We are going public in these events to demystify the process," he said. "It's a new day."

The Gift of Lifts

Folks shopping for plastic surgery in the post-Baywatch era will find a new marketplace, where doctors are working at a pace reminiscent of a drive-thru McDonald's. Dr. Leonard Roudner of Florida told the Associated Press he averages five breast jobs a day and is widely known as "Dr. Boobner" for his steady business. His office says he's booked solid for the next few months.

And some men think nothing says "I love you" better than a gift of saline breast implants.

"Over the years, I've had a steady stream of boyfriends and husbands coming into the office to purchase a breast implant procedure for their spouse or girlfriend for Valentine's Day," said Dr. Franklin Rose of Houston.

"This year looks to be an especially busy year," Rose added. "It's been a cold, rainy winter and I think people are looking forward to putting on a swimsuit and heading to the beach."

Rose, who has performed more than 4,000 silicone and saline-gel breast implant procedures, says it's almost always the women who suggest the gift. But it's a delicate matter. If a guy brings up the subject at the wrong moment, his sweetie may end up performing ad-hoc surgery on his face.

Still, other women may be grateful to have the subject on the table. "For many women, breast implants are something they secretly want but they're just too embarrassed to take the plunge and get them," Rose said. "In many cases, it's the fulfillment of a lifelong dream."

Were these ladies traumatized by the sight of perfect bods on *Baywatch*? Rose says women were bombarded with bodacious body images long before *Baywatch* hit it big. The show, however, did have an undeniable impact.

"The big-breasts, small-hips, perfect-buttocks look goes back to Barbie and before," he said. "*Baywatch* was a part of that, however. A big part."

The Man Who Wanted Canine Cajones
Testicular Implants Available for Dogs, but Not Humans

MARCH 2000

Jim Webb says he's not the only guy who wants an artificial dog testicle implanted in his body. And to prove it, he doesn't care if he becomes a national joke.

Webb—a 42-year-old United Airlines employee—became known on late-night TV talk shows as "The Man Who Wanted Canine Cajones."

He put up with the jokes, because that's the only way to get the message across. "I have a serious problem that thousands of other men share," he says.

An estimated 8,000 men lose one or both of their testicles each year because of cancer, injuries, or other misfortunes. Up until the mid-1990s, testicular implants were available.

But several years after the public scare involving silicone breast implants, the Food and Drug Administration halted the manufacture of prosthetic testicles until they could be proven safe and effective.

"It's ridiculous," says the San Francisco resident, who lost his left testicle in 1988 after a severe infection. He says he feels better, but the deformity has left him feeling embarrassed, especially in intimate situations.

"All these plastic surgeons willing to do penis enlargement and weird plastic surgery. All I want is reconstructive surgery to look normal and so do a lot of men in my predicament."

Going to the Dogs

Last fall Webb contacted the makers of Neuticles—artificial testicles for dogs, cats, and other animals—and the company offered him their product, free of charge.

Unfortunately Neuticles aren't FDA-approved, and Webb soon found he had no other choice but to take to the airwaves.

"I was prepared to achieve freak-of-the-week status," he says, and indeed, Jay Leno mentioned Webb's proposed surgery in his opening monologue twice in one week last fall.

"It was a little embarrassing. But I figured if I stepped up, other men would speak up and we would get some results."

Webb said he considered getting artificial testicles overseas. He had even received advice from a female-to-male transsexual who had gone through the process in Canada. But he wanted to be aboveboard. And he wasn't afraid to be a test case.

Restoring Fido's Manhood

While Webb was searching for answers to his problem, business was booming for Gregg Miller, the inventor of Neuticles.

Since the mid-1990s, more than 36,000 animals, mostly dogs, can now hold their shaggy heads high—and so can their owners, who often feel "post-traumatic stress" from neutering their pets, Miller says.

"It's an inexpensive, simple procedure, and if it helps owners feel more willing to do this, isn't it worth it?" Miller says, pointing out that twenty million unwanted pets are destroyed annually.

The Neuticles slogan: "Looking and feeling the same."

The doggie models come in three sizes and a variety of styles, all FDA-approved for animals. The low-end models are plastic shells with the company's trademark etched in the side, available to vets for less than $100.

But if a pet owner wants to splurge on "Natural" Neuticles, Fido gets rubbery, solid silicone prosthetics. And now there's the "Ultra" line, new to the market this month.

"It's marshmallowy soft," Miller says. "Lots of pet owners want to give their animals the most comfort possible."

A Neuticle Necklace

When President Clinton had his black Lab Buddy neutered two years ago, Miller sent the White House dog a free pair along with a souvenir Neuticle necklace.

The company reached a milestone this February when a man bought

Neuticles for his bull. If inquiring minds want to know: Each lifelike bull orb is 5 inches high and 2½ inches wide.

"The guy didn't want to say much about the purchase. . . . He didn't let us use his name in a press release," says Miller. "But at $695, it's a great direction for us."

All the publicity caught Webb's eye. He surfed over to the Neuticles Web site last September, and Miller immediately offered him a set of collie-size Neuticles and helped identify a doctor in Kansas who would perform the simple procedure for about $400.

Miller loves offbeat marketing. He even sells Neuticle key chains, with real prosthetics attached. The chance to help Webb had "PR juice," he said.

Unfortunately for Webb, medical officials weren't ready to let Neuticles be man's new best friend. So the jokes continue, but so does Webb—one man on a comic mission in the name of science.

P.S. By late 2002 Neuticles had sold its 100,000th pair of testicular implants. They're now available in seven different sizes, including custom moldings. Humans can now get prosthetic testicles, too, opening the way for Webb and other men. Interestingly, Webb declined to give an update of his condition, pleading for privacy, a completely reasonable request.

Happy Birthday, Thong
An Underwear Legend Is Born

AUGUST 2001

It's time to honor the underwear that nearly brought down a presidency. It's the twentieth anniversary of the thong.

Back in 1981, when Frederick's of Hollywood began

mass-marketing thong underwear—then known as "scanty panties"—who knew it would become the fastest-growing segment of the multibillion-dollar women's under-apparel industry and a cultural phenomenon?

R&B star Sisqo celebrates "That Thong th-thong-thong-thong" in song, and women of all ages and sizes have come to appreciate the magic power of the thong's thin strap in back—popularly known as "butt floss"—in their never-ending quest to hide those visible panty lines.

Of course, there's the "wedgie" factor. But what's a little discomfort in the name of looking good?

"These days, a woman comes into Frederick's of Hollywood and she buys maybe one corset. But she'll buy six, seven, eight thongs," says Frederick's spokeswoman-model Lee Ann Tweeden.

The lingerie giant sells an astounding 75,000 thongs a week—accounting for 90 percent of its sales—and it carries more than 100 different colors, styles, and fabrics, from low-rise to the "Rio," from cotton to charmeuse.

"It used to be scandalous," she says. "Now it's a necessity. Clothing is form-fitting, and nobody wants lines."

For Every Woman, There Is a Thong

To think, the thong started out as a novelty item, something sold alongside crotchless and edible undies. Now one fashion research group estimates that thong sales have more than doubled since 1997 while sales of regular panties have only grown about 10 percent.

Only the most daring dressers are donning thong beachwear. But they've found their way into millions of women's underwear drawers—and virtually every woman's apparel store. The cheapies go for less than $15 at Target, while Calvin Klein or Tommy Hilfiger can ask for $200 or more for theirs.

Indeed, the thong is turning up everywhere, even in the Whitewater investigation. The infamous Bill Clinton–Monica Lewinsky White House affair began with a steamy thong moment, according to Independent Counsel Kenneth Starr's report.

"In the course of flirting with [President Clinton]," the report states, "[Lewinsky] raised her jacket in the back and showed him the straps of her thong underwear."

The scandal didn't affect the sales trend, says Tweeden, age twenty-eight, who has been a Frederick's underwear model for ten years, "more than a lifetime in my business."

"I can't even tell you the last time I wore full-bottom panties, and I think a lot of women who work everyday jobs in offices would say the same thing."

At on-line retailer Stephanna's Curves, full-figured women can find titanic teddies, and, yes, thongs to fit a size-22 rear end. The proprietors say that "sex appeal does not come in a size-2 package."

If you're the crunchy-Granola hippie type, there's the all-natural, eco-friendly hemp thong. "You'd be surprised how well they sell," says George Bates of Shirt Magic in Lewiston, California.

"This is for the woman who has one eye on the environment and the other eye on impressing her boyfriend."

From Loincloths to G-Strings

Historians debate the true origin of the thong. Some trace it all the way back to the cavewoman's first loincloth. Others point to the 1939 World's Fair in New York City, when Mayor Fiorello LaGuardia decreed that the city's nude dancers cover up a bit. Thus, the G-string was born. And the G-string begot the thong.

Six years later the orbit of the Earth was brought to an abrupt halt when French designer Louis Reard unveiled the bikini at a Paris fashion show. It was named after the Bikini Atoll of the Marshall Islands, where some of the first atomic bombs were tested, and since then, it's had a similar effect on men.

Then in 1974 fashion maverick Rudi Gernrich married the thong bottom to the bikini top. Gernrich was the man who pioneered unisex fashions. In the disco era he unveiled clothing that made a woman look nude under the flashing lights of a dance club.

While traveling in Brazil the owner of Frederick's of Hollywood, Frederick Mellinger, spotted some ladies in beach thongs. He decided it was to be "the next big thing" in America.

In a stroke of genius, Mellinger decided the thong had a future not only as a bikini bottom but also as underwear. Some women may have thought it was sleazy—but not for long.

As a thong model, Tweeden says she's happy if she's contributed to the

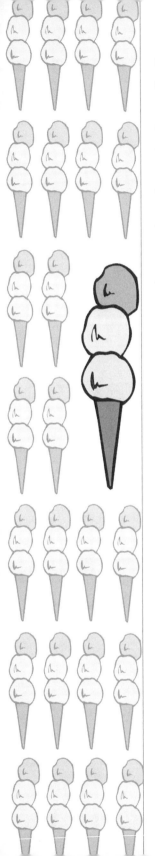

underwear revolution. "My family is proud of what I do," she says. "It's modeling in Frederick's. It's not *Hustler*."

But what about thongs for men? "I've seen them on guys," she says. "But not willingly . . . I just want to shout out, 'Get a towel, cover up, please!' "

You Are What You Eat . . . for Dessert
Flavorology Reconsidered

M A Y   1 9 9 8

Are you irritable, pessimistic, and suffering from low self-esteem? You might like strawberry ice cream. "It was amazing to discover how distinct personalities corresponded with ice-cream flavors," said Dr. Alan Hirsch, a neurologist at Chicago's Smell & Taste Treatment and Research Foundation.

Dreyer's and Edy's Grand Ice Cream hired Hirsch to conduct a study on whether certain personality types prefer certain flavors. But executives probably didn't expect to get results that depict strawberry ice-cream eaters as unsavory losers.

In its current "Flavorology" advertising push, the ice-cream company tells their customers that double-chocolate-chunk eaters are "lively, creative, dramatic, charming, enthusiastic, and the life of the party."

But Dreyer's leaves out the report's most startling results, that double-chocolate-chunk eaters tend to be "followers rather than leaders" and "flirtatious."

If you want to know the official results, *The Wolf Files* has them. But be warned, dessert lovers, you may never look at your favorite flavors the same way again.

A Little Too Accurate for Dessert

The ice-cream maker flat-out admits candy-coating Hirsh's study for their press release.

"We put a spin on it. We are in the ice-cream business to make people happy," said Dreyer's spokeswoman Jill Kasser. "This is supposed to be fun, not upsetting. We never tried to deceive anyone.

"Of course we didn't include all the information," she said. "You are not supposed to look at our Flavorology and say, 'My favorite flavor is strawberries and cream. I must be a loser.'"

However, Hirsch confirms that Dreyer's commissioned a serious report and that his results have scientific validity. He declined to criticize how the frozen dairy conglomerate used the information, saying only that his full report is "more complete."

The Banana Cream Pie Factor

Hirsch was asked to investigate whether people can be characterized according to six of Dreyer's most popular flavors. "We collected a representative sample of sixty subjects, gave them a series of psychological tests, and used accepted research methods," he said. "I stand behind the accuracy and reliability."

Among the institutes' findings: Just because you like vanilla doesn't mean you're bland. Vanilla lovers tend to be impulsive risk takers who set high goals and have high expectations of themselves, and they enjoy close family relationships.

Butter Pecan fans are hardly nutty. They tend to be logical and ethical, if not socially reserved and a little tight with a buck.

Even though personality types might gravitate to a particular flavor, Hirsch can't explain why. "Very simply, you can't make yourself a better or worse person by switching your favorite flavor ice cream," he said. "But wouldn't it be nice if it were that easy?"

Still, he sticks by the correlation he found between you and your ice cream of choice. "If your spouse suddenly switches flavors," he said, "I'd watch out."

Curiously the most flattering personality profile belongs to lovers of banana-cream-pie-flavored ice cream. These folks are said to make "the perfect husband, wife, parent, or child." Banana cream pie also happens to be Hirsch's favorite flavor. "It's a coincidence," he said. "But it's true!"

Blondes Have More Fun . . . and More Mosquito Bites

Skeeter Idiosyncracies Revealed

JUNE 2001

Just like gentlemen, mosquitoes prefer blondes—especially at evening weenie roasts. Professor Andrew Spielman, coauthor of *Mosquito* and one of the world's foremost experts on mosquitoes and the diseases they carry, says blondes and redheads might be more attractive to skeeters for the same reason they tend to turn heads at cocktail parties—they stand out in a crowd.

"Mosquitoes are attracted to contrasts," says Spielman. "If you have one blonde person with long hair wearing bright colors at a picnic held in the shade, where the other people are dark-haired, you know who is going to get the attention."

But mosquitoes look for more than good hair when choosing a target. A variety of research has shown that ovulating women, people with smelly feet, and those who sweat a lot are also good eatin'.

"Some people are clearly more attractive to mosquitoes. The precise reasons are unknown. But various research has shown that skin temperature, contrasts of color, lactic acid, and other conditions make a difference."

While this difference shouldn't really prompt blondes to buy extra bug spray—or feel at greater risk for a mosquito-borne disease like West Nile virus, it says a lot about one of man's smallest, yet deadliest foes.

Book Has Good Buzz

Spielman's book, cowritten with Pulitzer Prize–winning reporter Michael D'Antonio of *Newsday*, takes a look at how the mosquito has shaped our lives and, to some extent, world history. This summer as you gather 'round to roast weenies and the insects gather 'round you, keep a few things in mind:

The More You Swat, the More You Get Bitten: When you flail your arms to shoo away skeeters, you're probably just attracting them.

The sweat from your effort merely tickles the mosquito's antennae. Your movement catches her eye. The lactic acid from your overworked muscles whets her appetite. The heat of your skin tells her, "It's feeding time."

Humans Often Play a Role in Mosquito Sex: When it comes to biting humans, it's the females who do the dirty work. A pregnant mosquito will sink her pointy proboscis into your hide just before she lays her eggs.

Of course there are some 2,500 varieties of these mini-vampires. Only a few feast on human blood. Still, a human often comes in handy in egg production. If you are scratching, itching, and a little too red, just remember that you're helping someone's mother.

Insect Politics: The mosquito has made its presence felt. Through malaria, yellow fever, and other insect-borne diseases, our little winged foes have claimed the lives of Alexander the Great, Oliver Cromwell, and various popes and world leaders. They've held back Roman legions, helped defeat the Spanish Armada, and thwarted Genghis Khan's attempt to conquer the world.

Think of the mosquito as a protector of the weak. When spears and guns won't stop a would-be band of plunderers, mosquito-borne illnesses will often do the trick. "In Africa and Asia you'll find that explorers contracted malaria and other diseases that the locals were immune to," Spielman says.

Many historians believe Africans were able to rebel on the *Amistad* slave ship because the crew had been stricken by yellow fever. Not bad for a critter the size of a grape seed.

It wasn't until 1890 that scientists suspected the bug's role in the spread of many diseases. But even today malaria kills more than one million annually, or one person every twelve seconds. And when you consider the international problems caused by West Nile virus and various strains of encephalitis, you realize that not much has changed.

That Sexy Buzz: Does that buzzing sound turn you on? It drives male mosquitoes into a swarming frenzy. A female achieves an extremely high "C" note by flapping more than 500 times a minute. Spielman notes that a power station in Canada that made the same note began malfunctioning. Turns out it was gummed up by tens of thousands of mosquitoes, all males, apparently sexually attracted to the hum of the machinery.

The Swarming Sex Party: When you walk through a swarm of mosquitoes, you're not just at risk of swallowing a bug, you're crashing a sex party.

The female is drawn to the swarming guys. But after this big buildup, the end might sound depressingly familiar to those of us who look to nature for inspiration.

Once a male and female pair off, it's over in seconds. The female usually ends up pregnant, never wanting to have sex again. And the male often flies away with his sex organ chopped off.

Bug Zappers Don't Work: Forget electronic bug zappers. They merely kill moths and draw more mosquitoes to your backyard than they kill. Ultrasonic sound repellents? Dr. Spielman says they're unproven.

Spielman says at his outdoor events he uses sprays and oils with DEET. "You should be careful when you apply it," he says. "There are a few reports of people who have gotten neurological damage by grossly overexposing themselves. It's rare."

Citronella candles and some other oils also work.

Do Bugs Bug a Bug Expert?: On a summer night that annoying buzzing can drive Spielman out of bed with the warnings about West Nile Virus running through his head. "I know as much as anyone, the chances of getting it are remote," says the seventy-year-old. "But I hear the warnings, too."

Back at work at Harvard University, he's happy to stick his hand in a mosquito cage to let the little critters feed. "I'm immune to a few species," he says. "It doesn't really help when I go to the park, unfortunately—it's a different kind of mosquito there."

But not everyone thinks his job is so thrilling. "My granddaughter thinks what I do is gross," he says. "I tell her you can learn a lot from insects. I'm sure she will."

Mutilating Barbie
Scientists Play Rough with Dolls

FEBRUARY 1999

Barbie might not be anatomically correct—but her legs make great fingers.

A prosthetics specialist at Duke University Medical Center is converting

Barbie's knee joints into the knuckles of realistic-looking fingers.

"About a dozen people who lost part of a hand are living fuller, richer lives because of this fantastic, plastic ratchet joint," says Jane Bahor, who began dismembering America's favorite doll three years ago in the hope of helping the disabled.

My Office, the Playpen

Bahor claims it was the first time she came close to playing with Barbie. "I might be the only little girl who never had one," says Bahor, a forty-eight-year-old technician. "Then, suddenly, my office looks like a playpen."

Jennifer Jordan, an engineering student, helped Bahor come up with the idea. Jordan had suffered an amputation and was working on a senior project to invent a movable joint for hand prosthetics. She was also a Barbie girl.

It turns out that Barbie's knee moves much like the metacarpal joint of the finger—the knuckle that sticks up when you make a fist.

Bahor incorporates the doll's joint in a silicon glove. A pull-cord lets the wearer change the position of the prosthetic finger, letting a person hold a pencil or a cup.

"We had been using wire," Bahor says. "But Barbie's knee snaps into place, and that makes it much more lifelike."

Barbie Graveyard

The Barbie knee joint transfer certainly flies in the face of feminists who say the 11-plus-inch, polystyrene temptress (with a 4-inch bust) distorts little girls' images of their bodies.

"We're overjoyed," says Barbie's spokeswoman, Lisa McKendall of the Mattel toy company. "We are generally against the mutilation of our dolls, but in the interest of science, we condone it."

This has been a tough year for the plastic-haired blonde. Having been introduced at the 1959 toy fair, she turned forty. Last month the Barbie Hall of Fame was evicted from its home in Palo Alto, California, leaving nearly 21,000 dolls temporarily homeless.

You older folks might think Barbie couldn't bend at the knee. She could wear a wedding dress around her dream house, but she wasn't flexible enough to pull stockings up her disproportionately long but sexy legs.

Nevertheless, modern incarnations—such as Super Gymnast Barbie, WNBA Barbie, and Woman's World Cup Soccer Barbie—can snap their legs in a variety of positions.

Of course just like any office gnome, Working Woman Barbie still can't flex her knee—even if her plastic life depended on it. And Barbie's boy toy, Ken, is also a stiff.

While Barbie critics say the doll puts an unrealistic expectation on little girls, toy maker Mattel quickly seized the PR initiative and donated a large supply of plastic joints. "Thank God I don't have to dissect dolls anymore," Bahor says. "It was sad, having a little Barbie graveyard."

Batgirl and Fat Men
Undying Lust for a TV Superhero

JUNE 2000

Fat, middle-aged men are always reminding Yvonne Craig, "You were my first love." That's what happens when you thrill a generation of pubescent boys as Batgirl—they never forget.

"I was bouncing around in a spray-on costume, and these guys must have been twelve-year-old boys with the early stirrings of puberty," Craig says, recalling her role on TV's *Batman* in the 1960s.

Craig, age sixty-two, always has a huge crowd of graying male baby boomers around her at nostalgia shows—she reminds them of the boys they used to be.

"I see these guys line up with their sons and daughters," she says, "and they rarely are shy about it."

Craig has a few claims to fame. She played the savagely sexy green-skinned space alien who seduces Captain Kirk on *Star Trek*. And in real life she briefly dated Elvis Presley. But she never hit it big.

After she went claw to claw with Catwoman and kicked Penguin's butt, her show-business career petered out. Craig went into the real-estate business and later sold prepaid telephone cards, after ever-decreasing TV appearances on the likes of *Fantasy Island, The Six Million Dollar Man,* and *Kojak*.

Now retired, Craig is on the comic book and nostalgia convention circuit, promoting her book *From Ballet to the Batcave and Beyond*, a look at her slice of celebrity.

"Grown women actually say to me that I was their hero," says Craig. "It's a kind of funny statement on the state of TV back in the 1960s. There really weren't too many female characters who stood up to men. Girls had Batgirl."

Hot Bat Sex

Strangely, the filming of the campy TV show has been the subject of controversy. The man who played Robin, Burt Ward, blew the lid off the Bat Cave in his 1995 tell-all memoir *Boy Wonder: My Life in Tights*, claiming that the show was a never-ending sex party, with "thousands" of women waiting outside the superheroes' trailer, hoping to get into their Bat skivvies.

Batman star Adam West once shouted to his groupies, "On your knees, girls, and stay in line!" Ward writes, as the show reached new heights in "Batutsi" sexual self-indulgence.

West, now age seventy-one, was furious with the book, denying all the salacious details. He's spent the last few years assuring fans that he's not a Bat Pervert.

Batman was a break-out hit when it hit the air in 1966. The half-hour show ran twice a week on ABC, with Wednesday's episode leaving the dynamic duo in cliffhanger peril, the announcer urging viewers to tune in Thursday, "same Bat Time, same Bat Channel."

With stars Vincent Price, Joan Collins, Ethel Merman, Eartha Kitt, and Cesar Romero clamoring for parts as guest villains, the show will be remembered as the first to hold two spots in the season-end Nielsen top 10.

Craig, for her part, claims she never knew of sex orgies on the *Batman* set. Producers had brought her in for the third and final season to fight declining ratings the old-fashioned way—with sexy outfits.

"Burt did spend a lot of time in his trailer," she says. "But I don't really know what he was doing. I really hung out with the writers."

Playing with Elvis's Monkey

The Ohio-born actress tries to keep up her humor. Her first marriage, to actor-singer Jimmy Boyd, famous for an early 1950s hit recording, "I Saw Mommy Kissing Santa Claus," ended after two years. Back then Craig took work in any form, including a part in *Mars Needs Women*, which is on many film critics' short lists for worst movie of all time.

She's now married to venture capital businessman Ken Aldrich of Santa Monica, California, and proudly boasted a few years back, "He had never seen me in anything but *By Love Possessed.*"

But having just finished her memoirs, she is now ready to relive her past. Meeting up at fan events, she helps keep the peace between Batman and Robin, although Robin is less likely to show up these days now that he and his wife have started a Great Dane rescue service in Northern California.

Of her leading men, she recalls Elvis most fondly. "You never really go out with Elvis. You went in with Elvis," she says. "He was a homebody. We'd watch movies at his place, and he was a perfect Southern gentleman."

Elvis claimed many times that he had slept with all his leading ladies—except for one. Earlier this year actress Mary Tyler Moore, who starred with Elvis in *Change of Habit*, claimed it was her—joking with a Florida audience, "What was I thinking?"

But Craig, who appeared in *It Happened at the World's Fair* and *Kissin' Cousins*, says, "I didn't sleep with him either."

"We spent a lot of time just watching his crazy pet monkey. I swear."

High Hopes
World's Tallest Woman Vows to Rise Again

J A N U A R Y   2 0 0 0

You may as well know, Sandy Allen wears a size-22 shoe. Sooner or later, everyone asks.

On New Year's Eve at a physical rehabilitation center in Indianapolis, Indiana, Allen—the world's tallest woman—has three resolutions: "I want to laugh. I want to be around children. And I want to get back on my feet."

The Guinness Book of World Records certifies Allen's height at 7 feet, 7¼ inches. But it's been more than a year since she's stood up. Suffering from a severe bladder infection, atrophied muscles, and a variety of ailments, she vows that she will walk again. "Don't laugh," she says, "but I have high hopes."

'Life's Short, I'm Not'

At age forty-six, Allen has outlived many other giants. Unusual growth can trigger a variety of health issues. The world's tallest man, Robert Wadlow, who was 8 feet, 11 inches, died at age twenty-two. The tallest woman, the 8-foot, 2-inch Zeng Jinlian of China, was just seventeen.

"My time could be running out," she says. "But I'll go down fighting." She has a nightshirt that says it all: "Life's Short, I'm Not."

Allen's whole life has been a fight, from being an outcast in Shelbyville, Indiana, to working in what she called a "glorified freak show" in Niagara Falls. Her favorite memories are doing assembly programs for elementary-school children, teaching the simple lesson, "It's OK to be different."

"I felt so much like an outcast, a space alien, someone who didn't belong," she says. "I feel I have a duty to help others who stare up to the sky and say, 'Why me, lord?'"

One Size Fits All . . . But You

Imagine a world several sizes too small. Terror lurks in the bathroom. She once got her 400-pound frame stuck in a tub for several hours. "Showerheads," she says, "hit me in the belly button."

Try washing dishes when the sink comes up only to your thigh. Try finding a pair of panty hose that fit. If anyone could complain, "I haven't a thing to wear," it was she.

Allen suffers from "acromegaly," commonly known as "giant's disease." She was a normal 6 pounds, 5 ounces at birth. But a tumor in the pituitary gland triggered unusual growth. By the sixth grade, she was 6½ feet tall and towered over her teacher.

"We had a graduation party at a skating rink and I was the only kid who couldn't participate," she said. "My feet were too big to rent skates. I just wanted to be like other girls."

Allen couldn't get behind the wheel of a car when it came time to take driver's ed. No boy would dance with her.

"They called me a beanpole, a monster, a freak. And that's what they said to my face," she said. "I could only imagine what they said behind my back."

'Why Not Go on TV and Make Some Money?'

Some people turn the other cheek. Not Sandy Allen. "I try not to have anger. But I give it to them back when I need to," she says. "I've learned to pity mean people.

"You can laugh off some of those jokes. But how many times do you want to hear 'How's the weather up there?' Especially if they are being mean about it. Sometimes you want to spit on those people and say, 'It's raining.'"

She credits her grandmother for teaching survival instincts. Sandy's mother abandoned her, and she never knew her father.

In 1976, only a few years after high school, she was working as a secretary when Guinness recognized her as the world's tallest living woman and a high-school pariah turned international celebrity.

"Suddenly, my height became an asset. I was getting invitations everywhere," she says. "I figured why not go on TV and make some money?"

Over the next years she worked for Guinness at a museum and traveling exhibit and became a familiar face on the talk show circuits, speaking with the likes of David Frost, Phil Donahue, Merv Griffin, Oprah Winfrey, Leeza Gibbons, Maury Povich, Jerry Springer, and Howard Stern.

"Most of the time people were nice, and I got to travel the world," she said.

One high point, she says—famed filmmaker Federico Fellini flew her to Europe to appear in his version of *Casanova*. In case you missed it, she played an arm-wrestling giantess who, at one point, takes a provocative bath with two dwarfs.

"I was definitely proud of what I did and to be a part of a critically acclaimed filmmaker's work," she said. "When it played in Shelbyville, I was the toast of the town."

Michael Jackson and the Giantess

While working at a *Guinness* exhibit in San Francisco in the mid-1980s, a man came up to her one evening and introduced himself as Michael Jackson. "Of course, I didn't believe him," she said. "I shot back, 'Yeah sure, and I'm the next president of the United States.' "

But, she says, she and Jackson saw each other several times. He came back the next day with autographed copies of his albums, and she later sent him an autographed copy of the *Guinness Book of World Records*. "I was truly impressed with his humble kindness," she said. "I still can't believe he sought me out."

But life on the road had low points. In Niagara Falls, tourists paid a few bucks to pose with her and that grew old fast.

While she's always tried to maintain her dignity, it's not always easy. When talk show host Howard Stern tried to get her to talk about her sex life, she finally admitted on the air that she was a virgin.

"I don't want to hurt Howard Stern's reputation," she says. "but he's actually a nice guy. A little strange, but aren't we all?"

She talks a little more openly in her book: "A man once pursued me for a relationship, but I found out in no time that he was married and he was just curious.

"I'm sure a man would marry me," she now jokes, "but what man could afford a diamond that would fit on my size-16 ring finger?"

Post–September 11 Compassion

By the early 1990s Sandy found herself working as a secretary again and speaking at elementary schools. "I started to hate traveling. I had trouble getting in and out of planes and cars," she said. "The most satisfying work was speaking to children."

But the death of her grandmother and the loss of her job hit her rather hard in recent years. Her health has since been in decline, and she's had money issues. At one point she tried selling signed paint-by-number portraits for $45.

While in physical therapy, she heard about the September 11 attack. "I was scared and devastated," she says. "But it also made me want to go forward. It made me feel so close to other Americans, and that we are a country that's compassionate.

"I've really struggled with depression, especially recently," she says. "The trick is to get yourself to realize that you can be compassionate and that you can find compassionate people. The idiots and the mean people, you can just ignore."

P.S. Sandy's health stabilized in 2001; although she can no longer walk, she continues to answer fan mail. Friends in Indianapolis held a fund-raiser in November 2002 to help her pay for medical expenses.

Patriot
Games

Bushisms 'Resignate'
A Fortune in Mangled Language

JANUARY 2003

Don't "misunderestimate" President Bush's "embettered" English. Bushisms are big business and worthy of "analyzation." A talking Bush doll, a Bushisms calendar, and several best-selling books celebrate the president's unique gift of gab.

Whether it's pronouncing nuclear as "NOO-kyuh-luhr," botching speeches, or coining new words like "Hispanically," Bush just seems to "resignate" with Americans.

President Rivals Dilbert

The 2003 George W. Bush Quote Calendar has became a national sensation, selling more than 110,000 copies in the last two months and joining such perennial powerhouses as *Dilbert* and *The Far Side* on Barnes & Noble and Calendars.com's Top 10 lists.

Bush's mangled words are even finding their way into the English language. "Misunderestimate" tops the list of 2002's new words, according to YourDictionary.com.

There are more than 10,000 references to "misunderestimate" on the Internet. Even if the word is often used as a joke, the president's impact is unmistakable, editors say.

For those of you not fluent in Bush-speak, the Web site offers these definitions. Examples of their usage are offered here as documented by Jacob Weisberg's best-sellers *Bushisms* and *More Bushisms*.

- **Misunderestimate:** To seriously underestimate. Usage: "They misunderestimated me." (Bentonville, Arkansas, November 6, 2000)

- **Embetter:** To make better. Usage: "I want to thank the people who made the firm and solemn commitment to work hard to embetter themselves." (Washington, D.C., April 18, 2002)

- **Resignate:** To resonate. Usage: "This issue doesn't seem to resignate with the people." (Portland, Oregon, October 31, 2000)

- **Foreign-handed:** To understand foreign policy. Usage: "I will have a foreign-handed foreign policy." (Redwood, California, September 27, 2000)

- **Analyzation:** Analysis. Usage: "This case has had full analyzation and has been looked at a lot. I understand the emotionality of death penalty cases." (June 23, 2000)

There's a blooper reel for every modern president—even those hailed as master communicators. It's no wonder. Every word they publicly utter is recorded and dissected. But Bush is on his way to becoming the Yogi Berra of American politics.

It's a talent that's been apparent since he set out on the campaign trail. "I know how hard it is for you to put food on your family," he told supporters in January 2000 at the Nashua Chamber of Commerce, shortly before the New Hampshire primary.

Bush addressed education policy in South Carolina: "Rarely is the question asked, Is our children learning?"

Then, debating rival John McCain, Bush made overtures to unite his party. "I think we agree, the past is over," he said, after complaining that the Arizona senator "can't take the high horse and then claim the low road."

How to Push the President's Button

Toy merchant John Warnock and his family struck gold just before Christmas with a talking George W. Bush doll—a $30, 12½-inch action figure that demonstrates the president's way with words with seventeen "powerful and patriotic phrases."

Push the plastic president's button and he says all your favorite things, such as, "I don't need to be 'sublim-in-able' about the differences between our views."

More than 12,000 Bush dolls sold in less than a week, when supplies ran out, Warnock says. In the days before Christmas, they were selling on eBay for $250, making the commander in chief this year's Tickle Me Elmo.

Through it all, Bush laughs off his critics. "You have to admit in my sentences, I have gone where no man has gone before," he joked at his own expense at the 2001 White House Correspondents Dinner.

But if we laugh at Bush, we should remember that he's not the only national politician who's been roasted for his malapropisms. Al Gore certainly has been known to trip over his tongue.

On the campaign trail in 1996, Gore visited a school in a largely Hispanic section of Albuquerque, New Mexico, and decided to use a little Spanish. He tried to say "muchas gracias" ("many thanks"). Instead he waved and told the crowd, "machismo gracias" ("manliness thanks").

Then in 1998 after Michael Jordan led the Chicago Bulls to their sixth NBA championship, the vice president offered this assessment of the game: "I tell you that Michael Jackson is unbelievable, isn't he? He's just unbelievable."

P.S. Even the greatest political orators make mistakes. With Cold War tensions brewing, John F. Kennedy gave a dramatic address at the Berlin Wall to show America's commitment to Eastern Europe. He meant to say, "Ich bin Berliner."

Instead he botched his German, saying "Ich bin ein Berliner," which translates into the affirmation, "I am a cream-filled pastry."

Top Dogs in Politics
Furry, Four-Legged Washington Wags

JULY 2002

Harry Truman once said, "If you want a friend in Washington, get a dog." But it's more than a matter of canine companionship—a pet is virtually a presidential prerequisite.

Ask President Bush how his family is doing, and he probably won't talk about his twin daughters, who have had some scrapes over underage drinking. But he'll just rave about his pooches—a thirteen-year-old English springer spaniel named Spot and a 1½-year-old Scottish terrier named Barney.

"The family's doing well," Bush told a crowd recently in Little Rock, Arkansas, according to the *New York Times* wire service. "Barney, the dog, is in great shape. Spot, the dog, who was born in the White House when Mother and Dad were there, is getting a little up in the years, but she's doing well, too. She's used to the confines of the South Lawn. And I invite her every morning into the Oval Office to start my day."

At a political fund-raiser this year in Kansas City, Missouri, Bush called Barney—a gift from Christine Todd Whitman, the former head of the Environmental Protection Agency—"a fabulous little guy." He even referred to the terrier as "the son I never had."

Pets humanize a president. Millard Fillmore, Franklin Pierce, and Chester Arthur were the only chief executives who failed to provide the White House with animal occupants. Not all of them have been dogs. Thomas Jefferson kept grizzly bears in a cage in his garden. John Quincy Adams let his alligator reside in a White House bathtub. And Calvin Coolidge had a virtual menagerie that included a bobcat, two raccoons, a donkey, and a wallaby.

In all some 400 beasts have lived at 1600 Pennsylvania Avenue, according to Carl Anthony, author of *America's First Families*. No matter how fuzzy-wuzzy, or how exotic, they do one thing—they humanize a president, and they serve as a moment of distraction in times of strife.

About 60 percent of all American families have a pet, and taking one inside the Beltway only makes the first family seem more in touch with average Americans.

As the Clinton administration careened from scandal to scandal, the president turned to his faithful Lab Buddy for support—and a photo op.

The new top dog in Washington is clearly Spot Bush, the elder of the president's two dogs. Spot comes to office with a presidential lineage—just like her master. She is the daughter of Millie Bush, whose dog-eyed account of White House life, *Millie's Book* (as told to then–first lady Barbara Bush), became a best-seller, raising nearly $1 million for literacy programs and outselling the elder President Bush's memoirs.

At the height of her fame, Millie graced the cover of *Life* magazine, and George Bush père had a dog biscuit dispenser shaped like a gumball machine at Camp David.

But life in the White House is not all caviar and kibble. Like any savvy politician, you have to watch your tail. The late Mama Millie could have told Spot that. *Washingtonian* magazine once voted Millie the "Ugliest Dog" in the capital.

Dog House Scandals

The president is supposed to have more to worry about than the antics of his pets—but that's not always the case.

Theodore Roosevelt's bull terrier, Pete, caused a wee bit of an international scandal when he tore a leg off the French ambassador's trousers during a White House function, according to Roy Rowan, author of *First Dogs*.

Lyndon B. Johnson provoked a firestorm of animal-cruelty accusations when he picked up his beagles, Him and Her, by their ears so that photographers could get a better shot. Dog owners complained, but Johnson had a characteristic answer: "To make them bark is good for them."

Calvin Coolidge's vast array of critters didn't help his reputation for being a misanthrope. Presidential historian Carl Anthony reports that Coolidge's collie, Rob Roy, once menaced a senator at lunch. "Senator," Coolidge said, "I think he wants your sausage." The senator gave in.

Even Franklin Roosevelt, the only president to be elected to four terms in the Oval Office, took political heat after he boasted that he had a naval destroyer fetch his Scottish terrier when she was accidentally left behind on the Aleutian Islands.

Republicans tried to turn the Fala Roosevelt rescue operation to their political advantage, claiming it cost taxpayers $15,000 in dog biscuits.

The Assassination of Lincoln's Mutt

Abraham Lincoln's mutt, Fido, suffered a shocking fate, much like his master: He was knifed to death in the street by a drunk who became angry when the dog jumped on him with muddy paws.

Rowan recounts the story of John Roll, Lincoln's neighbor from Springfield, Illinois, who wrote the Lincoln family in Washington, reporting that the "poor yellow dog was assinated [sic] just like his illustrious master."

Maybe it's just true that some dogs and masters take on each other's lives. John F. Kennedy's terrier, Charlie, had a notorious Cold War romance with the Soviet dog Nikita Khrushchev gave the president—resulting in a litter of four pups.

Of course, master politicians can use their pets effectively. Richard Nixon effectively used his dog Checkers to deflect accusations that he had received improper campaign gifts during his vice-presidential campaign in 1952.

"Someone in Texas had sent us a little black-and-white cocker spaniel puppy. My daughter had named it Checkers . . . and I said that regardless of what anyone said about it, I was going to keep it," Nixon said.

Unfortunately, the dog died before Nixon became president.

Clinton 'Fesses Up to Sleeping with Dog

Late in his second term, with his sex life in the news and his wife Hillary on the campaign trail, President Clinton even kidded with reporters that he had a new bed partner.

"I've got a friend," Clinton told White House reporters. "He sleeps with me when Hillary's not here. He's my true friend. We have a great time."

Buddy got special treatment when Clinton left office. While Clinton's cat, Socks, was handed off to his secretary, Betty Currie, Buddy got to romp on the former First Couple's $1.7 million estate in Chappaqua, New York.

Unfortunately, several months ago Buddy was stuck and killed while chasing a car in what the former president described as "by far the worst thing" to happen to him since he left office.

But Clinton contacted a Maryland breeder and ended up with one of Buddy's great-nephews. The new pup is named Seamus, the Gaelic form of James. The two reportedly are very happy together.

Monica Lewinsky's Royal Roots
Clinton Scandal Touches the Late
Princess Diana

AUGUST 1998

Even if Monica Lewinsky never took a White House internship, she'd still have some claim to fame—through an accident of marriage, she's related to Princess Diana.

Lewinsky's stepfather, Ronald Peter Straus, can trace a blue bloodline that runs through railroad tycoons in the Vanderbilt family, Wall Street powerhouses at Lehman Bros.—and ultimately to heirs of the British throne.

ABCNEWS.com has confirmed the research of New York genealogist Jon Speller, who has identified seventeen blood and two marital ties that unite a Jewish girl from Beverly Hills to British royalty.

Many genealogists agree that at least one in five Americans can find royalty in their family if they search back far enough. But Lewinsky's path is more direct than most.

"Most people think if you are Jewish, or a member of another minority, you can't possibly be connected to royalty," Speller said. "Here's proof we are a lot closer to a global family."

From Beverly Hills to Windsor Castle

The authority on British aristocracy, *Debrett's Peerage and Baronetage*, indicates that Diana's mother, Frances, was one-quarter American. Her father was the grandson of Frank Work, a poor man who one day helped a stranger who slipped on the streets of New York. That man happened to be railroad tycoon "Commodore" Cornelius Vanderbilt—and Vanderbilt sure knew how to say "Thank You."

Vanderbilt hired Work, who eventually became the family's stockbroker and one of the most powerful men on Wall Street.

Work hated the notion that his daughter married into British aristocracy. He disowned the child until her divorce and, under the terms of his will, threatened to disinherit any family member who set foot again in Britain.

But Diana's grandfather, Edmund Maurice Burke Roche, defied the will and claimed his title, becoming the 4th Baron Fermoy.

Edmund's sister, New York socialite Cynthia Burke Roche, married iron manufacturer Arthur Scott Burden, whose family developed a process to manufacture nails about the time of the Civil War and parlayed it into a fortune.

Enter Joan Rivers

Arthur's brother, James, who ran the company, was prominent in New York society. He entertained the Prince of Wales at his home in 1924 during an international polo match. And his wife was a daughter of Cornelius Vanderbilt.

The rest, as they say, is history—and well documented through New York's society pages. The Vanderbilts married the Lehmans. The Lehmans married the Strauses. And in April, Monica's mother, Marcia Lewis, married into the Straus family.

The line turned from Christian to Jewish with the marriage of Wendy Vanderbilt and Orin Lehman—whose family founded the Lehman Bros. financial empire.

Now divorced, Lehman recently became engaged to comedienne Joan Rivers, raising the possibility that she, too, would take a spot on the Lewinsky-Diana family line.

Relatives You Don't Brag About

Of course, many people fear what they might find if they dig into their past. Even in this line of crème-de-la-crème lineage, there are members you wouldn't brag about at the family picnic.

Arthur Scott Burden, for instance, suffered a mental breakdown in 1913 after he fell off his polo pony. A sheriff's jury declared him incompetent and he died in a White Plains, New York, mental hospital. James Abercrombie Burden told the *New York Times* that his brother Arthur was "a victim of brain atrophy."

More appropriate table conversation might be the tale of Alfred Gwynne Vanderbilt, who died heroically in the 1915 sinking of the *Lusitania*. A front-page *New York Times* headline read: "Vanderbilt Saved Woman, Gave Life Belt Though He Could Not Swim."

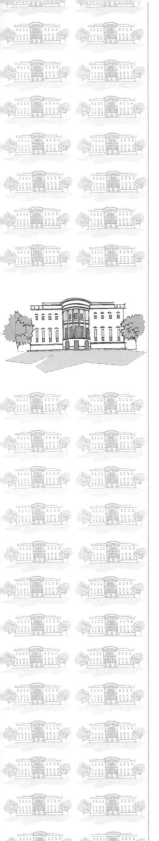

"A woman came up to him, and I saw him place the belt around the woman," said *Lusitania* survivor Thomas Slidel. "He had none for himself."

P.S. Speller also proved that such notables as Al Gore, Drew Barrymore, and even the Marx Brothers, can be linked to Princess Diana. But those genealogies have many more links in them. In this sense, at least, Monica Lewinsky is closer to royalty.

Excuse Me, Officer, My Dad's President
Growing Up in the First Family

JANUARY 2001

If President Bush now has his hands full with daughters Jenna and Barbara, he should be happy he's not Chester A. Arthur—his son got caught skinny-dipping in a White House fountain with the prince of Siam.

Having a dad for president has a few advantages. Police let Alan Arthur off the hook when they found out who he was. But if White House history has taught us anything, it's that being leader of the free world doesn't exactly make you all-powerful in controlling your kids.

"My children give me more pain than all my enemies," lamented John Adams, the nation's second president.

Theodore Roosevelt—who took office with six children under age seventeen—put it even more bluntly. He said he could either be president or control his kids, but "couldn't do both."

"First families are under fantastic scrutiny," says historian Carl Anthony, author of *America's First Families.* "It's amazing that anyone can grow up under those conditions. The whole world is watching."

Still, only ten presidents and first ladies had no living children while in the White House—and many had to raise children while trying to keep world peace.

That 'Indolent' Little Wash

Roosevelt's eldest, Alice, had quite a reputation, dancing on cars in Newport, jumping into the White House pool fully clothed, screaming when the staff refused to serve champagne. When she left home, her stepmother Edith snapped, "I want you to know that I'm glad to see you leave," adding, "You have been nothing but trouble."

Even the first president had problems with a step-grandson, a party-hardy Princeton University student known as "Little Wash."

President Washington noted that his namesake had "an almost unconquerable disposition to indolence in everything that did not tend to his amusements." Princeton eventually gave the boy the boot for "having endeavored in various ways to lessen the authority and influence of the faculty."

Everyone knows that Adams had a son, John Quincy Adams, who also became president. But no one talks much about his son Charles, an alcoholic who died while his father was in office.

In true White House fashion, John Adams used the tragedy for political advantage. Rather than receive Thomas Jefferson at the Executive Mansion after Jefferson defeated him in a reelection bid, Adams snubbed him, claiming he was still mourning his dead son.

"It was a lame excuse, considering that Charles had been buried three months earlier," Anthony writes. "Adams hadn't attended the burial, but he had appeared at numerous public events since then."

If It's Not the Kids . . .

Just about each of the recent presidents has had to deal in public with family squabbles. Patti Davis, President Reagan's daughter, bared her body in *Playboy* and admitted to having used cocaine, even as her mother was promulgating the "Just Say No" antidrug campaign.

The elder President Bush had a real problem on his hands with his son Neil, who became embroiled in a federal investigation of the 1988 collapse of a savings and loan that ended up costing taxpayers an estimated $1 billion.

Yet it's wrong to simply blame the children. Presidents are always having family problems, just like the rest of us. Who doesn't have a relative whom he would just as soon forget? There's a Roger Clinton or a Billy Carter swinging from every family tree.

Jimmy Carter had to resign himself to the fact that his brother was a self-described beer-guzzling "redneck." The president once publicly thanked him for doing his share for the nation's economy by "putting the beer industry back on its feet."

"I wish Billy would have gone along with my plan to involve him in the government," President Carter once told an audience. "I was going to reorganize and put the FBI and the CIA together. But Billy said he didn't want to join any agency he couldn't spell."

It's Good to Be the First Kid

Growing up with the whole world watching is sometimes rough. Still, look at the upside of being a First Kid: You're living in a 132-room mansion complete with swimming pools, a movie theater, bowling alleys, and a putting green. And then of course, there's Air Force One and weekends at Camp David.

Also, you don't have to worry about the usual kid chores. The White House comes with a domestic staff of ninety-one servants. That might seem a little excessive. Just keep in mind the White House has 31 toilets to scrub, 147 windows to squeegee, and 18 acres to mow.

Now do you remember why little kids want to grow up to be president?

Jimmy Carter's Killer Bunny
A Hare-Raising Political Scandal

SEPTEMBER 1999

All presidents face confrontation. The media attacks. The opposing party attacks. And twenty years ago, as Jimmy Carter found, a bunny rabbit can also attack. The so-called "killer bunny" that came after Carter as he was fishing near his home in Plains, Georgia, in mid-1979 marks an interesting moment in the history of White House controversy. Certainly his staffers will never forget it.

"I think a lot of people in politics have gone to school on this bizarre little event," recalls former press secretary Jody Powell.

"More than anything else, it shows the extent to which an insignificant incident can snowball and end up in newspapers and news shows across the country."

The Start of Bunnygate

Most people simply couldn't believe a rabbit could swim. But this was no Easter Bunny cutting across the pond. It was an ornery critter, hissing and gnashing its teeth, Carter said.

Could this have been an imaginary bunny? Do you think the president guzzled too much Billy Beer? Not likely. A photo shows the president swatting an oar into the water to chase off the little beast.

Certainly this was no Watergate, arms were not secretly traded with a country that supports terrorism, and the president did not have to deny having sexual relations with a White House intern. Nevertheless, the Carter administration had to go into a deep huddle to figure out how to respond to reports that the leader of the free world had to fight off a belligerent bunny.

"It was a nonstory, but they had to respond," says presidential biographer Douglas Brinkley.

"It just played up the Carter flake factor and contributed to his public persona as something less than a commanding presence. I mean, he had to deal with Russia and the Ayatollah and here he was supposedly fighting off a rabbit."

When Rabbits Swim . . .

Brinkley says Ronald Reagan knew how to shrug off what he calls "tabloid attacks." But Carter lacked that media savvy. He had simply mentioned the incident to staffers over a lemonade out on his porch, and suddenly he had to do some explaining.

In an interview with ABC News shortly after the incident, Carter stuck to his guns, telling Sam Donaldson, "Rabbits swim and that one was swimming without any difficulty at all. I can certify to that."

But today the incident still strikes people as odd, even outdoorsmen. "I've heard of some strange things," says Lee Salber of Ducks Unlimited, a national hunting organization, "but I've never heard of that. Maybe it was a Republican bunny."

Salber says that a hare, when attacked, will run in a circle to look for its burrow or a thicket to hide in. He theorized that it might attempt to swim if its path is blocked or if it has rabies.

Looking back on it, Powell says he wishes the whole thing had never got out. "Did we screw that one up?" he says. "You bet."

Powell recalls that he "leaked" the story to Associated Press White House correspondent Brooks Jackson thinking it was nothing more than lighthearted conversation. That title of that chapter: "A Grave Mistake."

Carter, on the other hand, chose to leave the rabbit incident out of his 1988 book, *Outdoor Journal*, when he recounted scads of other experiences with nature.

But the incident still follows him. At a Carter administration reunion two years ago in Atlanta, the former president was presented with a broken oar and a giant stuffed animal. Carter just laughed and stood in front of it, allowing folks to take pictures of him with it.

"After writing my Carter biography I can tell you," Brinkley says, "more people ask about the bunny than about the Camp David Accord or the Panama Canal Treaty. Strange."

P.S. Reagan was not only better at responding to such attacks, he could also instigate them. The picture of Carter and the attack bunny surfaced only after his staffers found it in 1981 in White House files.

Sideshow Stars Hate Florida's Political Circus
Election Recount Irks Clowns and Blockheads

NOVEMBER 2000

Who won the presidential election? Gore? Bush? You can call the never-ending Florida recount a fiasco. You can call it chaos. But the people of Gibsonton are pleading with fellow Americans to please, please, please stop calling it a sideshow.

The people of this seaside town just outside of Tampa take sideshows and circuses very seriously. This is the winter home where Lobster Boy, the Human Seal, and other sideshow legends once lived. Even today thousands of carnies reside here—and they don't think it's fair that this tainted presidential election is being compared to their profession.

"I've been in circus life for forty years, and let me tell you, a circus is highly organized and efficient. This election is chaotic," says Jackie Le Claire, a retired white-face clown who traveled with Ringling Bros. and Barnum & Bailey Circus.

"You ever try to manage dozens of clowns, acrobats, and wild animals? Don't use 'circus' when you mean 'disorganized,'" Le Claire says. "Everything needs to be precise. We could teach these election officials a thing or two."

Gibsonton is hardly your typical American city. It's the winter home for several circuses and traveling shows. Residents affectionately call the place "Freaktown, USA," a description that was more apt fifty years ago, when folks wouldn't bat an eye when a bearded lady, hermaphrodite, or three-legged man ambled down the street.

Sideshows that exploit human deformity have, for the most part, gone the way of the minstrel act. Only a few elderly residents ever made a living as "professional freaks," as they were once called. Still this town of 7,000 people, who largely live in small houses and trailers, remains the largest concentration of circus folk.

Blockhead: 'We Deserve a President'

Gibsonton's last remaining human blockhead, ninety-three-year-old Melvin Burkhardt, is having a good laugh over the

election chaos. "I wouldn't honor those election officials by calling them block-heads. At least I made an honest living at what I did. I entertained thousands of people all over the world and on TV," he says. "I've been on *Jerry Springer* four times."

Burkhardt's routine, which he still performs on occasion, involves leaning backward and hammering nails, spikes, screwdrivers, and ice picks up his nose. A boxing injury as a teenager resulted in several bones being removed from his nasal cavity, allowing him to thrill and amuse audiences around the world.

"I invented the blockhead routine. I did it at the Chicago World's Fair in 1933, and I've been perfecting it ever since," he says. "There are other people banging things in their head. But not everybody does it with style."

Burkhardt lives with his wife, Joyce, on the outskirts of town in a trailer that bears the bumper sticker *God Bless This Mobile Home*. He loves to talk about the glory days of the sideshow business and the honor among the fat ladies and geeks he called colleagues.

"We're simple working folks, or retired folks," he says. "We deserve a president."

Burkhardt remembers a time more than twenty years ago when there were many so-called freaks in Gibsonton. Al Tomaini, a hulking 8-foot, 4-inch giant, was the police chief. A dwarf named Colonel Casper served as the fire chief, and the post office had a lower table so that little people could sort their mail.

Tomaini married Jeanie "The Half Girl"—a woman born without legs—and the two toured the country as "The World's Strangest Married Couple" in the 1930s before settling down. Until she died a few years ago, Jeanie ran the town's bait and tackle shop, perched on a stool behind the cash register.

The Saga of Lobster Boy

Many in the town are reluctant to talk to the media. In many ways, Gibsonton is still recovering from the Lobster Boy saga.

Lobster Boy was a sideshow sensation. His real name was Grady Stiles Jr., and, like his father, he was born with a genetic condition that caused his fingers and toes to fuse into two-digit claws. He propelled himself with flipperlike legs.

By the 1950s he was one of the hottest acts in the business. But he was said to be a violent alcoholic who even drank onstage. He was convicted of killing his daughter's boyfriend. But due to favorable testimony from two carny neighbors—a bearded lady and a fat man—he was spared a lengthy prison term.

Stiles was later murdered by his wife and stepson (a human blockhead), who paid a hit man $1,500 to shoot him. They are both now serving time.

Stiles's son by another marriage has the same condition as his father and is also trying to make it in show business. He recently had a public access show on cable TV in Tampa. He's also tried to sell tracings of his hands on eBay.

Most Gibsonton residents don't want to talk about Lobster Boy with outsiders. But they're more than willing to talk about other subjects.

The Last Sideshow

"These people could joke about who they were, but they had pride," says legendary carnival impresario Ward Hall, who runs one of only two remaining traveling sideshows. His "World of Wonders" attraction has an upcoming gig at the Florida State Fair in February.

"I don't think anything that is going on in this election shows that the politicians have pride."

Hall, age seventy, once acted as the carnival barker, standing in front of the theater with a straw hat and cane, shouting, "Hurry, hurry, hurry, see the most amazing sights in the world with your own two eyes. . . ." But now that patter is delivered via a tape recorder, and a good part of the World of Wonders exists as a wax museum. The show still features "Howard Huge," a 712-pound fat man; a fire-eating dwarf; a woman who dances the cha-cha over broken glass; and "Tough Titties," a man who pulls a wagon of sledgehammers by hooks in his nipples.

"It was a way of life, and a good one," Hall says. "They got paid and they stuck together. That's why so many of them lived in this town. It was a brotherhood."

Hall says it took more than political correctness to put most of the sideshows out of business. Medical science provided corrective surgery and other treatments for many people born with deformities, reducing his potential stable of talent. But the real killer, he says, was economics.

"We sideshows used to work on a 60-40 split with the carnivals," Hall says. "But then the carnivals started investing in big rides. Once you have a ride, you

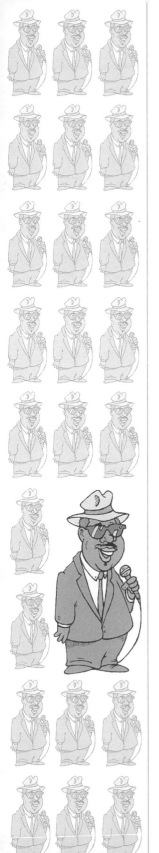

get all the money and you don't have to worry about the split."

Sideshows hit a high point in the 1950s, when more than one hundred traveling acts toured the country. States began cracking down on sideshows in the 1960s. Pete Terhurne, Hall's 3-foot, 7-inch fire-eater, and a man known as "Sealo, the Seal Boy" (he had hands growing out of his shoulders) challenged a Florida law against exploitation of deformed people, and in 1972 the state supreme court struck it down as unconstitutional.

Hall has since gone on the offensive to defend the sideshow life. In 1994 he denounced experts who wrote about exploitation shows, telling the *Chicago Tribune*, "Until you've sat up all night with the fat lady in a hospital room or consoled a brokenhearted dwarf, you're no expert."

The Covert Comic
Joke and Dagger Games

A P R I L   1 9 9 9

If you believe John Alejandro King, he's the biggest joker at the CIA. King claims he's a fifteen-year CIA veteran who builds computer databases and is privy to classified information. But after quitting time, King puts down the cloak and dagger and picks up his rubber chicken, calling himself "The Covert Comic."

"As a CIA employee, whenever I hear that the agency is programming people's minds I have to laugh," he says. "I don't want to laugh when I hear this, but I have to because that's the way the CIA programmed my mind."

At least that's part of his shtick. Like all newbie comics, King never really steps offstage. His act right now is confined to a Web site, www.covertcomic.com, which he launched a few months ago, much to the ire of his bosses, he says. But he hears the stage calling.

Is he really a spook? The rule in show business is "anything for a laugh." For that matter Woody Allen might not be Jewish; you never know.

For now it is a bit of a mystery. Keeping to its image, the CIA won't confirm or deny whether King is one of theirs. "I'm aware of an article about him," says spokesman Tom Crispell. "But it is our policy not to comment on employment status."

Crispell is referring to a January 28 *Washington Post* article in which an unnamed intelligence source is quoted as saying that King works for the agency and that he's gotten in trouble with his bosses for matters unrelated to his punch lines.

"That said," the source told the *Post*, "his jokes are not funny and, in many cases, tasteless."

King says his bosses went through the roof when he began publishing, and they are just looking for an excuse to dump him. "They tried to fire me," he says. "But I got a lawyer to reinstate me."

King isn't the only comic who has claimed to work for the CIA. Chuck Barris, the host of *The Gong Show* and creator of such TV institutions as *The Dating Game* and *The Newlywed Game,* claimed that he secretly worked as a CIA-trained killer-for-hire, killing thirty-three people on assignments all over the world.

If King is for real, his Web site certainly does dish the kind of gossip that would rankle the squares. It reveals bizarre secrets about other CIA agents, including a female agent who keeps male "sex slaves" and a male agent known as "Jesus Jr." who performs faith healings in his spare time.

"Why would I risk it?" King says. ""Because national security is too important not to be joked about."

A former bass player in the disco bands Sylvester and The Weather Girls, King, age forty, says he entered the CIA as a career trainee and has received technical training on, among other things, chemical-biological weapons. He claims to have a GS-14 classification and an annual salary of $72,000.

But everybody wants to be a comedian. Should he keep his day job? You judge. Here are some bits:

On Alien Abduction: "I don't think the CIA is abducting aliens."

On Experimental Surgery: "Ever since he got that complete body transplant, it's like my father isn't the same person anymore."

On Meddling in Foreign Affairs: "The two criticisms we at the CIA hear most frequently are, first, that CIA intelligence is inaccurate, and second, that CIA officers are selling CIA intelligence to foreign spy agencies. . . . So what's the problem?"

America's Bunker Mentality
Carroll O'Connor Remembered

J U N E   2 0 0 1

Carroll O'Connor is gone, but The Bigot of Hauser Street lives on—and he still has some choice words for you pinko liberal fruitcakes out there.

If you've forgotten just how important O'Connor's Archie Bunker was to America, settle into your favorite armchair, pop open a "beah," and "stifle yah self" for a minute.

From Gomer to Bunker

When *All in the Family* premiered on CBS in 1971, Archie Bunker—a loud-mouthed working-class Joe from Queens, New York—lambasted every minority and every white person who didn't share his reactionary ways.

There was nothing subtle about Bunker. He called African Americans "black beauties," Puerto Ricans, "Spics," and Jews, "members of the tribe." (Unless, of course, they were religious. Then they were "off-the-docks Jews.")

Yet somehow *All in the Family* was simultaneously the most popular and controversial TV show of the early 1970s—with fifty million people tuning in each week in the second season to hear Archie pontificate.

O'Connor, age seventy-six, who collapsed in his Culver City, California, home and died of a heart attack Thursday, somehow managed to satirize racism yet still give his character some redeeming qualities.

At a time when TV viewers were accustomed to such pap as *Gomer Pyle, U.S.M.C.*, Archie Bunker was squaring off with his unemployed liberal son-in-law, Mike Stivic, as played by Rob Reiner, on premarital sex, the Vietnam War, and abortion.

While the subject matter might have been highbrow, the fighting often degenerated to the sort of name-calling that you'd expect at a playground. Bunker, for instance, always addresses his son-in-law as "Meathead."

"Sticks and stones may break my bones," Bunker tells Stivic. "But you are one dumb Polack."

What's to Like?

Perhaps the key to O'Connor's Bunker is that he always seems to get things just a little bit wrong. In an Italian restaurant he'll order the "veal scalapeepee." His wife, Edith, will have to see the "groinocologist" about her "mental pause." And his oversexed son-in-law and daughter will engage in "floorplay."

Bunker, ultimately, is not malevolent as much as he's just ignorant. The world's changed just a little too much since he came back from "Dubya-Dubya Two." He's painfully slow to let go of the prejudices that he embraced as a kid, even though, somewhere deep inside, lurks a heart of gold.

In a classic confrontation, Sammy Davis Jr. once found himself at the Bunker residence.

"Now, no prejudice intended," Bunker tells the famous entertainer. "But I always check with the Bible on these here things. I think that, I mean if God had meant for us to be together he'd a put us together. But look what he done. He put you over in Africa, and put the rest of us in all the white countries."

Davis replies, "Well, he must've told 'em where we were because somebody came and got us."

But Davis later decides that Bunker, for all his failings, isn't the sort who would burn a cross on your lawn. "But if he saw one burning, he's liable to toast a marshmallow on it."

As we bid good-bye to O'Connor, here then are some of the most enduring

Bunkerisms—those moments when Archie is trying to prove a point. And he does. Only it's not the one he's trying to make.

On Gun Control: His daughter tells him that guns cause 60 percent of all deaths in America. "Would it make you feel any better if they was pushed out of windows?" he asks.

On Crime: "All the airlines have to do to end sky-jacking is arm the passengers."

On Homosexuality: "I never said a guy who wears glasses is a queer. A guy who wears glasses is a four-eyes. A guy who is a fag is a queer."

On a Typical Day: "Yeah, it was a beauty, coming home I was held up thirty-one minutes in the subway. Packed in like sardines, we were. No lights, no fans, just me pressed up against a 300-pound Italian man, half of which was pure garlic."

On Affirmative Action: Archie reads off the names on the slate he's voting for: "Torre, Feldman, O'Reilly, Nelson," he says "That's an Italian, a Jew, an Irishman, and a regular American. That's what I call a balanced ticket."

On the Difference Between Richard Nixon and Franklin Roosevelt: "Well, I'll tell you one thing about President Nixon. He keeps Pat home. Which was where Roosevelt should have kept Eleanor. Instead he let her run around loose until one day she discovered the colored. We never knew they were there. She told them they were gettin' the short end of the stick, and we been having trouble ever since."

On His Memories of Carrying His Wife across the Threshold on Their Wedding Day: "I says to her, 'Watch your head, Dingbat, or you'll knock your brains out!' "

On Premarital Sex: Archie tells his son-in-law that he never, ever had sex with his wife until they were married. "Yeah," Edith adds, "And even then . . . "

On God's Words to Adam and Eve in the Garden of Eden: "Get your clothes and get the hell out of here."

It's O'Connor's genius that he could deliver such material with humanity. Folks say he was as nice and kind as they come. May he rest in peace.

The Patriotic Way to Burn the American Flag
Old Glory Deserves a Proper Funeral

JULY 2001

If you're a red-blooded patriotic American, you'll retire your worn-out flag properly this Fourth of July—and burn it.

With the national argument over flag burning still smoldering, the National Flag Foundation is reminding folks that flags soiled or ragged beyond repair should be respectfully incinerated.

"Some folks think you should bury the Stars and Stripes—that is just plain wrong," says David White, the group's executive director. "Congress laid down guidelines of how to dispose of a flag, and a conscientious American should follow the rules."

According to the Flag Code, enacted by Congress in 1942, "when a flag has served its useful purpose, it should be destroyed, preferably by burning."

You begin a flag funeral with the Pledge of Allegiance and the patriotic songs of your choice. Ignite the red and white stripes first, and then the blue field of stars. The Veterans of Foreign Wars or even a local Boy Scout troop will do this for you, free of charge, if you don't want to do it yourself.

White says that the idea for burning the flag dates back at least as far as ancient Rome, when a general's remains were laid upon a funeral pyre.

When Doing the Laundry Becomes a Banner Day

Before you give up your old Old Glory, White says you

may want to try washing it by hand or sending it to a dry cleaner. Today's flags are largely made of polyester or nylon, which means they're a lot easier to launder than the cotton, woolen, and linen banners of yesteryear.

"Some dry cleaners will even do it for their steady customers for free," White says.

Unfortunately, even modern flags don't come with cleaning directions. But take it from a pro, don't put the Stars and Stripes in the dryer. "Just hang it on a clothesline to drip-dry," White says.

Just remember, no matter how often you wash your flag, America will never be washed up.

Donald Duck Politics
Swedish Voters Quackers for Disney Duck

NOVEMBER 2002

If you don't think of Donald Duck as a political figure, you haven't lived in Sweden very long.

With apologies to Bugs Bunny, SpongeBob SquarePants, and even Mickey Mouse, Donald Duck has a fine tradition of scoring high in Swedish national elections among those who favor the joke vote.

In fact, over the last twenty years, the Donald Duck Party has scored enough write-in votes at points to theoretically be the country's ninth-most-popular political organization. That's quackers!

The Donald Duck Party—better known in Sweden as Kalle Anka—dukes it out with the Tax Evader's National Party, the Beer Party, and the Professional Bachelors Party for seats in the Riksdag, Sweden's 349-member parliament.

Nonexistent Candidates Disappear

About one in twenty Swedish voters cast their ballots for unofficial, write-in candidates. That's about 26,000 votes.

Donald's best showing in recent years came in 1985, when he took 291 votes. Perhaps in a country of 9 million, that's not that impressive. But let's remember—

he's a cartoon duck and he frequently gets more votes than living, breathing politicians.

Sadly for Donald, the joke won't go on forever. Swedish politicians are changing election rules. By 2006 voters will be prohibited from choosing nonexistent candidates, eliminating the potential embarrassment of leaders having to open an embassy in Tomorrowland.

Momentum is already starting to shift. In national elections on September 15—when Sweden's Social Democrats garnered 40 percent of the vote—the Donald Duck Party had one of its worst showings in years, earning just fifty-eight write-ins.

Perhaps that's bad for a human politician. It's still pretty good for a cartoon duck. This strange expression of Donald's popularity is hard for many Americans to understand.

"Donald's an Everyman and he's very popular abroad, in many cases more popular than Mickey," says Hollywood historian Stephen Schochet, author of *Fascinating Walt Disney*. (The Walt Disney Co., by the way, is the parent company of ABCNEWS.com, which publishes *The Wolf Files*.)

"Mickey was always the model citizen. But Donald was the one with the temper. He argues. He gets angry. He's always played better with adults, especially in Europe."

Cartoon Duck Beats Lame Duck

Donald Fauntleroy Duck isn't exactly a novice in U.S. politics. Even though he's never registered as a candidate, he regularly receives token support in virtually every state—gleaning countless votes, even in presidential elections.

Unfortunately, cartoon characters have trouble establishing residency in a voting district and are frequently disqualified from office. That's a handicap—but there are still a lot of voters who wish upon a star.

In the controversial 2002 election, Donald Duck proved his political prowess once again. He beat out both George W. Bush and Al Gore for district director of the Marion Soil and Water Conservation Board in Salem, Oregon.

Okay, maybe that's not such a great job. It comes with no pay. In fact nobody ran for the job—all 4,570 votes were write-ins and very few people took the election seriously.

Donald Duck received the most votes, although they were all immediately discounted. Embarrassed officials didn't even announce the tally.

Instead, Gore—who came in second with twenty-three votes—was declared the winner. In a curious political footnote, after the 2002 election Gore could have bought land in Salem and remained in American politics by taking Donald's place.

But perhaps the outgoing vice president felt being a lame duck is much better than beating a cartoon duck—especially on a technicality. Gore decided to return to private life, at least for now.

Donald Pays Taxes, Mocks Hitler

Still, Donald Duck is a proven force with the electorate. His reluctant membership in The Mickey Mouse Club only proves his status as an outsider. His current work in *House of Mouse* on the Disney Channel reconfirms his enduring fame. And the sailor suit reminds voters of his commitment to the military.

Indeed, Donald has served this country. In World War II the Roosevelt administration commissioned him to appear in *The New Spirit,* a 1942 film that stressed that paying your taxes promptly was the job of every patriotic American.

Ducks usually like their bills—but not their tax bills. However, when irritable Donald sees the terrible threat of the Nazi war machine, he hightails it to Washington to personally deliver his share to the Treasury Department (which paid for the film).

Later, in the Oscar-winning *Der Fuehrer's Face* (originally titled *Donald in Nutziland*), our hero is forced to work as a virtual slave in a Nazi munitions factory, where he gets beaten up for not saluting Hitler.

Donald wakes up to find that he's no Nazi. It's all been a nightmare, and he is still living in Disneyland.

But if Donald ever has to leave, it's comforting to know that he has a home and political future abroad. If you throw in some meatballs and an Ikea discount, he might even bring Mickey and Goofy.

Feral
Beasts

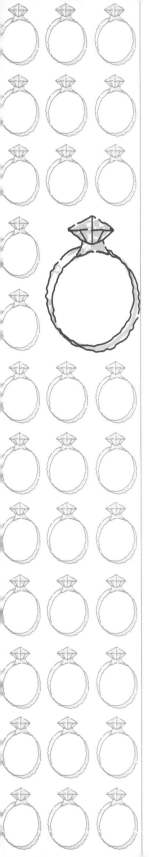

With This Yak Grease, I Thee Wed

Let's Be Grateful These Ancient Marriage Rituals Didn't Stand the Test of Time

FEBRUARY 2003

If you think getting married is tough these days, be grateful you don't live in ancient Persia. Couples back then declared their intentions by publicly drinking each other's blood.

The betrothed couple would slit their arms in dramatic fashion as villagers gathered around to celebrate, according to sex historian Lance Rancier, author of *The Sex Chronicles: Strange-but-True Tales from around the World*, a look at courtship rituals in more than 300 ancient cultures.

Of course, oddity—like beauty—is purely in the eye of the beholder. Why did ancient Britons break bread over the bride and groom? Why did Tibetans splash newlyweds with yak grease? For the same reason we throw rice: to wish the bride and groom luck and fertility.

Weddings Are Always a Gamble

Brides who aggressively diet, fearful of the wedding photographer's unforgiving lens, might welcome how the Nigerian Ibos of West Africa showed off their wealth. A bride spent most of her engagement in a fattening house. If she wasn't plump enough, the groom could reject her.

"A plump bride is valued in [many] cultures, particularly when food is scarce," says J. Christopher Kovats-Bernat, an anthropology professor at Muhlenberg College in Pennsylvania. "Thinness as a desired trait—a sign of wealth and power—is much more of a contemporary idea."

It's safe to say marriage has always been a gamble. Wedding and wagering evolved from the same Anglo-Saxon word—*weddian*, which means "to vow."

"In a sense, the groom was gambling the future of his family on a woman," says J. Joseph Edgette, resident folklorist at Widener University in Pennsylvania. "He would pay the bride's family for the woman's hand in marriage, and on that union hung the economic future of his family."

Talk about a money-back guarantee: The Anglo-Saxon groom often stipulated that the bride's family return his payment if his wife didn't conceive in the first year. Consider it early evidence of prenuptial agreements.

Cross-Dressing Masai Prove Marriage a Drag

Women's rights didn't enter into the picture until the last century, though there are notable exceptions. In parts of ancient Greece, a man could divorce, but he could not remarry to a woman younger than his ex-wife.

The Masai tribe of East Africa required a groom to wear his wife's clothing for one month after the marriage, to give him insight into her life.

But as much as wedding rituals have varied, marriage has been an institution in nearly every society since the dawn of civilization. We humans have an innate need to publicly declare the union of husband and wife (or wives, in some cases).

Future archaeologists might laugh out loud trying to explain today's customs. Even over the last twenty years, we've seen a dwindling of such customs as throwing the bouquet and applauding the groom as he inches the garter up the bride's thigh.

But if marriage is so universal, then why is it so universally difficult?

"You can think of marriage as a form of fraternity hazing," says Kovats-Bernat. "It's a trial by ordeal. You have to prove yourself."

So if you're not mixing blood, like in the good old days, you might be forking over $6,000 for an engagement ring.

This Valentine's Day, if you're getting ready to rent a hall, buy a dress, send out invitations, and open a bridal registry, don't let the ordeal overwhelm you. Just be happy that these traditions didn't stand the tests of time.

Ancient Marriage Rituals

Here's Mud in Your Eye: Women of some Amazonian tribes, such as the Chorowti, expressed their love by spitting in their partners' faces—either as a greeting or a sexual overture.

The Groom Got Cold Feet: In ancient Britain, women married in their finest dresses but the groom wed "skyclad"—in the nude. This practice might explain the tradition of June weddings.

No Guts, No Glory: In ancient Rome a marriage was not valid until the sacrifice of an animal, typically a pig. The entrails were examined for signs of a bad omen.

Who Needs a Guy?: In southern India the Mysorian Lambadis did not allow males at the wedding ceremony, except for the Brahman priest. Even the groom was excluded.

It Pays to Marry a Stiff: Ancient Persians who died as virgins were married before burial. The corpse's spouse received a fee.

Make Love, and War: In central Europe a Teutonic woman prided herself on standing by her man, even on the battlefield. According to superstition, she proved she was marriage-worthy by killing one of her beloved's enemies.

Look before You Leap: In north Wales, peasants once had to jump over a broom before taking their vows. If either bride or groom failed to clear the cleaning appliance, the marriage was off.

Ironclad Commitments: The Greeks and Romans believed that a vein ran from the fourth finger straight to the heart, and many believe that's how the custom of wedding rings developed. But Romans' wedding rings were made of iron, even though they valued precious metals and gems.

"The iron was the preferred metal because of its durability," says Holt Parker, a classics professor at the University of Cincinnati. "What did it say when the ring rusted?"

Unchain My Heart: In many ancient cultures, when there was a scarcity of nubile women, men raided other villages for wives. Some cultural historians believe the wedding ring was symbolic of the shackles worn by these POW brides.

Bachelorhood at a Price: To encourage marriage in Colonial times, Connecticut levied a special tax on bachelors of twenty shillings a week.

A Youthful Crush: Polynesians sometimes held sacrificial weddings. Matchmakers chose a young man and woman to marry. Immediately after the couple exchanged vows, villagers pulled out the legs from the nuptial canopy, killing the newlyweds in an avalanche of rocks and wooden debris. Even for Jennifer Lopez, that's a short marriage.

"The ceremony was supposed to bring good luck," says Pamela Jaye Smith, a Hollywood consultant on myths and ancient civilizations. "At least they didn't have to worry about a prenup."

Are American Men Getting Smaller?
Let's Hope Size Doesn't Matter

M A R C H   2 0 0 1

Men of the world, rejoice! If you feel shortchanged with your anatomy, check out some recent studies that show the average length of a particular organ is shorter than scientists once thought.

A study by Lifestyles Condom Co. shows that the average length of an erect penis is 5.877 inches. Compare that to the landmark Kinsey Sex Report in the 1940s, that put penis length at 6.2 to 6.4 inches.

"Our results show that about three-quarters of men fall under the average quoted by Kinsey," says Simon Joseph, a spokesman for Lifestyles. "A half-inch or less might not have anything to do with how you perform sexually, but it might make a difference in how you feel about yourself."

Men aren't diminishing physically. Modern researchers give a simple reason for the loss in penis size: In the old days, men got to measure themselves and report the results.

Alfred Kinsey's researchers simply gave men stamped postcards. Each one simply held a postcard against his erect penis, marked how long it was, and slipped the results in the mail.

"They never had to hold a ruler against themselves," says Kinsey spokesman Jennifer Bass.

The revelations brought out in newer studies only confirm what most women could have told you—guys lie.

What Some Guys Will Do for Beer and a T-Shirt

Measuring an erect penis is no easy matter. Kinsey, Masters and Johnson, and various urology groups have been satisfied with either letting the men do it themselves or with surveys of a few dozen volunteers.

But in the age of safe sex, condom companies have been competing for better-fitting products. Researchers for Lifestyles say they did the largest and most accurate measure of penis size ever just three weeks ago.

Company representatives went to Cancun, Mexico, at the heart of spring break, hoping to get 1,000 guys to drop their trousers, get aroused, and let a team of nurses measure them individually.

The guys got to go into a private tent outside Daddy Rock nightclub, where they found girlie magazines and other items to put them in the mood. Then came the doctor and two nurses. Each penis was measured by two of the four nurses.

"It was a highly professional operation," said Dr. Francisco Ordonez, who supervised the research. "The nurses wore disposable latex gloves and the men were all good-humored and well-behaved."

It's amazing what some college guys on spring break will do for some free T-shirts, condoms, and other prizes. The researchers thought holding the testing in such an environment, where guys tended to cluster in bunches, would help get true variety.

"In other tests, guys responded individually, and perhaps only guys who were proud of their penis size would respond," says Joseph. "In this test, we thought peer pressure would help coax guys who wouldn't ordinarily do such a thing into doing it."

Still, when it came time for measuring, about 25 percent of the guys weren't up to the job and had to face a little humiliation in the name of science.

Ordonez and his team had to be satisfied with 300 respondents. That's far fewer than they hoped for. But it's nearly twice as many as a similar study in Brazil last year, which had similar results.

The Long and the Short of IT

According to the survey, about two-thirds of the 300 college-aged men ranged from between 5.1 and 6.2 inches.

For those of you who don't like to deal in raw numbers, at 5.877 inches, the average penis is about the size of a Nestle Butterfinger candy bar (unwrapped) or a grande (medium) cup of coffee at Starbucks (with the sip lid). Most men vary in size between a Twix bar and a Peter Paul Mounds (with the wrapper extended).

"It's absolutely important that we have the best information to make the best-fitting condom," said Carol Carrozza, Lifestyle's vice president of marketing. "If a condom is too tight, it constricts circulation. It's uncomfortable, and it reduces sensitivity. If it's too loose, that's dangerous."

Carrozza says the circumference of the penis—otherwise referred to as girth—is often more important than length when new condom sizes are considered. "Because of the way condoms unroll, it's really not the case that they are not long enough."

According to the study the average erect penis had a girth of 4.972 inches. About 75 percent of men were between 4.5 and 5.5 inches.

"We already have a larger condom," says Carrozza. "What our research shows is that 17 percent of erections measured under 4.5 inches, and there might be a market for that."

Of course, once again, the frail male ego comes into play, and while condoms come in large, studded, ribbed, and flavored varieties, you don't see small or petite models. Maybe the condom business will just have to follow Starbucks logic. Go to a restaurant and look at the menu: An average-size cup is a "grande," a big cup is a "vente," and a small cup is "tall."

Guys will just have to learn not to be embarrassed for being "tall."

Feral Beasts

Makin' Whoopee at Zero Gravity
Tourism Industry Prepares for Sex in Space

NOVEMBER 2000

There's no doubt earthlings will be vacationing in space. The big questions are—how soon, who will cater the gourmet meals, and how great will the sex be at zero gravity?

Several companies are investing millions and promising service on "floating hotels in the sky" in the later half of the decade. Frommer's has already published a travel guide to the moon. And New York's Rochester Institute of Technology now offers a ten-week, two-credit course in space-tourism development.

"We all saw Stanley Kubrick's *2001: A Space Odyssey*, says Frommer's writer Werner Kustenmacher. "Soon we will live it. We will go to space as tourist-adventurers to marvel from afar at the blue pearl that we can all call our home."

Kustenmacher says Frommer's saw a "joke value" when it published the moon guidebook. But there's also a reckoning of the reality of space travel. "Everybody knows this is the future," he says. "And we are all pioneers at heart."

Space Tourism 101

How do you serve wine in a weightless environment? Can you smoke in a space capsule without destroying the air regenerators? The students in Rochester want to know.

At first glance you'd think "Space Tourism Development" is the sort of class the football team takes to keep up their grade point average. But the school has a sound reputation, especially in engineering, and the school is dead serious about hoping to send the first hotel managers and caterers where no leisure professional has gone before.

"The students are taking on problems that now challenge the industry, and they are looking for solutions," says professor Clinton Wallington, who says about fifty students have taken his class over the past year, including future engineers, marketers, and tourism executives.

"Students break into teams for projects . . . the marketers are asking questions about who will go into space and at what price. Others deal with details like food-service packaging, insurance, safety, and comfort."

In mid-February, Gene Meyers will speak to the school about the Space Island project. His lofty plans involve raising money to buy Boeing's space shuttle division and having a commercial space station ready by 2007.

The key to the project is the large, orange external fuel tanks NASA uses to carry its shuttles into orbit. Instead of letting them burn up in the atmosphere, as they usually do after launch, Meyers plans to save them, link a bunch together, and form a giant wheel—similar to the space station in *2001*—where 500 people will work and vacation.

The station would orbit about 300 miles above the Earth, high enough to enjoy the view without serious radiation dangers or the threat of crashing into a satellite.

"In the first wave of travelers, you will see adventurers and people for whom money is no object," Meyers says. "The same people who look at Mount Everest and say 'Been there, done that' need a new thrill—and here it is."

Each space shuttle fuel tank is as large as a jumbo jet. Meyers envisions vacations at this floating hotel, complete with restaurants, health clubs, and game rooms. (Don't worry about the smell of these tanks, the liquid oxygen and hydrogen fuel is odorless.) By 2012 he projects that a week at Space Island will cost about $12,000, allowing a slew of folks to see the heavens.

That might be quite a reach, considering it costs NASA an estimated $10,000 for each pound it launches into orbit. And Meyers still has to raise about $2 billion annually over the next few years to finance his dream. But he believes in his project. Unveiling new details of his project for the first time in Rochester will be a good test of what the science and business communities think.

"Think of what we do today that was impossible twenty years ago," he says. "I think you have your answers."

Sex in Space

It doesn't take a Madison Avenue genius to tell you that sex sells, and folks who have an eye on tourism in space are sure that weightless whoopee will be one strong motivator to commercialize the galaxy.

"Hasn't everyone fantasized about it?" says Kustenmacher. "Imagine nothing

but the touch of your sweetheart. No bed, no breeze, just floating in a cozy cabin. That's a freedom anyone would want."

But wait, it gets better. Zero gravity does some amazing things to your body. Suddenly your blood is no longer pulled downward by gravity. Wrinkles in your face disappear. Your face becomes fuller, younger looking. Your chest expands. And you grow taller. Early astronauts noted that their space suits were a little smaller on the moon. Once they were free of the Earth's gravity, their spines stretched out a few inches.

"If you look at astronaut pictures from before liftoff and from mid-flight," Kustenmacher says, "they look like father and son shots."

Now, floating around might create some problems in those intimate moments, but Meyers and others are thinking of solutions to save frisky folks from bouncing off the capsule walls. "I see couples floating and tied to each other with bungee cords," he says. "So you could snap your sweetheart back into your arms when necessary."

Family-planning advocates take heart: Many experts think it would be impossible for a woman to conceive in a weightless environment, which would make birth control absolutely free.

Of course many astronauts have complained of nausea, and that the capsule's smell was less than enticing. But we hope future technology will address those issues.

At Rochester, students are looking at all human life in space. "When you look into commercialization of space, you have to keep your eyes open and think out of the box," says Wallington. "Some folks have kicked around the idea of televising sports from space. Up there, the average man might jump higher than Michael Jordan. It might make for fantastic TV."

Was That in the Brochure?

The space-travel option might be at least a few years away, but folks love to sit and fantasize. "I knew there would be a market for it," Kustenmacher says of the Frommer's guide. "It's still my dream vacation."

As it does with almost every other tourist destination, Frommer's points out the downsides to space travel, along with a crater-by-crater rundown of all the can't-miss sites. Just as in a lot of exotic locales, it might not be so easy to find a toilet in space that you'd be comfortable using. The astronauts used a vacuum apparatus that might scare off the squeamish.

Meyers says Space Island will have public areas that have one third of Earth's gravity, which might help them address the downside of weightlessness. In such a situation you could drop the fork from your plate, wipe your chin, say "excuse me," and still grab it before it hit the floor.

While you might not be the first one into space, you may hear about it soon. The money-starved Russian Space Agency reportedly has a paying customer—financier Dennis Tito of California. According to news reports, he's paying $10 million to $20 million to swing from the stars.

Of course the Russians' orbiting home away from home, the Mir space station, is supposed to return to Earth in a controlled crash. There's always International Space Station Alpha, but that might require U.S. approval. So like a lot of travel adventures, Tito might be one more flight-weary tourist who arrives at his destination only to find his reservations lost and a No Vacancy sign in the window.

P.S. Boy-band star Lance Bass tried to follow Tito into space, but has thus far been unsuccessful. Russia was reportedly charging $20 million a ticket for out-of-this-world vacations.

The Columbia *shuttle disaster slowed space tourism. But Netherlands-based Mir-Corp. and U.S. Space Adventures say space tourism will live.*

In one plan, would-be adventurers would compete for a seat on a spacecraft as part of a reality TV show.

Growing Demand for U.S. Sperm
World Clamors for All-American Export

DECEMBER 2000

When I tell you the United States is sending a lot of semen abroad, I'm not talking about sailors.

There's talk that America can't make anything anymore. The rest of the world doesn't respect our goods and services. The French bomb McDonald's. Asia now controls vast sectors of the international high-tech business. Our foreign-trade deficit has ballooned to a record annual rate of $425 billion.

But whatever economic problems America may have, we can at least raise our fists and tell the world with pride that we are the No. 1 exporter of human sperm.

That's right; the French may be the leading authorities on romance, and Latin Americans may take pride in their *machismo*, but foreigners are nonetheless buying our semen. Four of the five largest sperm banks are based in the United States, and they control an estimated 65 percent of a burgeoning international business believed to be worth between $50 million to $100 million.

That's chump change to a hard-core macroeconomist, and, to be sure, I'm not suggesting sperm dollars will ever be able to correct the trade balance or make up for all the foreign-manufactured DVD players we're importing. But this is a psychological boost that we Americans should savor.

Squiggling to Canada

While former Republican leader Bob Dole does TV ads for Viagra, and Hollywood stars are pumping up with steroids and human growth hormones, it's nice to know this country can still produce in one area where it counts. And in great quantities.

Yes, American sperm is squiggling into Western Europe, Asia, and the Middle East at record levels. In recent weeks Canada has announced that it has a sperm shortage, and it will be turning primarily to the United States for help.

How'd that happen? An inspection of Canadian fertility clinics last year—

ordered after a woman who received semen from a sperm bank became infected with chlamydia—uncovered widespread irregularities in the mandatory testing of semen samples.

Now thirty-five of Canada's forty-nine sperm banks and clinics have been ordered to quarantine some or all of their sperm, leaving an inadequate supply for the 2,000 women and infertile couples expected to seek assistance this year.

"The stocks have decreased dramatically," fertility specialist Roger Pierson, president of the Canadian Fertility and Andrology Society, told Reuters.

Much of that demand is now being met by U.S. firms, Pierson said, because they can adhere to the tougher new standards.

"It's an opportunity for us. Right now, we are having trouble keeping up with demand," says David Towles, spokesman for Xytex Corp. in Atlanta, a major U.S. sperm bank. A third of all Xytex's foreign orders come from Canada, and the company recently opened a subsidiary in Toronto.

According to the World Trade Center Institute in Baltimore, a private, non-profit trade promotion group, the export of human glands and secretions to Canada topped $1.5 million in the first nine months of 2000, up 139 percent compared to the same period last year.

Towles estimates that in the next year, Canadians will be plunking down $3 million to $5 million for high-grade, U.S. sperm.

Spermatozoa with a Pedigree

Now let's define "high grade." It means the sperm has been screened for disease, has a high level of motility (that is, the sperm swim fast enough to reach their target), and comes with background information on the donor.

This reporter was saddened to learn that despite being in excellent health and holding two master's degrees from an Ivy League university, he is at least an inch and a half too short to donate highly desirable sperm. How humbling.

Although I didn't make the height requirement (you have to be at least 5-foot-8), it might have made a difference if I were a classically trained musician or a medical doctor. (Advanced degrees in journalism don't count.) Xytex claims only about one in ten men make the grade.

"People are very choosy," Towles says. "We've had requests for Brad Pitt's semen."

Celebrities and politicians have used Xytex's services, although Towles can't name names. And while folks can be very specific in their requests, you can't yet purchase sperm of the stars.

However, if you want a donation from a blue-eyed, 6-foot, blond doctor who is Catholic and likes the outdoors, many sperm banks can deliver. And that's one reason U.S. sperm banks have a competitive advantage.

"America is a big country, with a diverse population. It's easier for us to get what people want than for competitors in homogenous countries," Towles says.

The Laissez-Faire Semen Trade

You might think foreign countries wouldn't have to look abroad for sperm. You should be able to count on domestic production. But American companies benefit because the United States has fewer restrictions on the buying and selling of sperm than in other countries.

Denmark also exports a lot of human sperm. But donations there and in many other countries are anonymous. And these days, customers want semen with a pedigree.

Xytex often provides clients with photos of the donor and the offspring he's helped produce, along with a detailed biography.

Middle Eastern and Asian sperm is harder to come by, for cultural reasons. Towles says it's quite common for a Japanese couple to travel to the United States for fertility assistance.

Lauren Owenby of the Georgia Department of Industry Trade and Tourism helps promote U.S. human sperm abroad. "It's funny collecting information on this," she says. "When I called the Danish Consulate, the man there thought I was asking him for his sperm. Then I had to explain, I just wanted his country's regulations."

Georgia has eleven foreign trade offices, and Owenby has gathered trade information. "Because it is unusual to export sperm, we investigate local laws and trade practices," she says. But the practice is becoming more acceptable.

For American men who qualify, becoming a sperm donor can be somewhat lucrative. You earn about $50 for each vial you fill. Xytex has 10,000 samples on hand, and each one contains about 15,000 sperm.

Some might call it a commentary on society that human sperm and cattle sperm sell for about the same amount on the open market. It's interesting to note

that the United States is a leader in the sale of both com-
modities. Sperm from a pedigreed bull can sell for $200.

"A specimen of that caliber is really hard to come by.
The animal has been carefully bred and almost considered
a one-of-a-kind creature," says Brenda Hastings of Worldwide Sires in Visalia, California, which ships bovine genetic
material to seventy countries.

"I don't think they can measure humans that way. Not
yet, anyway."

Planet of the Love Monkeys
Humans Bear Striking Resemblance to Sex-Crazy Apes

A U G U S T   2 0 0 1

What if superintelligent talking apes really did take over
the world? It might be one big sex party.

Scientists are amazed by the sexual antics of the
bonobos, who are as close to humans as the chimpanzees.

The bonobos share more than 98 percent of the same
DNA as their human cousins, and they party like hairy little
Hugh Hefners. Their society literally revolves around elaborate, recreational sex. They typically resolve a group con-
flict with a nice, long orgy.

"The bonobos are the free-sex hippies of the animal
world," says primatologist Franz de Waal of Emory
University in Atlanta, author of *Bonobo: The Forgotten
Ape*. "They make the sexual revolution of the 1960s and
1970s look quite tame. You'll see two bonobos hanging
upside down and copulating—and groups of them doing
likewise."

Indeed, a *Planet of the Apes* run by the promiscuous bonobos would be a whole lot different from what we'll see at the movies. It would certainly have given new meaning to Charlton Heston's immortal line from the original film: "Take your stinking paws off me, you damn, dirty ape."

Chimps Don't Monkey Around

In a bonobo-dominated world, Mark Wahlberg, the star of the new *Ape* flick, might slip back into his Dirk Diggler porn-star role from *Boogie Nights*.

In the new film, Wahlberg actually shares an onscreen kiss with his chimp counterpart, Helena Bonham Carter—an actress who looks pretty darn good with long sideburns, a hairy chest, and knuckles that drag on the ground.

In our world, when it comes to making love, real chimps don't monkey around. It's all business, with rarely any foreplay. A typical lovemaking session lasts under ten seconds. The bonobos, however, are connoisseurs of recreational nookie.

If two males get into a fight over food, they will do a little more than kiss and make up. "They practice homosexuality much more than other species—and they do it just for pleasure," says de Waal.

"They do it in every combination imaginable. They do it face-to-face, with some French-kissing thrown in. And they do it often just to relieve tension."

A Society of Mama's Boys

Not much is known about the bonobos, also known as the pygmy chimpanzees. They are few in number and were only identified as a distinct species in the ape world in the 1930s. They are only known to live in the wilds of the Congo region of Africa.

Compared to chimps, the bonobos have longer legs and smaller heads. They're more slender and tend to walk erect on two feet—much as humans do.

And unlike the male-dominated, sometimes warlike chimps, the bonobos are all mama's boys. In fact the males depend on their mothers for protection all their lives and derive their status by being the son of a dominant female.

Only about 120 bonobos are in captivity. A zookeeper in Cincinnati learned just how different a bonobo is from other primates a few years ago. "The bonobo grabbed him and kissed him, open-mouthed," says de Waal. "That guy probably never expected to get a tongue stuck in his mouth.

"A chimp wouldn't engage in 'French-kissing,' but certainly, that's just the beginning for a bonobo."

The political maelstrom in what is now the Democratic Republic of the Congo has made it nearly impossible for scientists to do more research on this endangered species.

In recent years animal-rights activists have complained that bonobos are being hunted and eaten as "bush meat." Scientists fear as few as 10,000 still exist in the wild.

"We can only assume the worst," says de Waal. "It would be so tragic to lose them. Yet the risk is very real."

We can only hope that the situation in the bonobos' homeland will improve, that they will soon get the protection they deserve. Maybe we all have to consider that we're a little more like the bonobo than we care to admit.

Fishy Orgasms
What Lady Trout Don't Tell Their Lovers

JULY 2001

Bad news for boy fish: Female fish are known to fake orgasms. Who even knew that fish had egos? Sweden's National Board of Fisheries watched trout in an aquarium and found that females faked orgasms in 69 out of 117 couplings, according to Britain's *New Scientist* magazine.

How did these fish learn the dubious art of sexual deception? Did they catch Meg Ryan in *When Harry Met Sally*?

It actually takes more than a little conspicuous moaning. Researchers say the female trout trick their partners into premature ejaculation, most likely to give them some choice over who will father their children.

As a couple begins to spawn, both fish quiver violently with their mouths open. Egg and sperm are released simultaneously. (You could call it the caviar of sex.)

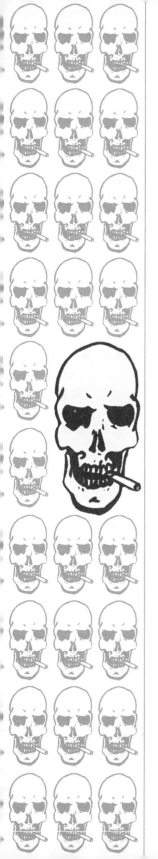

But researchers noted that female fish often quiver without releasing their eggs. Of course those dumb male fish fall for it every time—hook, line, and sinker.

It apparently pays for fish to fake it. Researchers noted that the more false orgasms a female had, the more other males were attracted to her. With a bigger pool of eligible bachelors, she'll have a better chance of hooking up with a fertile guy when she finally does have the Big O.

And who do the lady fish ultimately choose? It often turns out to be the male fish with bigger fins and jaws. Forgive me for being a short man, but isn't that always the case?

Thousands of fishermen flocking to the twenty-seventh Annual Brown Trout Festival in Alperna, Michigan, this weekend were hardly surprised by the news.

"These are wily fish," said festival director Ken Kolasa. "To hook one, you need lots of skill and patience."

Screamin' Jay Hawkins' Illegitimate Family Reunion

The Legacy of a Blues Legend and Lothario

FEBRUARY 2001

With bones up his nose, a vampire cape, and a cigarette-smoking toy skull named "Henry," Screamin' Jay Hawkins put the cool in ghoul. Now the legendary blues man and womanizer is being celebrated posthumously in a way only he could have appreciated: His illegitimate children—and he claimed to have more than fifty of them—are getting together to throw him a party.

Call it the Screamin' Jay Hawkins' Illegitimate Family

Reunion. At least twelve of his offspring are coming to Los Angeles—making pilgrimages from as far away as Paris, Cleveland, and Honolulu—to celebrate the bizarre showman on February 12 at L.A.'s House of Blues.

Love Children Galore

Hawkins, best known for the hit "I Put a Spell on You," died in Paris last February of multiple organ failure—a condition presumably not related to supporting his prodigious extended family. His was a storied life of stage antics and skirt chasing. One girlfriend even stabbed him in the back when she found he was cheating on her.

But that episode occurred some forty years ago, and the Cleveland native lived to the ripe old age of seventy, singing, dancing, and dressing like a ghoul right up to the very end.

"He led a fast life, a hard life—and he said without exaggerating that he had fifty-seven children," said his friend Maral Nigolian, a banker and film producer who is working on the singer's life story.

"He wasn't boasting," she said. "He was just sad that he didn't get to know many of the people who should have been more present in his life."

Hawkins left behind a thirty-one-year-old French widow—his sixth wife—and thousands of admirers, who packed European venues for his concerts up until his final years, when he was residing in Paris.

Nigolian recalls meeting Hawkins after hearing "I Put a Spell on You" in the Jim Jarmusch movie *Stranger Than Paradise*. For days they sat in his living room as the old man chain-smoked, gazed at the TV, and rued the fact that he was not close to his offspring.

He had three children with his first wife and was certain that he had fathered more than fifty other children (with girlfriends and groupies), some of whom he had met. At some point he estimated that there might be seventy-five Hawkins love children out there.

An old man's boasting might not have a lot to do with reality. But in the weeks after Hawkins' death, Nigolian started the Jayskids.com Web site and now believes she has identified thirty-three of the so-called Hawkins 57.

"It wasn't like an FBI investigation—no DNA tests," Nigolian says. "But I ask for documents. The locations, dates of births, and stories check out. There is, also, a family resemblance."

Shock-Rock Granddaddy

Hawkins, who had a tradition of beginning shows by jumping out of a flaming coffin, might rightfully be dubbed the granddaddy of shock rock. Indeed, Ozzy Osbourne, Kiss, and Marilyn Manson have pulled rubber snakes and fake tarantulas out of Hawkins' bag of voodoo tricks.

With a dad like that, the kids might not be your typical suburbanites. But you never can tell. "Two of the kids are in bands, one in Washington, the other in Calgary, and they have acts that would make their papa proud," says Nigolian.

But for many of the supposed children, the event at the House of Blues is the closest they've come to a stage.

"It's a little scary meeting a whole new family for the first time. But I'm really excited about it. I can't wait," says Melissa Ahuna, a thirty-one-year-old hula dancer, hotel store manager, and nurse.

Hawkins had a high-school yearbook photo of Ahuna in his Paris home at the time of his death. But father and daughter lost contact in 1993.

"He had been a presence in my life," Ahuna says. "He'd call every few weeks when I was in high school. And he was proud of me. We always got along well."

Ahuna is of Hawaiian, Chinese, Portuguese, and African ancestry. "When this reunion comes off, it will be the first chance I've had to get in touch with my black roots," she says.

She has a younger brother, another Hawkins kid, who was put up for adoption, and she hopes this reunion will help them find each other.

Of his three legitimate children, Hawkins had the closest relationship with Irene, now a puppeteer in Cleveland. "He saw a lot of his work in hers," Nigolian says.

Constipation Blues

Biographers don't even bother counting Hawkins' string of lovers, the most notorious of whom, Pat Newborn, stabbed him in the back—literally—when she caught him two-timing her.

But apparently his suffering was in the name of true love. The other woman in that relationship—Virginia—became his wife in 1961, and the union lasted twenty years.

In fact it was in an Hawaiian hospital that Hawkins wrote one of his most outlandish tunes, "Constipation Blues," 4½ minutes of bathroom hell set to music, complete with Hawkins moaning and groaning, albeit not much like Muddy Waters wailing for a lost love.

Ironically, Hawkins—so famous for his coffin stage entrance that a society of morticians derided him—insisted on cremation.

"He figured he'd spent enough time in a coffin," Nigolian says. "He wanted his ashes cast upon the water."

Truth is, Hawkins never really liked coffins all that much. Famed New York DJ Alan Freed had to pay him $2,000 in 1956 to lure him into his first box. But it was an instant hit, not to mention a career-defining moment. . . . And it sure seemed to have gone over big with the chicks.

P.S. Ahuna was one of five women to show up for the Hawkins family reunion in February 2001. Perhaps that's a disappointing turnout, but Nigolian says she positively identified thirty-six children—and that's a lot of Screamin' kids.

Sex and Drugs— Brady Bunch—Style
The Not-So-Squeaky-Clean TV Family

M A Y   2 0 0 0

Here's the story...
Of a show called Brady
A sitcom family,
The kids had perfect lives,
The girls had blond hair,
The boys were hotties,
That's the way they all became a swingin' bunch!

"Extra, extra! Hot *Brady Bunch* Sex!" Now there's a gold-plated headline that everyone wants to read about. Cut to Greg and Marcia's late-night swimming-pool rendezvous. She steps from the shadows in a supercool, 1970s-style bikini, her lustrous blond locks running wild. His pubescent eyes, with those luscious lashes, melt into the chlorine waters.

Sure they played brother and sister on TV. But off-camera, the kids playing groovy Greg and perfect Marcia Brady were real teenagers, with real hormones.

Did actors Barry Williams and Maureen McCormick "hook up," as they say? And will the actors who portray them in the TV flick—Adam Brody and Kaley Cuoco—whitewash the story or shatter the illusions of TV purity?

After all, you could drive a Hummer down the space separating Mr. and Mrs. Brady in bed. Even Lily and Herman Munster got cozier in the sack.

In fact the producers never fully explain how two adults with three children each formed this *Bunch*. Apparently Mike Brady was a widower and Carol was divorced, although sticky situations like that never came into play.

The Brady Kids' lone bathroom—the sight of many domestic skirmishes—didn't even have a toilet. But some wild antics apparently went on behind this antiseptic backdrop.

The Wolf Files has screened the TV movie, and for those of you who can't wait, it's Williams's account. And, as set forth in his autobiography, he and his Hollywood sis never went all the way, but their on-screen sibs, Peter and Jan, sure did.

'Florence Was Playful'

Sex was definitely in the air at Paramount's Studio 5, where the Brady family made TV magic. Williams even made a play for his TV mom, Miss Wessonality Florence Henderson, in what could have been a very Brady Oedipus complex.

"Florence was playful," Williams tells *The Wolf Files*, recounting the magic night he took her out to dinner. "But she was not thinking of the possibility of waking up with me in the morning."

Hollywood gossip has rumored otherwise. But that's not what you're going to see in this special. You also won't see the time Williams came to the set stoned—a 1972 incident recounted in the book and written into the movie but left on the cutting-room floor.

Williams, then age seventeen, had a rare day off, and he says his older brother's friends turned him on. They were listening to Buffalo Springfield, Fleetwood Mac, and the Moody Blues when the studio made a surprise call.

It was the episode when the Bradys get a boat. Dad drives up with the surprise gift strapped to the family station wagon's roof, and Greg is supposed to lead the chorus of cheers.

"I flubbed my lines a few times and got through it," Williams says. "A lot of funny stuff went on in my head." Alas, Brody's re-creation of that chemically enhanced moment had to be sacrificed due to the length of the film.

Maybe it's just as well. After all, Williams says it was an isolated incident—as far as he knows, that was the only time anyone ever showed up on the set high.

Brody says he suspects NBC might not have been happy with the drugs. But Williams says he wasn't trying to sanitize the story. "We were certainly playing it for humor. But we weren't going to leave it as drugs being a good thing."

Brady Turned Bundy

While the Brady actors weren't as unblemished as their characters' pimple-free faces, they didn't exactly end up with rap sheets like the kids on *Diff'rent Strokes*. Michael Lookinland, who played Bobby Brady, pleaded guilty to drunken-driving charges related to an accident two years ago in which his Bronco rolled over.

But in the age of Hollywood bad boy misbehavior, what is that?

Susan Olsen, who played Cindy, has had to confront rumors that she had a secret life as a porn actress. But as *TV Guide* reported last year, Olsen merely resembles the star of the 1986 X-rated skin flick *Crocodile Blondee*.

For Williams, life as an ex-Brady has been a mixed bag. He's had steady work, appearing on Broadway in the title role in *Pippin*. At one point he agreed to play serial killer Ted Bundy, but the film's financing fell through. "Let's face it, after playing Greg Brady, all-American kid, anything I do is a departure."

Williams doesn't resent the Brady nostalgia industry. Good parts come and go, but the Brady gravy train chugs along quite nicely.

The Brady Bunch had a five-year run that ended in 1974. Three years later the cast—minus Eve Plumb (Jan)—reunited for a disastrous variety show. That was followed by three TV specials, a TV movie, and even two big-screen take-offs on the original show.

Brady Bunch reruns still air in at least fifty-five countries. "I can't explain it," Williams says. But his on-screen counterpart has a theory. "I think it's the theme song. . . . It's so damn catchy."

Men Are from Mars . . . Musicals Are from Vegas
Self-Help Set to Music

S E P T E M B E R   2 0 0 0

You've read the book, watched the video, and played the board game. Now America's most popular recipe for a happy marriage has been set to music. Get ready for a Las Vegas stage version of *Men Are from Mars, Women Are from Venus*, opening September 28 at the famed Flamingo Hotel.

One can only imagine what legendary gangster and Flamingo-founder Bugsy Siegel would say if he saw actors dancing and singing about their lackluster, codependent sex lives. Is this what Bugsy envisioned for Sin City?

Here's a sampling from a number called "Dysfunctional":

Woman: He told me he was healing his inner child.
Chorus: Child, child
Woman: He showed such empathy that it drove me wild.
Chorus: Wild, wild
Woman: And as a woman who loves too much,
I failed to see the codependency when we touched.
I couldn't tell he was dysfunctional!
Chorus: Dysfunctional! Dysfunctional!

In another couplet, a woman croons, "There's no joie de vivre in my libido." To which her partner replies, "I think my libido has gone incognito." In another, one man advises, "Make time to please her," only to have his friend retort, "Max out your Visa."

What Planet Are You From?

It's not exactly Andrew Lloyd Webber. But love guru and author John Gray must know what he is doing. Gray's *Men Are from Mars, Women Are from Venus* was the best-selling hardcover of the 1990s, unless you want to count the Bible.

Since 1992 *Men Are from Mars* has sold more than 11 million copies, not to mention 2 million audio cassettes and 300,000 videos. It's been translated into forty-three languages, and it even hit the best-seller list in Bosnia.

"There was war in Eastern Europe and people told me it was a sensation there," Gray tells *The Wolf Files*.

"I think it will work on stage," he says. "When I do my seminars, people are rolling in the aisles laughing. I can't wait to see the reaction to this."

For those of you living on another planet, *Men Are from Mars, Women Are from Venus* attempts to explain the classic disconnect between the sexes with the help of a little science fiction.

As the metaphor goes, men come from Mars, where the inhabitants are goal-oriented and need respect. When faced with stress, they withdraw into a cave to heal in silence.

Women are native to Venus, where they value communication and beauty. They need to be cherished.

When the Martians and Venusians meet, it's true love. But they travel to Earth and soon forget their origins. Instead of appreciating their differences, they try to change one another. The result: unhappiness, divorce, and, presumably, a lifetime of searching bookstores for instant solutions.

Some call it psychobabble. Feminists grouse that Gray only reinforces traditional sex roles. But millions swear by it. Gray has trained more than 500 Mars and Venus counselors to counsel the lovelorn worldwide, and he now stands as a one-man media empire, with a syndicated column in more than 200 newspapers.

The book has spawned such offspring as *Mars & Venus on a Date, Mars & Venus in Love, Mars & Venus Starting Over*, and *Mars & Venus Together Forever*.

In mid-October Gray will spin off his franchise into a syndicated weekday TV show hosted by Cybill Shepherd and available in many markets on NBC stations. Gray will appear only occasionally, but his love philosophy will be omnipresent.

"I don't worry about overexposure," he says. "I believe in doing what I love, and the rest will take care of itself."

Sorry Guys, No Cave

The musical tracks the lives of five couples, some young, some old. Seniors Harry and Bea recount struggling through twenty-five years of marriage in a ditty called "Suppress Yourself."

Frances and Rex represent a Mars-Venus role reversal. She is incommunicative. He just wants to be held. New Age fad lovers Paul and Sylvia have steeped their herbal teas with all the right infusions. But they, too, need more. And youngsters Mitzi and DuPree have a great thing going physically, but they have a lot to learn.

The play centers around the courtship of Mandy and Nelson, who have been burned many times. Of course, this is a musical comedy, where all endings are happily ever after.

"It has an irreverent spin," Gray says. "It's sometimes seems like it's *Saturday Night Live* doing a spoof on me."

Gray fans might even be disappointed that there is no cave on the set for actors to hide in when the women are singing their ears off. "The characters just talk about the cave," he says. "Showing it might have been too obvious."

A Music Teacher's Dream

One can only imagine what will happen if this play succeeds, and the publishers of *Sex for Dummies* and *The 7 Habits of Highly Effective People* take their message to the Great White Way.

Still, Gray says he never envisioned the American theater as the next bastion of multifaceted marketing. The idea for setting *Men Are from Mars* to music came from Rita Abrams, who was teaching piano to one of Gray's three daughters.

"I brought it up several years ago. John encouraged me, so I started working on it," she says. "I didn't spend a lot of time with John. But I was very familiar with his work, and he gave me a lot of feedback."

Mars and Venus on a Diet

For Gray, it seems, the Venus and Mars juggernaut will roll on indefinitely. His new book, *Practical Miracles for Mars & Venus*, dispenses mind and body health tips, including a natural-energy diet that emphasizes drinking lots of water and avoiding refined sugar.

In a market glutted with self-help recipes, Gray's continued success is astounding, especially considering he got his doctorate from a correspondence school (the Columbia Pacific University in San Rafael, California).

Gray, now age forty-eight, studied under the Maharishi Mahesh Yogi, famous for tutoring the Beatles in meditation. He lived as a monk for nine years, and he was in a prolonged period of celibacy when he decided to devote his life to helping couples communicate.

Just to prove that pop psychologists don't have all the answers, he and his first wife, Barbara DeAngelis, author of *Secrets about Men Every Woman Should Know*, ended their marriage in 1984.

Now the Houston native lives in San Francisco with his second wife, Bonnie. He says humor has helped them overcome life's difficulties, and that's why allowing his counseling theories to be turned into musical comedy isn't as strange as it seems.

P.S. Men Are from Mars, Women Are from Vegas enjoyed a modest, ten-month run at the Flamingo. Gray is still developing his franchise in all manners, and so are his detractors. Susan Hamson calls the book sexist, patronizing, male-centered invective, in her book The Rebuttal from Uranus.

Mundane
Thrills

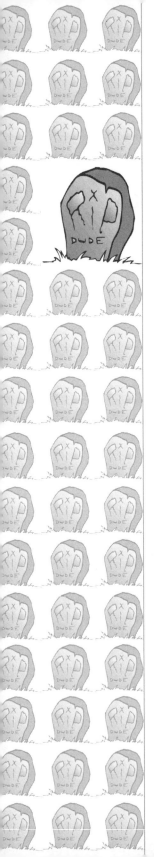

Baby Boomer Funeral Fun
Last Laughs for TV Generation

JANUARY 2001

If a funeral had to be a sad affair, the word wouldn't begin with F-U-N. A growing number of graying baby boomers want to celebrate life when they say that final good-bye. The generation that gave us fast food and ATMs now desires to put a personal touch on last rites. And if that means replacing "Amazing Grace" at the memorial service with "Stairway to Heaven," amen.

Going in Style

"The boomers are reinventing the funeral. They don't think a funeral has to be all sad to remember their loved ones with respect," says Joe Weigel, spokesman for Batesville Casket Co. in Indiana, the largest North American coffin maker.

The folks at Batesville have seen it all in the last few years. One family had exotic dancers at their loved one's funeral because the deceased was "that sort of guy." A golf lover was buried with his lucky Callaway Big Bertha driver.

And then there was the guy on the West Coast who had a "boxing-themed" memorial. The funeral parlor was decked out like a boxing ring, complete with a drop-down microphone. Mourners actually stepped between the ropes like prize fighters to deliver eulogies over the sound system.

Recently the family of Paul Wellener of Mount Lebanon, Pennsylvania, bought a pair of plastic seats from the old Three Rivers Stadium, former home of the Pittsburgh

Steelers. Wellener had season tickets for more than forty years. The seats will now be mounted on stone, along with an inscription, to serve as a grave marker.

Batesville surveyed 500 baby boomers over the last few years. Asked about what should happen after they die, 14 percent said they wanted mourners to "visit their grave." In comparison, 41 percent said they wanted friends and relative to "throw a huge party."

"This is all a throwback. A hundred years ago most funerals were in the home, so mourners immediately had the sense of the deceased when they arrived to mourn," Weigel says. "Now we want to give mourners that atmosphere when they go to the funeral parlor."

At funeral directors' conventions, Batesville now helps undertakers create services with distinct themes. Batesville's "Cool Jazz" funeral calls for the casket to rest on two loudspeakers (presumably playing a meditative selection of Miles Davis) with a drum set nearby.

The "Outdoorsman" funeral calls for the area around the coffin to be festooned like a hunting lodge, complete with mounted elk antlers, bearskin rug, and gun rack.

Remember, every life is special. If you spent your spare time in a La-Z-Boy chair, you might be a candidate for a Sports Nut funeral. The coffin would come complete with a keepsake drawer, so that you could be buried with a bag of chips, a beer, and, of course, the TV remote control.

P.S. Batesville used John F. Kennedy Jr.'s burial at sea to launch a new product, the Floral Reflections scattering urn. When placed in water, the pressed cotton urn floats for several minutes, then slowly dissolves and sinks, releasing the deceased's ashes into a watery grave.

Dead Man Sparkling
Dearly Departed Loved Ones Can Live On . . . As Jewelry

FEBRUARY 2003

My wife is a real gem—now that she's dead. That could be the slogan for LifeGem—a company that turns the ashes of your late loved ones into diamonds.

The remains of a twenty-seven-year-old woman from Phoenix have been transformed into six precious stones that are to be delivered to her family and friends on Friday. LifeGem's first order could be the start of a new age in the funeral industry.

The woman, who died of Hodgkin's disease, had asked that her ashes be distributed to loved ones. To honor that last wish, her family turned to LifeGem, hoping to create something special from this tragedy.

"When I look at her ashes, I know what they are and they make me sad; when I look at her LifeGem, it is a very positive experience," her father says in video footage the company is releasing to document its first sale.

The father worked closely with the company, which was founded two years ago outside Chicago. The diamonds, certified by the European Gemological Laboratories in New York, have been set into rings and have "the same brilliance, fire, and hardness as any high-quality diamond you may find at Tiffany's," according to company literature.

Out with the Urn, in with the New

You might think that LifeGems are the ultimate in tacky jewelry. But the company claims it's working on more than fifty orders and is on pace to ring up more than $1 million in sales—many of their customers are grieving pet owners.

These sparklers aren't cheap. A quarter-carat diamond—the smallest LifeGem sells—has recently been marked down from $3,950 to $2,095. Even at the reduced price, that's more than twice the cost of a natural diamond, so don't get the idea that you're worth more dead than alive. You're still only worth something to the people you love.

Still, LifeGem is refining its process in order to create more spectacular gems, in various shades of red, blue, and yellow. The top-of-the-line, three-quarter-carat rocks go for nearly $10,000, and the company is promising "near-flawless diamonds of up to three carats in the very near future." LifeGem puts a new twist in the classic family feud—Who's getting Mom's jewelry when she dies? With the company's patent-pending process, a cremated human can yield 100 certified, high-quality diamonds—enough to mollify a Kennedy-sized clan.

Of course diamonds are already vested with meaning. They're a girl's best friend, the ultimate way to say I love you. Just try getting engaged with a cubic zirconia. But what does it say if you pass off a LifeGem as an engagement ring? I can already imagine a Hitchcockian thriller, involving a man who murders his wife, has her crushed into a LifeGem, and passes her remains off as a token of his esteem—to his next victim. Call it *The Man Who Proposed Too Much* or perhaps *Dial L for LifeGem.*

Despite the jokes, Dean VandenBiesen, one of the founders of LifeGem, is confident that diamonds can take on a new meaning in death. His brother Rusty came up with the idea three years ago, when he decided that he didn't want his final resting spot to be in a cemetery or an urn left on a fireplace mantle.

"If you think about it, carbon is the building block for all life, and that's what a diamond is made of," VandenBiesen said.

Frisbees . . . And Other Ash Alternatives

In nature, carbon crystallizes into diamonds—the hardest substance on earth—after millions of years of intense heat and pressure. In the 1950s General Electric developed a process to manufacture diamonds in a lab. These synthetic diamonds were first used for such items as drill bits and other cutting devices. Later on, synthetic diamond jewelry was introduced.

In an age when burial costs are climbing, more people are turning to cremation, and VandenBiesen sees that as an opportunity. The cremation rate is now 26 percent and forecasted to rise to 36 percent or higher by 2010.

One reason for the trend: Embalming, coffins, and memorial service expenses have pushed the average cost of a funeral to more than $6,130. A cremation can cost less than $1,000.

Just as many Americans make their own funeral arrangements, to spare their families that dreaded task, Jack French is planning a final resting spot on his wife Jackie's neck—as a necklace.

"Like everyone, I thought the idea was crazy at first, but now it's a great comfort," says the sixty-nine-year-old former plasterer from Joliet, Illinois, who is suffering from emphysema. And if French should survive his wife, she would live on as a diamond ring.

"The doctors gave me two or three years to live, but that was back in 1993," said French, who blames his illness on working with asbestos for more than 40 years, although he also says he regrets having been a smoker.

But if your late loved one wasn't the jewelry type, check out these ash alternatives:

Ultimate Frisbee: When Frisbee inventor Ed Headrick died last August at 78, family members announced that they would honor his wish and mold his ashes into a flying disc. That's great news for kids. Even after the memorial service, they can play catch with Grandpa.

Sponging Off Relatives: Eternal Reefs in Georgia is putting a new spin on burials at sea for ecologically minded baby boomers. The company mixes cremated remains with cement to form seabed habitats for sponges and ocean coral. Costs range from $1,500 to $5,000.

The Final Frontier: In September 1999 the ashes of *Star Trek* creator Gene Roddenberry, along with those of LSD guru Timothy Leary, boldly went where no urn had gone before—into orbit, via a U.S. satellite. After two years, the satellite was expected to re-enter the Earth's atmosphere, where it would be smashed to fiery bits.

Painted Love: The Eternally Yours company promises to make everlasting art of a loved one's ashes. For prices ranging from $350 to $550, your dead husband will hang around forever.

A Comic Ending: Marvel Comics editor Mark Gruenwald was a creative force behind such classics as *Captain America* and *Quasar*. In 1996 his wife honored his final request and mixed his ashes with ink during the printing of a comic book. There's a little piece of him in *Squadron Supreme*, a limited-run poster of Marvel characters that's popular with collectors.

Hail, Mighty SPAM!
A Hog-Wild Milestone
for the All-American Mystery Meat

JUNE 2002

There will be rapture in Austin, Minnesota. In less than two weeks, the 6 billionth can of SPAM will roll off the assembly line, and there's nothing snobbish culinary purists can do to stop it.

To many folks, SPAM is nothing more than a joke, immortalized in Monty Python routines and goofy haikus. But that doesn't mean the all-American mystery meat doesn't taste great.

SPAM is a throwback, and it refuses to change. Our modern-day obsession with health—the Tofuization of America—has taken much of the fun out of eating. "The land of the sugar-free and the home of the bland" might be an appropriate kicker as the Fourth of July holiday approaches.

But in Austin, better known in some circles as SPAMtown USA, the folks are acutely aware of the awesome, salt-laden, nitrate-packed power of canned pig meat.

Pink Pleasures for the Palate

Go to any SPAM party—a SPAMboree, if you will—and you will see America's fat-laden traditions honored in true fashion. What other luncheon meat is immortalized in song, tossed for distance, and sculpted into art, while being eaten for breakfast, lunch, and dinner? And there will be many such events this summer.

SPAM parties are perhaps the only adult gatherings where guests are expected—even encouraged—to play with their food. You haven't seen it all until you've seen a SPAM rendering of Stonehenge. Modeled to scale. And edible.

For the true believers the SPAMboree begins with SPAMbled eggs and launches into a SPAMorama of blackened SPAMfish, Greek SPAMikopita, SPAM étoufée and other dishes to keep the plates—and the palates—pink. You can wash all that down with SPAM wine and top it off with SPAMoni sorbet.

"I must say I've had the SPAM brownies," says Shawn Radford, curator of Austin's SPAM Museum, which cele-

brated its opening last weekend with a dedication from Tom Brokaw. The NBC anchor wrote about SPAM's unique role as chow for Allied soldiers in World War II in his book *The Greatest Generation.*

That war generated a huge sales boost for SPAM-maker Hormel Foods, which provided 15 million cans to the military. From 1939 to 1942, the company's overall sales doubled to almost $120 million.

These days Hormel boasts $4.1 billion in sales and the blue-and-yellow SPAM logo is now is trademarked in more than one hundred countries. It's canned in Britain, Denmark, the Philippines, Japan, Taiwan, and South Korea, where it's served with wine.

"One reason SPAM is popular in developing countries is a reason it was popular in America years ago—it doesn't require refrigeration," says Radford. "But even in other countries, it finds a place."

Inside the SPAM Museum, fans will find plenty to absorb. A 430-foot conveyor belt rattles around the ceiling, carrying about 850 cans of SPAM. Visitors can take a SPAM exam or can their own SPAM (not the real stuff). There's also a radio station—KSPAM—and a video screen that shows classic Monty Python skits slamming SPAM.

A SPAM-o-Meter tallies the cans of SPAM produced. Hormel expects to turn out its 6 billionth sometime between June 29 and July 3.

"It's inevitable at this point," says Radford. "But it's still a big deal."

With the world on the cusp of such a milestone, it's time to reflect upon the noble place SPAM occupies in U.S. history. Its rise parallels the geopolitical trajectory of the United States itself.

Khrushchev Contemplates Life without SPAM

SPAM came to prominence around the time we were developing the atomic bomb. Since then some people have stopped worrying and learned to love both.

Soviet leader Nikita Khrushchev and President Dwight D. Eisenhower each expounded on SPAM's effectiveness in beating the Nazis.

"Without SPAM, we wouldn't have been able to feed our army," Khrushchev said in his autobiography.

If war is hell and an army travels on its stomach, SPAM helped make it that way, Eisenhower suggested.

"I ate my share of SPAM, along with millions of other soldiers," he said in a 1966 letter to Hormel's then–chief executive, H.H. Corey.

"I'll even confess to a few unkind remarks about it uttered during the strain of battle, you understand," he continued. "But as former Commander-in-Chief, I believe I can still officially forgive you your only sin—sending so much of it!"

America's Pâté de Foie Gras

Ironically, Eisenhower and SPAM's manufacturer shared the same advertising agency, BBDO, when the former general began his political career.

"I must say," Eisenhower wrote in the letter, "I believe they [BBDO] had a tougher time with me than selling SPAM to ex-servicemen. Happily, we all succeeded together."

According to Hormel, SPAM-and-bacon sandwiches have graced the menu at the congressional dining hall, giving new meaning to pork-barrel politics. And several biographies say Elvis Presley was (and still is, by some sightings) a SPAM eater.

After the war, as American influence spread on a global scale, so did SPAM. Though culinary revisionists might snub their noses at it, SPAM might be to the United States what pâté de foie gras is to France. Americans purchase 3.6 cans of SPAM every second. That adds up to 216 cans a minute, 12,960 cans every hour.

The reality is stark: Either you or someone you love is hooked on the pink stuff. And that's not just a joke. That's lunch.

My Son's a Fruit
Parents Name Children After Food

A P R I L   2 0 0 2

My son is a fruit. My daughter's a tart. And if you think that's cheesy, tell it to my nephew, Gouda. In one of the more disturbing trends in parenthood, children are apparently being named after Mommy and Daddy's favorite foods.

The Global Name Registry—the company in charge of handling registrations for the new Internet domain extension ".name"—has registered 200,000

members, and some are for people with first names such as "Gouda," "Almond," "Cappuccino," "Veal," and "Bologna."

Topping this trend is Jamie Oliver, better known on TV as "The Naked Chef." His wife, Jools, gave birth March 18 in London to a 7-pound, 14-ounce girl named Poppy Honey.

'My Name Is Canon, as in Camera'

It's tempting to think "Cappuccino" and other names are fabricated. However, the dot-name domain requires registrants prove their identities. And an expert who analyzes census and Social Security Administration records is not surprised such names exist.

"Anything is possible, when you consider that last year alone, 298 girls were named Armani and another 10 boys were named Halston," says Cleveland Evans of Bellevue University.

"Every year, the list gets stranger and stranger. It's as if parents think they're guilty of abuse if there is another kid in the classroom with the same name as theirs."

About 2 million boys and 2 million girls were born in the United States in 2000, the last complete year for which records are available. The Social Security Administration reports that 33,957 boys were named Jacob and 25,714 girls were named Emily, making them the most common baby names.

But the number of strange names on the Social Security Administration's list is getting longer. There were seventeen boys named Ventura (as in Jesse), six boys named Timberland (as in the boot), forty-nine named Canon (spelled like the camera), and twenty-seven named Blue (as in little boy).

The girls' names were equally bizarre. Thirty-five were named Vanity. Another twenty-nine were named Whisper, while fifty-four sported the name Sincere. And twenty-four were positively Unique.

Imagine two mothers meeting in a mall: "Hi," one says. "This is my daughter, Unique."

"Well," says the other mother, her competitive fire sparked, "my daughter is also Unique."

Birth Certificates Need Spell Checkers

The strangest names aren't even on the list. The Social Security Administration releases only names chosen five or more times, in order to protect the privacy of parents with bad judgment.

You have to worry about the ramifications of such parenting. Do the thirteen girls named Wisdom feel even worse when they screw up? What happens when the ten guys named Truth lie?

Then there's the issue of spelling. Are the fifteen kids named Ruddy really that rosy-cheeked—or are they really just Rudys?

We also had seventeen kids named Sky, but also eighty-five named Skye (a Scottish island) and Skyy (a premium vodka). How do you tell your child, "Daddy wanted to name you after the heavens above, but he can't spell a three-letter word."

Name Your Kid after Your Favorite Station

If you're really looking for parents who make sport of their children, consider that at least two children were named Espn, after the ESPN cable sports network.

Jason Curiel of Texas told the *Dallas Morning News* that he thought his wife was kidding when she made the suggestion. But the Corpus Christi couple loves sports.

"I thought she was pulling my chain and was going to suggest other names," he said. "But then he came and she was still for it. Even though the nurses would give me dirty looks and turn to my wife and say, 'His name, please?'"

Espn (pronounced "Espen") Curiel was born September 24. His birth follows that in January 2000 of Espen Blondeel of Newaygo, Michigan, whose parents were also sports fans but decided to go phonetic.

My Boy Morpheus—*The Matrix* of Naming

In another case of life imitating art, five boys were named Morpheus, apparently after the hero of the sci-fi blockbuster *The Matrix*, portrayed by Laurence Fishburne. "I don't think there's a trace of that name existing before the film," Evans says (except for the Greek god of dreams). "But now it's on the map."

The lead female character, Trinity, is faring even better. Between 1999 and 2000, the number of Trinitys tripled to 4,553, making it one of the fastest-growing girls' names.

Neo, the name of Keanu Reeves's character, scored only 113 names. "It's really not fair to compare," Evans says. "The movie obviously had an impact on naming. Trinity just started out as a real name, whereas Morpheus and Neo didn't really exist."

Reeves is so popular that he actually caused a naming controversy in Austria, where parents aren't allowed to invent names. Instead, they must prove that the name they give their child once belonged to another person.

When one Austrian couple wanted to name their son after the actor, officials objected, thinking Keanu was just a stage name. But after doing some research, they discovered the name relates to the actor's Hawaiian ancestry.

Now, we Americans must debate the virtues of allowing parents to name children anything they want. Just imagine the playground torment some children must suffer.

"Hey, can you smell it? I guess Gouda must be coming."

"Don't listen to Bologna. She's full of it."

Unusual Names

Unusual Names for children named in 2000.

SOURCE: SOCIAL SECURITY ADMINISTRATION

For Girls

Chianti (9)	Sincerity (5)	Unique (24)
Dung (5)	Sonny (11)	Vanity (35)
Rayon (5)	Sparkle (23)	Whisper (29)
Reality (16)	Special (11)	
Sincere (54)	Sunshine (93)	

For Boys

Adonis (244)	Doc (5)	Ruddy (15)
Atom (11)	Famous (6)	Sincere (187)
Blue (27)	Gator (5)	Starsky (6)
Cannon (117)	Halston (10)	Timberland (6)
Canon (49)	Hutch (7)	Trust (5)
Casanova (6)	Legend (30)	Truth (10)
Cashmere (6)	Lucky (48)	Tuff (8)
Champion (7)	Magic (9)	Ventura (17)
Coal (8)	Maverick (211)	Wisdom (16)
Cotton (5)	Morpheus (5)	
Denim (7)	Nature (5)	

Beware the Coconuts
Ig Nobel Honors for Nutty Science

They laughed at Copernicus. They laughed at the Wright Brothers. And they laughed at Kligerman—who eventually laughed all the way to the bank.

Alan Kligerman gave the world Beano—a dietary supplement that helps folks who suffer from flatulence.

Beano can now be found in virtually every pharmacy. But when it hit the market in 1990, Kligerman was the butt of countless jokes. The media hailed him, among other things, as "The Vanquisher of Vapor."

"That's the way people deal with embarrassing subjects. So why not?" said Kligerman. "They laughed. But we got the word out."

Since then Beano has relieved thousands of gas-pain sufferers—not to mention their close friends, coworkers, and spouses. Kligerman sold his interest in the product for more than $10 million. Talk about the sweet smell of success.

Today Kligerman is focusing on other products—CurTail, a Beano product for gaseous pets, and CatSip, a milk product for lactose-intolerant cats. Laugh now, but Kligerman will probably be laughing later.

Laughingstock Laureates

Of course, not all innovators enjoy such vindication. Many remain laughingstocks, others just obscure.

You might have to prove your contribution to humanity to win a Nobel Prize. But if you just bring a smile to the world with a seemingly crazy, novel innovation, you could win the highly coveted Ig Nobel Prize—awarded annually at Harvard University, by students and the *Annals of Improbable Research*, a science-humor magazine.

In addition to Kligerman, past winners include Peter Barss of McGill University, author of the medical report "Injuries Due to Falling Coconuts"; George and Charlotte Blonsky, who invented a device to help women give birth by spinning them at high speed; the British Standards Institution, for publishing a six-page specification of the proper way to make a cup of tea; and Don Featherstone, the designer of the plastic pink flamingo.

If you scoff at coconut research, you probably don't live in Papua New Guinea, where the tropical trees grow more than 100 feet high and the coconuts fall with a force of up to one metric ton or more, Barss noted.

In the doctor's four-year study at one hospital, 2.5 percent of the trauma admissions were coconut-related. "Obviously, over there, it's no laughing matter," said Mark Abrahams, editor of the *Annals of Improbable Research*.

Of course most of the Ig Nobel attendees don't come from the tropics. They're happy to make coconut jokes, and so is Barss.

'We're Not Insulted'

Amazingly, Ig Nobel winners fly into Boston each year from all over the world—and they pay their own way.

A guy like Kligerman was obviously leveraging laughter to boost Beano sales. But other "honorees" are scientists who count on their professional reputation to secure grants. Why do they show up?

Some are undoubtedly out to prove they're not stuffy academics. Others come to defend research that—on the face of it—seems coconuts.

A few years ago three Scottish researchers flew into Boston to be honored for their report "The Collapse of Toilets in Glasgow," examining the physical collapse of toilets after people sat on them.

"We're not insulted," Jonathan Wyatt said. "Between us, we've published more than seventy research papers. This is the only one that's given us any publicity at all."

This year's event, on October 3, will be the second to be broadcast over the Internet (www.improbable.com). These days the festivities draw a crowd of 1,200 people, including many notables. But the show still aspires to be a small, prankish party. The audience can and will throw paper airplanes to express themselves.

As for this year's Ig Nobel winners, Abrahams says that's a closely guarded secret.

"Every year a theme or trend emerges, and this year we're all going to find out some interesting things about the intimate relationship between humans and animals," Abrahams said.

With the twelfth Ig Nobel festivities beginning, *The Wolf Files* took a look at past honorees. Here are some of the notables and their innovations.

Notable Ig Nobels

ENVIRONMENTAL PROTECTION

The Self-Perfuming Suit (1999)—When you work all day, party all night, and have a limited number of outfits, you might need a $400, self-perfuming suit, made of a special scratch-and-sniff fabric. The South Korean manufacturer, Hyuk-ho Kwon of Kolon, offers peppermint-scented attire that can be repeatedly dry cleaned without losing its special feature. Just rub the sleeves, and your B.O. disappears.

PSYCHOLOGY

Pigeons Learn Fine Art (1995)—When a pigeon leaves poo on a statue, is that a form of artistic criticism? Three Japanese psychologists at Keio University were honored for training pigeons to discriminate between the paintings of Picasso and those of Monet.

BIOLOGY

Airtight Underwear (2001)—If there's a market for Beano, there might also be one for Under-Ease, airtight underwear with a charcoal flatulence filter. Buck Weimer, a psychotherapist from Pueblo, Colorado, says he was inspired six years ago, after a huge Thanksgiving dinner, when his bedroom got a little gassy. "I don't mind the jokes," Weimer says, but folks like his wife, who suffer from inflammatory bowel syndrome, can really benefit from Under-Ease.

PUBLIC HEALTH

Nose Picking (2001)—If you are searching for a highfalutin' word for "compulsive nosepicking," it's rhinotillexomania. B.S. Srihari and another researcher at India's National Institute of Mental Health and Neurosciences received honors for their probing medical discovery last year that nosepicking is a common activity among adolescents.

"Some people poke their nose into other people's business," said Srihari, at his Ig Nobel induction. "I make it my business to poke my business into other people's noses."

PUBLIC HEALTH

Inflatable Doll Advisory (1996)—Most grown men don't play with dolls. But a few guys apparently play very intimately with the inflatable kind. However, before you get a little too familiar with "Rubber Rhonda," you might want to read a cautionary medical report from Ellen Kleist of Greenland and Harald Moi of Norway, "Transmission of Gonorrhea Through an Inflatable Doll," published in the medical journal *Genitourinary Medicine*.

MEDICINE

Intimate Zipper Injuries (1993)—Three doctors at a Navy Hospital in San Diego received their Ig Nobel for a 1990 research report, "Acute Management of the Zipper-Entrapped Penis." Unless you've had such an injury, you'll never know the importance of such research. Moreover, our boys in the navy deserve all the protection we can afford.

MANAGED HEALTH CARE

The Spinning Birthing Table (1999)—How can you ease labor pains? How about strapping a woman into a circular table and spinning her at high speed. Then you can pop out the newborn with centrifugal force. The late George and Charlotte Blonsky of New York City thought of this while observing elephants at the Bronx Zoo. Apparently, pachyderms spin when they're in labor. The Blonskys even patented their idea.

TECHNOLOGY

The Wheel (2001)—Maybe you've heard of the wheel. Well, last year, John Keogh of Australia patented it. Actually, he patented the "Circular Transportation Device" to demonstrate that, perhaps, there are some problems with patent laws.

It Pays to Be Ordinary—
Scholarships for the Rest of Us

SEPTEMBER 2001

It's that time of year when all kids feel like geeks: The first day of school. If you're feeling like a total loser who'll never get ahead in life, cheer up. There are people who will give you money for college simply for being left-handed—or fat.

When you're applying to college, having brains like Einstein never hurts. And if you're expecting a free ride to a top school, it's not a bad idea to be 6-foot-10 with a 45-inch vertical leap.

Still, the National Scholarship Research Center estimates that private charitable organizations donate about $50 billion to the U.S. educational system. About 3.5 percent of that money, almost $1 billion, goes undistributed, so it might pay to check it out.

If you think you have a future in harness racing, the Harness Tracks of America scholarship is worth up to $3,000. If you wish to advance in the field of shade trees, the International Society of Arboriculture wants to help you.

There are some scholarships that are ridiculously specific. For decades the University of California at Berkeley offered a $3,000 annual award to any Jewish orphan interested in a career in aeronautical sciences. The school had to appeal to the courts to broaden the scholarship because there were no takers.

Finally the courts said the scholarship could go to any flight-minded Jew—but a Jewish orphan would still be given preference.

Many more scholarships award money to people with average grades who don't have the sort of talents that would land them in the student newspaper.

Here are a few of the oddball scholarships that can help catapult a young mind to new heights.

Oddball Scholarships

The Fat Scholarship—If you are a fat high-school senior in the New England area, you can win a $500 scholarship to a two- or four-year college or university. Applicants must respond in writing to questions about his or her attitude toward fat people and size acceptance. Skinny folk who plan to gain a "freshman 15" in their first year need not apply.

David Letterman Scholarship—Ball State University's most distinguished celebrity grad, David Letterman has always supported not-so-gifted students. Grades are unimportant to the *Late Night* host. He wants to foster creativity. The David Letterman Telecommunications Scholarship Program gives awards of up to $10,000 to advance fertile minds. Two-time-winner Rich Swingley demonstrated Letterman-worthy work with the stop-action animation of a dancing penguin that scaled a beer bottle the size of the Empire State Building. Letterman's generosity is legendary on campus. Outside an audio room that bears his name is this dedication: TO ALL C-STUDENTS BEFORE ME AND AFTER ME—DAVID LETTERMAN.

Lefty Scholarship—It's great to be a southpaw at Pennsylvania's Juniata College. You can be awarded up to $1,000 if you are a lefty with sufficient grades. Applicants must be a junior or a senior. Winners of the Frederick and Mary Beckley Scholarship can also be ambidextrous. The admissions office couldn't tell me much about the origins of this scholarship, but they assure me that Fred and Mary were lefties.

Goodie-Goodie Scholarship—To qualify, a student at Pennsylvania's Bucknell University must not drink, smoke, chew tobacco, take drugs, or participate in "strenuous athletic contests." Joseph H. Deppen, class of 1900, donated the money for the scholarship in memory of his sister. It's unclear how they test applicants' virtue.

The Pot Scholarship—The National Organization for the Reform of Marijuana

Laws (NORML) gives out scholarships to students who write essays outlining a more "sensible" drug policy for the United States. Kevin Killough (pronounced like "kilo," strangely enough) received $650 last year for his essay, which suggests America follow the Dutch model of legalizing marijuana.

The Zolp Scholarships—Perhaps you or someone you know is named "Zolp." If so, this is your lucky day. The Zolp Scholarship at Loyola University in Chicago offers a four-year, full-tuition scholarship. Be prepared to present your birth certificate to the bursar's office.

The Amazing Hug Lady
Indian Woman Tries to Change the World One Embrace at a Time

JULY 2001

I was indeed witnessing a miracle in the making: thousands of cranky New Yorkers waiting in line for hours as if someone was giving away money—not hugs. The wait was for Mata Amritanandamayi—better known as "Amma," or "Mother"—who might be the most famous woman to come out of India since Mother Teresa.

Amma and an entourage of fifty assistants are touring the United States on a ten-city "Hugging Tour." In Los Angeles, Chicago, Washington, and Boston, it was the same scene. Thousands of people lined up, on their knees, and one-by-one she took them in her arms, cooed into their ears, and gently kissed them on the temple.

This cherubic Indian woman has supporters who call her "The Hugging Saint." In India she can reach out to 15,000 people. Many unwashed. Many in rags. When it is time to go home to eat her rice and curry supper, her white sari is often blackened from soot. This is her life, morning to evening, six days a week.

It's impossible to say how many people she's embraced since she began this practice more than thirty years ago. The claims are as high as 20 million. What's so special about Amma's embrace? It was now my turn to find out.

Swamis Direct Traffic

Amma has a publicist, and, as a result, journalists don't have to wait for the hugging experience. I arrived at Manhattan's Columbia University at noon and went to the front of the line, where folks had been kept waiting since 8:00 A.M.—all for a quick caress.

Swamis, clad in orange suits, direct the traffic in a room filled with chanting, drumming, and the twang of a sitar fill. I dropped to my knees.

Nobody can deny there is something magical about Amma. It's her energy, an unbelievable ability to work eighteen hours a day, often seven days a week. She works in two sessions—morning and evening—always smiles, and breaks only to meditate, eat, and sleep.

She has known poverty herself, and her rise to prominence is inexplicable. She came from the Indian state of Kerala. Born to fisherfolk in 1953, she left school at a young age to care for her family. In her early twenties, she began offering her blessing to others. The lines around her simply grew, and now she has millions of followers.

In 1993 Amma served as president of the Centenary Parliament of World Religions in Chicago. In 1995 she spoke at the United Nations' fiftieth anniversary commemoration.

At Columbia University many Hindu people kneeled on the lines. So, too, did Christians, Jews, and, presumably, people of other faiths. Amma rarely preaches. She says she embraces all faiths. It seems her doctrine is fairly universal—she hugs people as a mother hugs a child.

Her followers refer to this hug as a *darshan*—Sanskrit for an audience with a saint. Her U.S. spokesman Rob Sidon says, "Other holy people in India don't allow themselves to be touched like this. Amma breaks with tradition."

Some say she has supernatural powers. They tell stories of how she has cured lepers. But that is in India. In America it's simply a miracle that hundreds of people will wait in line for something that, theoretically, should be waiting for them when they get home—a simple hug.

I looked around me. Here were fellow New Yorkers—rich, educated, and hardened to flimflams.

"I'm not religious," a twenty-eight-year-old banker told me. I had disturbed the woman as she was meditating, preparing her self for her magic moment with Amma. Initially annoyed, she forgave me and continued.

"I saw her four years ago in Houston. Now, I just go to her every chance I get. She may be just an old woman who hugs. But there is some beauty in this. Maybe we have to appreciate our need to hug and be hugged—to care for each other."

The area around Amma was crowded, yet serene. Devotees followed an honor system. Those who had never participated in a *darshan* were allowed to move to the front of the line.

As I approached I saw her, sitting on a wooden chair adorned with flowers, caressing an age thrity-five-ish man, whispering into his ear. Her eyes closed, rocking the man back and forth. Trembling, I realized it was now my turn for the Amma experience.

A Hug and Chocolate Kiss

I kneeled before Amma and she smiled, pulled me to her chest, and rocked back and forth. I closed my eyes and listened to her whisper in my ear.

"My son, my son, my son, my son," she said, almost singing to me. "Love you, love you, love you."

She squeezed my elbows, smiled, and her assistant signaled that my time was up, handing me an apple, a rose petal, and a Hershey's chocolate kiss. That was it. I checked my watch—seventy-one seconds. In hugging time, that's an eternity.

Amma doesn't break for interviews. I speak to her through her swami-interpreter as she hugs and kisses the next in line.

I asked her where she gets her energy. "It takes no energy to love," she says. "It is easy."

Sidon, Amma's spokesman, compared her energy to that of a parent caring for a newborn. "A new mother or father will stay up all night," he says. "The love for the child is more powerful than the fatigue."

That seemed very nice. Too nice. I started to wonder if I was getting suckered. Her supporters sell books, videos, T-shirts, and souvenirs.

After you get your hug, you can buy an Amma Beanie Baby–type doll for $180, and she will bless it. That's a little pricey—even in the Big Apple.

But Sidon assured me that the blessings are always free. He couldn't say how much money they have raised. But literature that he handed out indicates the proceeds go to several charities begun in Amma's name. They include 4 hospitals, 33 schools, 12 temples, 25,000 houses for the poor, an orphanage, pensions for 50,000 destitute women, a home for senior citizens, a battered women's shelter, and various public projects.

I asked Amma if she will train others. Shouldn't there be an inspirational hugger in every city? She will not open a school, she said.

"What I did was spontaneous. I saw a need. It felt right, and I did it," she says. "You cannot teach love in a book or teach it. You can only show it."

Twenty million hugs. That's a lot. And yet Amma is still an oddity in most corners of the world, a humble proponent of the most primal form of communication. It's so simple, you could laugh at it.

Then again, it's so universal. Who couldn't use a nice big hug?

Useful Excuses to Do Nothing
Couch Potato Science

A U G U S T   2 0 0 2

If your spouse says, "Let's clean out the garage, it'll be a good workout," respectfully tell your beloved to take a hike. Far be it from me to instigate domestic quarrels. I'm just quoting medical research.

There's no evidence that housework improves health, according to a study of 2,300 elderly women at England's University of Bristol.

Dr. Shah Ebrahim, an expert on aging, concludes that a brisk walk is a much better health option than mopping floors, dusting, or cleaning windows.

"When we look at things that we think would go along with being physically active and fit, like pulse rate and obesity levels, they don't show any relationship with housework," he reported in a recent issue of the *Journal of Epidemiology and Community Health.*

Now, we're all aware that we live in the age of surveys and studies. You could probably dig up ten other reports that would suggest that Dr. Ebrahim should be piloting a Weed Whacker.

But why bother? In this hyperkinetic world, we need useful excuses to get out of work. We actually have to ask ourselves, "What do I have to do to do nothing?"

That's why *The Wolf Files* has compiled this list to help you avoid household chores, business obligations, diets—and any other activity more strenuous than slathering yourself with suntan lotion and sinking into a good book.

Useful Excuses for Adults

Excuse to work less: If your father tells you it wouldn't kill you to work a little harder, point him to this.

A study by Guys and St. Thomas' hospitals in London investigated the lifestyles of 700 men. The ones who had suffered heart attacks had spent more time at work. Those laboring sixty or more hours had twice the risk of men toiling fewer than forty hours.

Excuse not to marry: Just pick up the March issue of *Cosmopolitan.* According to a poll in the magazine, there's a lot of extramarital nookie going on. A whopping 59 percent of ladies admit they cheat, and so do 55 percent of so-called gents.

The statistics get even uglier, enough to shake any marriage-minded lover. Thirty percent of men and 23 percent of women have had sex with a friend of their girlfriend or boyfriend. Moreover, nearly 70 percent of both genders say they've lied about past sexual romps.

Excuse to drink beer: Dutch researchers believe they have proved that beer in moderation is better for men than red wine or other alcoholic beverages when it comes to preventing heart disease or even cancer.

The Dutch Nutrition and Food Research Institute studied 111 men and concluded that beer contains vitamin B6, which prevents the buildup of the chemical homocysteine, believed to be one of factors in heart disease. Wine and spirits did not have this effect to the same extent, they said.

Excuse to drink beer on dates: Beauty is in the eye of the beer holder, according to the research by Scottish psychologist Barry Jones.

In a study involving eighty Glasgow University students, he found men and women who had consumed a moderate amount of alcohol found the faces of the opposite sex 25 percent more attractive than their sober counterparts.

While the "beer goggles" concept is hardly a surprise to any drinker, it's nice to back that up with scientific research.

Excuse to stay in bed: Scientists have long known that adequate sleep is important for memory. Now German scientists are saying sleep is critical even for motor skills as simple as finger tapping.

Scientists writing in *The Proceedings of the National Academy of Sciences* taught students different finger-tapping sequences. Students who got eight hours sleep performed 35 percent faster and made 30 percent fewer errors than those who didn't get sleep.

If you can trust kids to tap their fingers on short rest, I'll just stay home and play tiddledywinks.

Excuse to sleep on the couch: Clearly good rest is critical to good health, and where do married men get their best rest? According to customer surveys from furniture giant Ikea, 72 percent of men claim they sleep better on the couch, as opposed to 27 percent who sleep best next to their wife.

Excuse to read in the bathroom: Some say it's bad manners. Some say it's uncleanly. Nevertheless, everybody's doing it. Research from the Quilted Northern toilet paper company reveals that 92 percent of Americans regularly read in the bathroom. The survey also shows that 48 percent of users spend potty time talking on the phone. Another 3 percent write letters on the commode.

Excuse for women to have sex: Women sprinters who have sex before competition generally perform better, top German trainer Uwe Hakus said. "We have scientific evidence that women who have sex shortly before competing run better. It boosts performance," he said. "With women, the testosterone levels rise when they have sex."

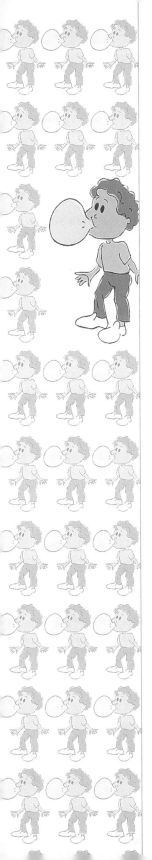

Unfortunately, Hakus says, male testosterone levels fall after sex, slowing them down.

Excuses for Little Children

Excuse not to mow the lawn: Kids, I know you love to help in the yard. But you should remind Mom and Dad that more than 9,400 youngsters under age 18 receive emergency care because of lawnmower-related injuries.

The American Academy of Pediatrics says children under twelve should not operate walk-behind power or hand mowers. And you shouldn't go near a riding mower until you're sixteen. I know you want to help, but safety first.

Excuse to chew gum: Chewing gum makes you smarter. Researchers at England's University of Northumbria concluded that chewing gum has a positive effect on cognitive tasks such as thinking and memory. Peppermint or spearmint? It doesn't make a difference. The key, researchers say, is the repetitive chewing motion.

Excuse not to kiss your sister: Little boys hate to kiss their sisters. Now there's scientific justification—they smell.

In fact all family members smell bad to one another, according to a team of scientists at Wayne State University in Detroit.

Researchers recruited twenty-five families with children aged between six and fifteen and gave them T-shirts. They were later asked to sniff two T-shirts, one worn by a family member and another worn by a stranger. The results: Volunteers far preferred the smell of the stranger's shirt. Why do people seem to think their families stink? Scientists concluded it might be nature's way of discouraging siblings from being attracted to one another.

Excuse to eat candy: Kindly remind Mom and Dad that, contrary to popular belief, the sugar in candy does not cause hyperactivity. That contention has been backed up by a

Vanderbilt University study. Other researchers have determined that chocolate, though tasty, isn't addictive. The National Confectioners Association even points to research at Penn State University that says chocolate may help lower cholesterol.

Excuse to eat ice cream: The typical American eats ice cream 2.2 times a week, according to a report by Mintel Consumer Intelligence. Unless you get ice cream more than twice a week, you're getting less than other kids. And that's good reason to whine, "It's not faiiiiir!"

Excuses for Bigger Kids

Excuse not to go to medical school: The school year is starting and career-minded parents want their kids to become doctors. But are doctors happy? Many are not, according to a survey published earlier this year in *Medical Economics*. The magazine says 33 percent of gynecologists have unsatisfying love lives.

There's also a good excuse not to marry a doctor. The same survey says 18 percent of married ophthalmologists say they've had at least one affair. Of doctors who do cheat, 36 percent of doctors who cheat do so with nurses, 9 percent with other doctors, and 7 percent with patients.

Excuse not to become an accountant: The book on accountancy is that it's the most headache-prone profession. A study by pain-reliever Excedrin shows almost half of all accountants suffer headaches during the workweek. About 42 percent of truck drivers and 38 percent of construction workers say their work causes headaches. At the opposite end of the scale, only 20 percent of home-makers say they suffer headaches while working.

Excuse not to go to college: The more you go to school, the less often you have sex.

A study by the University of Chicago's National Opinion Research Center finds that high-school graduates have sex fifty-eight times a year—a higher annual average than those folks with fancy diplomas.

College grads score only fifty-six times a year in the bedroom. And those with graduate degrees have the least sex of all—a mere fifty times a year.

The findings concluded that the most sexually active groups tend to watch more television, listen to jazz, and vote liberal. Now that sounds like the makings for a relaxing Labor Day, doesn't it?

Medium Mediocrity
My Predictions for National Psychic Week

AUGUST 2002

Here is my prediction for National Psychic Week: No medium will step forward to collect the James Randi Educational Foundation's $1 million prize for anyone who can prove they have supernatural powers.

The foundation isn't asking our psychic friends to change the course of a river or even pick who'll win the next installment of *American Idol*. In fact, if you can just bend a spoon, with your very own telekinetic strength—and under laboratory conditions—come and get it.

"This is easy money for the thousands of people out there who claim to have special powers," says paranormal investigator James Randi. "Prove it. Take our money. Please. Operators are standing by."

Mediums Rarely Face Scientific Scrutiny

You'd think today's top psychics—who make bold claims about their abilities on TV—would quickly step forward for the million-dollar payday. But John Edward, who relays messages from the deceased on the SciFi channel's hit series *Crossing Over*, has yet to accept.

Other such famous psychics as Miss Cleo and Sylvia Browne are also missing in action. Randi confronted Browne last September on CNN's *Larry King Live*, and she agreed on the air to be tested. But Randi says Browne has subsequently been uncooperative.

As for Miss Cleo, Florida's attorney general sued her earlier this year, alleging that the Jamaican shaman, among other things, wasn't even Jamaican.

Sparky the Psychic Dog

Who does go after the million-dollar prize? About three dozen people each month write, e-mail, or bang on Randi's door, claiming they have supernatural powers. Randi and his associate, Andrew Harter, have seen it all.

One California man insisted that his dog, Sparky, could read his mind.

A Chinese couple insisted their little girl could read what was written on a piece of paper inserted into the child's ear.

A dentist stepped forward to claim he could tell whether a battery was charged by holding it to his throat.

Another guy wanted to prove his telekinetic powers by jumping out of an airplane without a parachute and surviving.

About a third of the people who apply for the award claim to be dowsers—people who think they can find water, gold coins, or drugs using a tool such as a forked stick.

Many folks are stepping forward these days to say they can manipulate TV personalities to say whatever they want. "This one guy kept saying, 'I can make Oprah say Randi's name.' And you couldn't convince him otherwise," Harter says. "Self-delusion can be very powerful."

When a man from Mexico knocked on the foundation's doors one day, he was so certain he could glow in the dark that he even brought a suitcase to take home the million-dollar award.

"He tried a few times, but just couldn't glow. He said he was tired and that he'd come back later," Randi said. "He never returned."

Spoon-Bending Psychic Still in Business

With National Psychic Week approaching, *The Wolf Files* called the internationally famous "spoon-bending psychic" Uri Geller. Geller and I met through truly unbelievable circumstances—at a New York synagogue in 1999 when the fad-a-minute Michael Jackson decided to experience Judaism.

"I know you, Buck Wolf, you are going to write something sarcastic about me," Geller said.

Was he reading my mind? Yowsa! Maybe he really is psychic.

Then Geller said that he had no idea that National Psychic Week was coming. So much for intuition.

You would think that if you were endowed with telekinetic powers you could put it to better use than mangling silverware. Still, Geller was a 1970s TV sensation, wowing audiences by seemingly melting helpless eating utensils with one raise of his eyebrow—until his powers failed him in 1972 on the *Tonight Show*.

Nevertheless, Geller has eked out a career writing books and supposedly earning a fortune dowsing for gold and diamonds and hiring himself out to oil companies to locate petroleum.

You'd think that would be enough for Geller to relax. But he's also promoted a 900-number psychic hotline in an infomercial. He went on a media blitz promoting *Uri Geller's Mindpower Kit*, which included a book, a cassette tape, and a special crystal to nourish the purchaser's own psychic power.

Geller Turns to Moonwalking

On behalf of psychics everywhere, I asked Geller to claim Randi's million-dollar prize. "Would you mark National Psychic Week by proving, once and for all, that there really is such a thing as telekinetic power?"

"I have considered it," Geller said. But he says he's got nothing to prove. Many scientists have validated his talents, and he doesn't trust Randi's foundation.

"He's all about negativity. I want to concentrate on the positive."

Geller's big project now is helping the King of Pop travel in outer space.

"You will see," he says. "Michael Jackson will one day moonwalk on the moon. Imagine what an inspiration that will be for children."

Geller says he's been speaking to NASA officials to get the singer booked on a future space flight. He also says he's been mentally preparing his pop-star pal for blastoff.

"We train our minds to empower each other," Geller says.

Liar for Hire

Just like Geller, most psychics aren't even aware that National Psychic Week exists. How's that for intuition?

To all the uninformed professional soothsayers out there, here's a little lesson in psychic history.

National Psychic Week has been listed on calendars since 1965. It was created by show-business press agent Richard R. Falk, who had a flair for dramatic PR stunts. One of Falk's specialties was dreaming up spicy names for aspiring starlets—such as Suzie Sunshine, Sugar Cane, and Hope Diamond. One of his clients modeled an edible bikini made of frankfurters.

Falk also managed several celebrity psychics and perhaps he could have explained more about National Psychic Week in the book he was working on at the time of his death in 1994. It was to be called *Liar for Hire*.

"You need a press agent when you have something that's 50 percent real," he told the *New York Times* in 1991.

"You make it a little fantastic or humorous, bring in enough pseudo-facts and the papers will buy it. I always say that everything I write is guaranteed to be 50 percent true."

To all the psychics out there who are "50 percent real," have a great week.

Afterward

To find the true nature of National Psychic Week, I figured my only hope was to hold a séance and speak with Mr. Falk. Gail Summer, president of the American Association of Professional Psychics, thought it was a great idea, and we made an appointment to contact the dead.

As a working journalist, I had been speaking with PR folks for years—but all of them purported to be living. To me, it was a sketchy endeavor. Do people in public relations even go to Heaven? Summer told me not to worry and enlisted Barbara Gable, a Baltimore medium, for our telephone séance.

Gable told me to relax and began muttering in an otherworldly tone. It was hopeless, I thought. And then . . . success.

"I have a clear picture of him. I see a man with a great smile and intense eyes," said Gable. "This man has a great sense of humor. But he tells me he believes in National Psychic Day. . . . He is a believer in the paranormal."

Summer had told me that she founded the psychic

association in 1992 to certify psychics such as Gable and make sure they are ethically serving the public. The association, incidentally, has trademarked the term "Certified Psychic" and issues "accuracy certificates" to its members.

As I pressed for questions, Gable told me this visitation was brief. Unfortunately, Falk didn't mention whether he had ever finished writing his biography, *Liar for Hire*, or why we should believe someone who would.

Perhaps some things should be left unspoken, when you're communicating with the dead.

What's more, Gable and Summer promised me that I could speak with any dead friend or relative I wanted—absolutely free. While ABC News has a strict policy for reporters on what gifts they can and can't accept, this was one perk I couldn't pass up. I wanted to speak to my dear old Uncle Len.

Gable again slipped into her mystical tone. "I see a serious man, thin, shy . . . and he offers you a greeting," she said.

Len, of course, weighed close to 400 pounds, had a jolly laugh, and spoke only in punch lines.

Perhaps Len would have extended his visitation had this been a paid séance, and he could have explained how he managed to lose so much weight. Maybe he really was in Heaven, where all diets work. But why was he so quiet? What happened to his endless stream of dirty jokes?

Len, if you're out there and you can hear me, I hope you're laughing now.

About the Author

Buck Wolf is a founding staff member of ABCNEWS.com, where he serves as the entertainment producer, covering the film, TV, and music industries. He also writes *The Wolf Files*, a weekly look at pop culture and offbeat news.

As a member of *Us* magazine's Fashion Police, Buck has provided biting commentary on the wardrobe habits of celebrities such as Jennifer Lopez, Britney Spears, and Sarah Jessica Parker. He is also a regular guest on ABC radio shows throughout the country.

Buck holds master's degrees in journalism and international affairs from Columbia University. He pedaled a bike across the United States in 1989 and returned to New York City, where he lives, works, and plays blues harmonica.

MORE LAUGHS
FROM THE GLOBE PEQUOT PRESS

WHAT WERE THEY THINKING?
Really Bad Ideas Throughout History
By Bruce Felton
ISBN 0-7627-2667-9 · $14.95

This compendium of some 400 harebrained schemes, fool notions, and misguided obsessions both grandiose and mundane covers bad ideas in politics, science, sports, and more.

GULLIBLE'S TRAVELS
The Adventures of a Bad Taste Tourist
By Cash Peters
ISBN 0-7627-2714-4 · $16.95

Fans of Cash Peters' "Bad Taste Tours" on public radio hail this outrageously funny collection of essays about his experiences traveling to and reporting on the most bizarre and tacky tourist attractions across the United States.

THE CURIOSITIES SERIES
Quirky Characters, Roadside Oddities, and Other Offbeat Stuff

In this sassy series of more than twenty state-almanacs gone-astray, prominent humor writers, columnists, and media personalities comb their home states for the most wacky and outrageous people, places, and things. Discover places overlooked on school field trips, people with odd and amazing talents, history left out of the books—a wealth of weird wonders most residents never dreamed existed!

Available from your favorite bookseller or at www.GlobePequot.com